THE LETTERS PROJECT

"'The Holocaust,' Eleanor Reissa writes in this unforgettable and courageous book, 'is attached to me like my skin and I would be formless without it.' A very personal story that is also a fundamental one of a woman trying to make sense of her life and family and of the shadows that go back before she was born. There is plenty of feeling and sentiment but it never feels sentimental. Her inimitable wit leavens the sadder scenes. This journey of discovery is riveting, told with tender insight, at times heartbreaking and at times heartwarming just like the Yiddish songs that have delighted Ms. Reissa's audiences."

—**Joseph Berger**, *New York Times* reporter and author of *Displaced Persons: Growing Up American After the Holocaust*

"Among the great number of personal takes on the Holocaust, Eleanor Reissa's book really stands out, both for its intelligence and courage and for the unique way she braids the inter-generational stories together. In this brutal, poignant, and searingly honest book, Reissa simultaneously pieces together the unfathomable story of her Holocaust survivor father, reckons with the guilt she came to feel as his uncomprehending American daughter, and manages somehow to find insight and purpose in the ashes. This extraordinary account of two parallel journeys will stick with anyone privileged enough to read it."

—**David Margolick**, former *New York Times* reporter, author of several books, including, *The Promise and the Dream: The Untold Story of Martin Luther King, Jr. and Robert F. Kennedy*

"*The Letters Project* is a wonderful book—funny, heartbreaking, and ultimately transcendent. Eleanor Reissa's journey back into her family's past makes for a gripping—and very human—international mystery. I highly recommend it."

—**Tony Phelan**, TV Showrunner for *Grey's Anatomy*, *Doubt*, and *Council of Dads*

"Eleanor Reissa has written a gritty, fearless, yet funny memoir about herself, her family, and the Holocaust. Once I began reading it, I was completely swept away until the journey ended. I was moved by the power of this uniquely personal yet universal story."

—**Julian Schlossberg**, American motion pictures, theatre, and television producer

THE
LETTERS
PROJECT

THE
LETTERS
PROJECT

A Daughter's Journey

ELEANOR REISSA

A POST HILL PRESS BOOK

The Letters Project:
A Daughter's Journey
© 2022 by Eleanor Reissa
All Rights Reserved

ISBN: 978-1-63758-255-8
ISBN (eBook): 978-1-63758-256-5

Cover art by Bob Stern
Interior design and composition by Greg Johnson, Textbook Perfect

Post Hill Press
New York • Nashville
posthillpress.com

Published in the United States of America
1 2 3 4 5 6 7 8 9 10

For my parents
For my grandparents
For my brothers
And for Frida

"What is the meaning of life? It's the lineage and the connection to the past and the connection to the future. It's in our children. It's in our friends. It's in our work. It's all around us."

— PHILIP GLASS

"We have come here to remember. How and with what will we remember?"

— AHARON APPELFELD

"One of the most important things I had learnt in Auschwitz was that one must always avoid being a nobody."

— PRIMO LEVI

PREFACE

Thirty years ago, when my mother died at the age of sixty-four—the age that I am now—I went through all of her belongings. In the bedroom, in the back of her lingerie drawer, I found an old leather purse. Inside that purse was a large wad of folded papers in a plastic bag.

They were letters.

My First Project

I hadn't thought about this for many years, but when I was a kid in Brooklyn, I had to do a science project for my fourth-grade class. Science was not my strong suit, but I came up with what I thought was a very smart idea. I had recently been to the Museum of Natural History on a school trip and seen the miracle of the extinct dinosaurs brought back to life in the Great Hall: the ancient bones, enormous skeletons, pieced together to re-create a world gone by. Yes, that's what I would do too. I would make a dinosaur out of bones. Chicken bones. My grandfather was a kosher butcher, and I thought: *I've got this covered.*

I did not exactly think it through.

Did I mean to use the chicken bones to make a dinosaur or use the chicken bones to reconstruct the body of a chicken? I don't recall exactly what I was thinking except that it seemed like a great idea. Unique. I bet no one else would think of doing that.

I began by asking my family to save the chicken bones from their dinners for me. My family consisted of two uncles and their wives plus one set of grandparents, on my mother's side. Everyone else had been killed in the Holocaust.

Since they were sometimes kind and loving people, they agreed to help me. Of course, they laughed about it. I was a bit of a joke to them in general. They thought I was a weird kid—easy to laugh and easier still to cry. When I wept, my mother used to say, "You want a reason to cry? I'll give you a reason to cry," and then she would lift the back of her hand as though to hit me—which she never did—but it did make me stop crying.

Every week for nearly a month, they would give me little plastic baggies filled with the archeological remains of their Sabbath meals: bones from their kosher chickens. Sometimes, the bones would arrive intact, still attached to the greater skeleton of the chicken, with the knee bone connected to the thighbone, just like in the song. The chicken's skinny little rib bones would arrive either as separate calci-fied matchsticks or, when I was lucky, they would be attached to the sturdy spine of that sacrificial fowl. The neck bones—*di gorgl*, as we said onomatopoetically in Yiddish—might arrive connected too, so that you could actually visualize the spinal curve leading from the chicken's shoulders and narrowing up to the little pea-brain chicken head, not unlike the dinosaurs' at the museum. Or they would be loose independent little rectangular vertebrae that you could stack up on top of each other in size-place, like children's blocks. The smallest and most intricate bones were from the chickens' feet, a delicacy—at least to me. I loved gnawing on those juicy little feet and regretted that there were only two per chicken.

After their meals, my relatives not only washed the dishes—no one in my family had a dishwasher back then—but they also saved those bones for me, scrubbing them until they were nearly bleached white, bringing to mind the thoughtful care and attention given to a Jewish body when it is prepared for burial. A final act of kindness that is not usually afforded to chickens.

This science project seemed like a no-brainer to me, and ultimately, of course, it *was* a no-brainer—as in, there was no brain used in the execution of this project. My plan was to collect enough bones so that I would have all the pieces I needed to make a dinosaur. Or a chicken. I was still not quite sure which.

Had I ever studied the anatomy of a dinosaur? Or of a chicken? Did I investigate how to attach bones to each other? By glue or by wire or thread? Did I prepare in any single way? Do the slightest amount of reading or research?

No. I only collected the bones, week after week, baggie after baggie, emptying the contents into one large, black plastic garbage bag that rested on the floor of my bedroom closet.

The time was rapidly approaching for me to submit my project. A few days before it was due, I began the work in earnest. I covered the kitchen table with newspaper, took out the bag of bones, and spilled out its contents. It was impressive to see how many I had collected. Piled high, the bones looked like a mass grave of some kind. The Massacre of the Innocent Chickens.

And so, like Noah, I paired like with like. The leg bones in this corner, the wing bones there, spines and ribs here, feet, necks, and so on. I had a three-dimensional jigsaw puzzle.

I looked at all those bones on the table. I was ten years old. I stared at that mess and realized there was no way in hell I could do what I had set out to do, what I had told my family that I would do, what I pictured in my mind that I would do. I didn't have a clue about how to execute and complete that great idea that I had imagined.

Hastily, I bought one large six-volt battery, connected the ends of two wires to its anode and cathode and the other ends to a simple door buzzer, mounted the whole business onto a plank of wood with a couple of screws and—bingo!—my science project. The chicken bones were sadly and unceremoniously thrown away. A waste of time and effort.

Now, more than fifty years later, I'm taking on a project that reminds me of my dinosaur-chicken bone idea. The enormity of it is something I clearly have not thought through. My modus operandi has not changed. No research or scholarly preparation. Just imagination and hope for the best.

There is no reason to believe that the outcome of this project will be any different than the fate of that mound of bones on the kitchen table.

Ch. Schlüsselberg · Stuttgart

IMPORT

von Südfrüchten, Obst, Gemüse, Eier u. Geflügel

STUTTGART-W, den 28 September 49
Elisabethenstraße 5

Fernsprecher Nr. 69437

Bankkonto: Bankhaus
Anselm & Co., Stuttgart-

CHAPTER ONE

"It is not up to you to finish the work, but you are not free to desist from it."

— PIRKEI AVOT 2:16

The Letters

Both of my parents lived through the Holocaust.

My mother died two days after her sixty-fourth birthday in December of 1986, exactly one year after I married my first husband, Allen—a scrappy, Jewish, Brooklyn-born drummer who really did march to his own beat. I was in a hurry to marry at that time because my mother was dying, and I desperately wanted her at my wedding. It was, perhaps, not the smartest reason to get married but certainly well-intentioned.

My father also died in December, but in 1976, ten years earlier, when he was seventy-five. There was a twenty-year spread between my parents. He was born in 1901, and she in 1922. They separated when I was five, in 1958, but did not divorce until four years later in 1962 when I was in the fourth grade—the year I tried to make a dinosaur out of a chicken.

That year, my mother said she was going on a vacation. She, my brother Seymour, and I had recently moved across the street from the three-family house where we lived with my father into the top floor of a six-story walk-up apartment building where we lived without him. While my mother was away, I stayed with Seymour, who was twelve years older than me.

It was only when she returned home that I learned she had been to Mexico. The clue was a gift she gave me, a souvenir—a boxy leather shoulder bag that had the word "Mexico" embossed on it. Even then, I thought the quality of the leather was lousy. Hard and stiff, lacking any grace or artistry. I wanted to like it but I didn't. I don't think I ever used it, even though it was oddly reversible. So many possibilities and yet so…ugly.

I also learned that during that Mexican vacation, we had gotten a divorce from my father. That was what my mother said: "*we*," as though I was married to him too.

In those days, no one's parents were divorced except for movie stars. I remember that people would often express their regrets to me about my parents' divorce. "Oh, so sorry," they would say sympathetically. I would respond easily that "it was okay," "no big deal," "all for the best," and that I was probably better off.

When I think about that now, I wonder whose words those were.

From the time that they separated, I lived exclusively with my mother. I visited my father on most Sundays until I became a teenager, when I visited him less frequently. My time with him was an obligation that weighed heavily on me and one that I always felt ambivalent about. There was an uncomfortable gap between us. Maybe it was his age or his broken English or his love, which seemed too needy. To him, I was everything. To me, he was a chore.

On our Sunday visits, I would arrive around 11 a.m. and leave no later than 3 p.m. My father would make me lunch, always the same thing—a pre-cooked chicken from Meal Mart, the first kosher takeout place of its day. He always took the time to doctor-up the chicken for me, trying to make it seem homemade. Even though I was just a kid, I thought that he ruined a perfectly delicious, crispy rotisserie chicken. I knew enough not to say so, but there was something cloying and fatty about his newly sautéed, overcooked chicken. He also bought and doctored a side dish called *potato nik*, a kind of potato pie, which when homemade, is a fantastic delicacy: crispy on the outside, smooth and creamy on the inside. The French might call it a *galette*. But his version was mushy and soggy, more like a potato-sponge casserole.

We would eat, and he would wash up. We would play some chess—which he had taught me—and then he'd fall asleep on the couch while I watched TV, usually *The Bowery Boys* or *Abbott and Costello*. After that, I would find some excuse to leave and take the subway or bus by myself and go back home to my mother. He and I would speak on the phone a couple of times during the week in short, awkward conversations.

Everything changed in 1970 when I was seventeen and a freshman at Brooklyn College. My father had a stroke, followed by a series of other strokes, which left him with a paralyzed left arm and leg, and severely impaired speech.

My mother visited him in the hospital during those first few days. He wept deeply the minute he saw her. They hadn't seen each other for nearly a decade, since their divorce. It was painful for me to watch my father cry like that, like a child. So, believing that I was an adult who knew many things, if not everything, I asked my mother not to visit him anymore since it seemed to upset him so much. As the *actual* adult who might have known better but didn't, my mother agreed— and never visited him again. Unfortunately, at that time, I did not know that uncontrollable emotions are one of the side effects of a stroke.

After a few weeks, once he was medically stable, he was sent to Rusk Institute in Manhattan where they gave him physical, occupational, and speech therapy for nearly a month. He improved somewhat; walking—albeit unsteadily—with a cane, and his speech became minimally clearer. His left arm remained paralyzed, a dead weight around his neck, supported by a shoulder sling. The hospital declared that he had progressed as far as he could and that they would no longer care for him. As his only blood relative and next of kin, I would have to decide what would become of him—where and how he would live. Clearly, he would not be able to manage in his apartment without assistance.

I was very conflicted about what to do. He was seventy and I was seventeen. I had recently rented my first apartment, a one-bedroom flat near the college, and I was excited to be on my own. I came to the difficult conclusion that I could not, and ultimately would not, give up my newly independent adult life to care for my father. Another child might have done otherwise, but I did not.

I asked around for advice and was told—and believed—that a nursing home was the only logical option. I looked hard to find the best-of-the-worst nursing homes, which by its very nature, was a crappy solution. I found one that was new and seemed clean and less depressing than the others.

During the first two years of his nursing home stay, I visited my father every day because I believed his death was imminent. I was frightened for him. He seemed weak and, as usual, I imagined the worst—that he would not survive for long. I obviously didn't know him well enough.

I was able to visit him so regularly, either after my classes at Brooklyn College or before my waitress job, because just a few months before his stroke, my father brought me to the shiny dealership on Kings Highway and bought me a brand new 1970 Volkswagen Beetle. On my seventeenth birthday, I would have my own set of wheels—also known as freedom.

Many people thought it was wrong—or, at the very least, odd—for my father, who had survived Auschwitz, to buy a German car. He didn't seem bothered by it and, in fact, liked German products. I didn't question his decision for a minute. I thought VWs were cool, and I was happy as hell to have one.

My father lived in that nursing home for six years, minimally improving his speech and gaining additional movement in his leg. His left arm never recovered any of its mobility even though he believed it would and worked hard in physical therapy to try to resurrect it.

He died of a heart attack in the early morning hours on December 8, 1976. Alone.

Although she was only in her thirties when they divorced, and a very bright, beautiful, vibrant woman, my mother never remarried. She worked in a sweatshop for nearly all of her days in America and lived in a rented basement apartment in Canarsie, an ethnically diverse working-class neighborhood in Brooklyn. I lived with her until the end of my first semester at Brooklyn College, when I fled to my own apartment, just before my father's stroke. The decision to leave her was terribly conflicting for me. It was the '70s and I desperately wanted to be free and live my own life, but I was immobilized by my guilt at abandoning my mother. However, I was not *that* immobilized that I did not get the heck out of there as quickly as I could.

In 1980, when she was fifty-eight, my mother was diagnosed with multiple myeloma, a brutal cancer of the bone marrow. She went through six years of harsh chemotherapy and had plenty of pain and agony. She tried to maintain her dignity throughout her ordeal and died in Sloan Kettering Hospital, ten years after my father, on December 26, 1986.

During her long illness, she often instructed me on what to do after she died: Go immediately to the safe deposit box, she said, and empty it out. Withdraw all the money from the bank. Right away. Act as though nothing has happened. Don't tell anybody anything. "I don't want to know about that stuff now," I would say to her. But she didn't care; she knew better. And immediately after her death, devastated, I did my best to follow her instructions.

Weeks later, I went through all of her belongings in the apartment. I found bits of cash and tissues, mints and lipsticks in various coat and jacket pockets. Her closets were full of outfits that she had made for herself over the years, dresses she had not worn since she took ill because the disease had distorted and mangled her petite body. Some of those dresses fit me, and I would have them. Her delicate hand and sharp eye were evident in all of them.

I looked through a lifetime of her objects. I touched everything, caressed and smelled and lingered over everything. I wanted everything because she was in every single thing.

It was at that time, in her lingerie drawer, that I found the purse. The one with the letters.

It was not like the Mexican-divorce purse. No, this one had craftsmanship and style. It was beautiful. Classic. It was made of soft, warm chocolate-brown calf leather. On the front was a sterling silver medallion, now tarnished black, with my mother's initials "RH," for "Ruchale Hoff." I recognize the purse from a black-and-white photo of my mother, walking arm in arm down some European boulevard after the war with a woman who I believe was her aunt and who fiercely resembled my mother. More like an older sister, if only my mother had had a sister.

Inside that beautiful, worn, tired purse—a remnant from another world—I found a plastic bag from *this* world that contained a bunch of papers.

Handwritten letters. Many.

The letters were written on large, premium paper stock with a professionally printed business letterhead. In German. My father's name, "Ch.Schlüsselberg," ("Ch." for Chaskel) was centered at the top of each page in red block letters. In black ink below his name, it said

"*Import*" and listed a bunch of things in German that I didn't understand. On the right side of the page was an address in the city of
Stuttgart, Germany.

The letters were dated 1949.

I couldn't make out the handwritten portion of the letters. The
words swam across my eyes in long cursive waves that looked like
bunches of *mmmm*s and *wwww*s. I could only decipher the salutations, which were practically the same in every letter: *Tayere Ruchale
un Shamale*. That was Yiddish for "Dear Ruchale and Shamale." (The
Yiddish suffix "*le*" has a diminutive, affectionate quality when attached
to a name or a noun.)

Ruchale was my mother's Yiddish name. In America, she called
herself Ruth, even though "Rachel" would have been the literal translation. Shamale, my mother's son from a short wartime marriage, was
called Shamshin but became Seymour, even though "Samson" was
more accurate. Those salutations were all I could decipher. Except for
the signature. Those were the same too. They were all signed, *Chaskel
Schlüsselberg*. My father's full name. Each one of these letters, *Chaskel
Schlüsselberg*. That was also how he signed every single thing he ever
wrote to me. Every birthday card, every personal note, letter, book
inscription: *Chaskel Schlüsselberg*. Actually, what he wrote was, *Your
father, Chaskel Schlüsselberg*, as though I wouldn't know which Chaskel
or which Schlüsselberg or how he was related to me. The formality of
it, the distance of it, the "just-in-case-you-forgot-my-name," or the
"who-I-am-to-you," or the "I'm the guy that was your father, Chaskel
Schlüsselberg." That he had to spell out who he was filled me with
sadness and pity. There is very little about my father that didn't—and
still doesn't—make me sorrowful. In fact, I can't think of a single thing.

I counted the letters. There were fifty-six in all. Most of them with
writing filling up both sides of the long, legal-size paper; his words
circling around the corners of the pages with an urgency and hunger
for more room to say...what? What was burning in my father that
he needed to say? I had no idea. And why had my mother kept these

letters for so long—after the divorce, after my father's death—and never said anything to me about them?

In the thirty years since my mother's death, I often looked at these letters. I would take them out of their baggie from inside the ever-decaying purse, unfold them, and try to make sense out of them; squinting and staring to try to recognize some words, any words, maybe even a sentence. Impossible. They seemed to be written in German, but I wasn't sure; I didn't think my mother spoke German. Since the salutations were in Yiddish, I thought it was a Judeo-German dialect of some kind. I did show them to some friends over the years, but no one knew what to make of them. I didn't pursue it further. The whole thing gave me a headache.

Each time, I would just fold the letters back up, return them to their brittle plastic bag, replace the bag into the decomposing leather purse, and return it to my own sloppy lingerie drawer. Out of sight, out of mind. Perhaps that's what my mother thought too.

But this year, as my own age corresponds to that of my mother's last year of life on this planet, I decide to take another crack at them. I think of Hillel: "If not now, when?"

This year also brought with it an acting job on Broadway in the play *Indecent*, written by Pulitzer Prize winner Paula Vogel, directed by Tony Award winner Rebecca Taichman, and produced by the Tony Award winning producer Daryl Roth. Rebecca and Paula had worked on the play for nearly ten years—maybe more. They had faith in their vision, no matter how long it took. It was an idea Rebecca had during her college days at Yale—an institution not known for producing graduates with low self-esteem.

I have been working, making a living in the theatre for over forty years—even gotten my own Tony nomination—but still, I felt like an outsider, a fraud. Unworthy. Also working often in the Yiddish theatre for decades was problematic for me. Rather than believing it was unique and valuable, I found it marginal, limiting, and ethnic. I wanted to be blonde and mainstream.

But if Paula and Rebecca included me in their creative universe, perhaps that meant that I, too, was an artist of worth. Perhaps I, too, could encourage my own imagination, nurture my own creative notions. That, plus the Broadway paycheck—six months' worth— could give me permission to feel financially entitled to spend money on my vision.

Entitlement, to a child of Holocaust survivors, is not a part of our vocabulary. Our parents had nothing. Everything and everyone was taken away. Literally. Except for being alive, what is it that we, their children, were actually entitled to? Basically, nothing. The minimum would do. In fact, the minimum was more than enough. I used to say, proudly, that I could make soup out of rocks. Who were we to want or expect more? When I was a girl and asked my mother for something not particularly essential, she would say: "Who do you think you are, the Queen of Sheba?" Who did Rebecca Taichman think she was, the Queen of Sheba? Maybe she did. And at sixty-four, maybe I could crown myself queen, too.

I took my mother's purse out of the drawer again. It was a beautiful piece of work, that purse, but the leather had become dry and cracked. Some of the corners were splitting apart and the stitching was coming out. I seemed to be in the mood to repair the past, so I brought the purse to my local Greek shoemaker. He looked at it and shook his head, like a doctor over a terminally ill patient.

"Can't you do anything?" I begged.

"Not much," he said in his rich, thick Greek-accented English.

"Please," I said, "it is very old."

"Yes, I know," he said sadly. "I will try to glue it. If I sew it, that will only tear the leather and make it worser."

"Thank you so much," I said.

"I will polish it and bring it back to life. It is beautiful bag," he said. "You should have taken better care of it."

Yes, I know.

Before I brought the purse to the shoemaker, I took the letters out and really looked at them. For the first time, I took notice of the dates. The very first letter was dated 24 July 1949, and the last said 13 January 1950. Six months' worth of letters. Many were sequential or separated only by a day or two. Or three. 11 August 1949, 12 August 1949, 15 August 1949, etc.

Suddenly, I understood that I needed to not only take care of the purse, but I also needed to take care of the letters. I needed to have them translated. Now.

And that's when I thought about the chicken bones.

CHAPTER TWO

The Translations

I didn't know where or how to begin. I wasn't even sure in what language the letters were written. It looked like German, but that didn't make any sense to me. Why would my father write to my mother in German? I knew *he* spoke German, but I never heard *her* speak German. She spoke Yiddish, Polish, Russian, and English. Maybe it was some kind of Yiddish-German jargon, using Latin letters rather than the Hebrew letters in which Yiddish is written. I didn't know whom to ask for help. Then I realized I knew some people who were fluent in both Yiddish *and* German.

Yeva Lapsker

I knew this guy, a fellow performer, who was an expat Yiddish singer living in Berlin who sometimes visited New York. I thought of him and wondered if perhaps he could be a potential translator. Coincidentally, I heard that he was in town. Then bizarrely, I ran into him on the street the day after I thought of him.

When I saw him, I asked if he'd be interested in looking at these letters. It was not his thing, he said, but his girlfriend, Yeva, was a German translator by trade, and as luck would have it, she was also in New York.

He gave me her contact information and we spoke. She was intrigued by the project but was scheduled to return to Berlin that week. We hastily arranged a meeting.

ELEANOR REISSA

Yeva was about thirty, beautiful in a soulful Soviet way; intense and dark. She had been a dancer—tango, she said. She was lithe and lean, with an air of sadness and romanticism, as though she had just stepped out of a Chekhov play.

We decided to test the waters. I gave her a single letter to translate. In an email a few days later, I received her translation. She sent it as an attached document that looked like this:

Ch. Schlüsselberg • Stuttgart
IMPORT von Südfrüchten, Obst, Gemüse, Eier u. Geflügel

Elisabethenstraße 5
Telephone No. 69437
Bank account: Bankhaus
Anselm & Co., Stuttgart

24th July 1949

My very dearest Ruchale!

Please don't cry, it has to be this way. I'm longing these several weeks now to talk to you so that I can find some peace. I was happy about your detailed letter and I hurried to answer you, so that you would have a sign of life in front of you, my love, as you begin your big journey.

Yesterday, I had a boring Sabbath except for the letter from you. It was very, very empty here. Write to me often, my beloved Ruchale, as only this one joy remains for me. And we don't want to lose this. Please keep this last fragment of our lives safe. I don't want to overwhelm you with big letters, but they serve as a reminder that I am alive and that you are my only light.

Send my warmest regards to your beloved parents and Shamale.

I am sending you greetings and kisses with all my heart,

From your loving Chaskel Schlüsselberg

I read the letter again and again. I felt like the ground had opened up and my father, who had been silent for over forty years, was now speaking. Poetic words of love, no less. His voice was unrecognizable to me. It was from a time long before he was my father. I only knew him during the last twenty years of his life—and just barely at that. By then, most—but not all—of the damage had already been done. I had believed that I was the daughter of an "Other": a never-belonging, never-accepted, factory working, illiterate-in-English, immigrant-greenhorn-misfit. That's who I thought he was and consequently from whom I was descended. I never had any reason to believe otherwise.

Okay. I decided to make a deal with Yeva Lapsker, whoever she was. Translating that one letter had whetted her curiosity, and she could certainly use the extra dough. She was about to go back to Germany, and I was leaving New York as well. I was heading to the rugged shores of New England to spend time with John, my sixty-nine-year-old über-WASPy boyfriend, a man I was in love with and deeply attracted to but who was ambivalent about my company and kept me a heart's length away—which didn't stop me from knocking on his door, waiting to be let in.

Yeva and I settled on a too-small payment per letter. But even at that low fee, the translations would cost me thousands of dollars. Her job was complicated. First, she would have to decipher and transcribe my father's cursive writing into legible German text. From that, she would translate the German text into English. It was a challenging, time-consuming task. Deciphering someone else's handwriting was hard enough, especially with unfamiliar names etc., plus I was told that my father's writing style was old-fashioned and not how modern German was spoken or written. Thankfully, Yeva was game.

Although she seemed trustworthy, I wanted her to sign a nondisclosure agreement (NDA)—which said more about me than about her. I admit to being fairly suspicious, secretive, fearful, and probably selfish by nature. These letters were my family's legacy, and I felt possessive of all of it, as though the Holocaust was my own exclusive history. I didn't want Yeva to share any of the contents or information about my parents' lives with anyone. I had no idea what we would find in those letters; what confessions, admissions, or embarrassments we would uncover of those no longer able to defend themselves. I had inherited my family's secrecy gene—never tell anyone anything. The less people know about you, the better. Knowledge is danger, deceit is smart, and the truth is nobody's business.

Another reason for the NDA was that I imagined that these letters might contain creative possibilities. Perhaps an idea for a major motion picture? Or a play? Or a one-woman show where I play everyone—written, directed, and starring…me! I just wanted to be careful. And prepared. At the very least, not stupid.

Yeva agreed to everything. We were off and running. I gave her a cash advance along with photocopies of the first ten letters from 24 July 1949 until 31 August 1949. I expressed my good fortune at finding her, and then we both went our separate ways. I gave her an October deadline.

That was in August of 2017.

A number of emails were exchanged over the next weeks, mostly about delays. It was going slower than she thought it would. Computer problems, lost texts, a variety of excuses and mishaps. Had I done the right thing with the right person? I didn't know, but she was all I had.

That Labor Day, at a dinner party, I saw an old friend who, when I told him about these translations and the number of letters still needing to be done, mentioned a German friend of his, Knud Lambrecht, who was a professor emeritus of Romance Linguistics at the University of Texas at Austin. Having a second translator suddenly sounded like a really good idea. If ten letters were taking Yeva two months, the remaining fifty could easily take more than a year.

I wrote to Knud. He was interested and agreed. He had the time to work on it and would get them back to me in the next couple of weeks, he said. Great. I sent him the next ten letters, dated from 7 September 1949 to 28 September 1949. I offered him what I was paying Yeva. He said he would do it for free, but I insisted on paying him. I didn't want his translations to fit into the "you get what you pay for" category.

That was the first week of September 2017.

Eventually, Yeva's letters started dribbling in. She thoughtfully gave her translated letters the look of my father's business stationery: bolding his name, sizing it larger than the body of the letter, putting his address, bank information, and phone number along the right margin of the page just like it was on his original documents. She also translated the heading itself, which I hadn't paid any attention to. It read:

Ch. Schlüsselberg • Stuttgart
IMPORTER of Tropical and Local Fruits, Vegetables, Eggs, and Poultry

Elisabethen Street 5
Telephone No. 69437
Bank account: Bankhaus
Anselm & Co., Stuttgart

My father was an importer? Imported from where? Sold to whom? Was that the address of his store? His house? Office? He had a phone number *and* a bank account?

Well, yes, of course he did. My ignorance was appalling, even to me. There was so much I didn't know and hadn't bothered to find out. When my family was alive, I accepted whatever incomplete slivers of explanations they provided. I didn't press them, although on more thoughtful reflection, I definitely had inquired. But their responses were fractured, scattershot. Speaking of the past was clearly painful. I was intuitively aware of that for as long as I could remember, and I didn't want to contribute to any additional heartache. They often wore a tearful coat of grief, especially on Sabbaths and holidays, when one might have expected joy and celebration. Those days were sad, introspective, and wet with mourning.

Most of what I had cobbled together about my family's past came from photographs; pictures of people I didn't know: that cousin or those aunts or younger brothers or sisters who were missing—meaning dead. Years later, by the time the Holocaust became dinner-table fodder and survivors were being interviewed by the Shoah Foundation, my parents were long gone and there was no one left to ask.

Over the years, when people asked me what my father did for a living in Europe after the war, I used to say, "He sold stuff." In Yiddish, it was explained to me as: "*Er hut farkoyft skhroyre.*" "*Skhroyre*" means "goods" or "stuff." A generic term. That's all I knew. No one ever told me what kind of stuff. I thought it was a euphemism for black market hanky-panky. I accepted that and assumed I would never learn anything more.

But now, thanks to Yeva, I know that my father was an "Importer of Tropical and Local Fruits, Vegetables, Eggs, and Poultry." At least it said so on his stationery.

The rest of that letter looked like this:

14 August 1949

My dearest Ruchale and Shamale,

Although I have not received a letter from you, I am writing to you nonstop. I understand that you have your hands full until everything is in place, but please realize how very happy it makes me to read some words from you, my love.

As to my coming to America, I can only tell you, my darling, that I would fly to you if I only had wings. We know, although it's been very difficult for both of us, we cannot lose faith, and the most important thing is that, if God will grant us both health and patience, we will very much cherish each other.

I hadn't realized how beautiful it was to get on the express train for each Sabbath, and that in a little more than an hour, we would see each other, be together, and talk. Now we are so torn apart, but in our thoughts, we are even closer than before. How much I thirst for you and all of our beloved ones to come to visit me, and for the train to come soon so we can be together again....

My father closes this letter—as he does every other letter—with regards to my mother's family, who are already with her in the States.

He begs her to write to him more often, and concludes "with love, from Chaskel Schlüsselberg."

"*I would fly to you if I only had wings.*" I did not know the man who wrote those words.

But here's what I did know—how their strained and painful relationship would end. I knew their future: Those letters filled with love and need and hope and fear would culminate in an ugly, reversible Mexican purse.

It was not long before Knud's letters started arriving. They had a different tone than Yeva's translations. My father's voice in Knud's translations sounded more matter-of-fact and detached. Knud didn't begin each letter with the business heading and end with the cursive signature as Yeva did in all of her translations. I suspect it didn't even occur to him, just as it hadn't occurred to me. Yeva tried to capture the conditions and feelings of the writer, as she imagined his circumstances. Probably because she was an artist, the voice in her letters seemed warmer, needier, more anxious. Knud's words were stark, more like reporting. But maybe his translated letters contained more actual businesslike content in them. They still included my father's never-ending longing for my mother, as well as his insecurity and dissatisfaction with her abridged, lackluster, tardy responses. Knud's letters were written a month after Yeva's, so my parents had been apart for longer—and my father had been alone (as he would be always) for longer—which added new qualities to his letters: cynicism, resentment, irony—which surprised me.

4 September 1949

My beloved Ruchale and Shamale,

After a long time, no letter has arrived from you, my dearest. But one must be able to wait, says my Ruchale, right? I am just a very demanding person and expect a lot from you, right? First, I let you travel alone through the wide world, and then I demand that you write me. A person like me, who has led a solitary life, doesn't need that either? Is that what you think? I need a letter from you, and if it's at all possible, please don't neglect it. Today's letter calmed me down a lot. The content was good medicine, like prescribed by a doctor. I was very happy to hear that you now have your own apartment. I wish you the best in the new home. May it be all that you wish for yourself. From your letter, I took careful note of everything you said, and I will do as you ask. About the woolen blankets, it would be better if I bought them here. They cost about 150 marks. Because even over there, one needs something to cover oneself. You have to stay warm, so please write me about that. As for the ring with 1.5K to 2K, I looked at one today with 2.5 karat, which costs 3,800 marks, if it doesn't seem too expensive to you. Please write me about it by return post. However, there is one with 3.5 karat which costs 5,200. Let me know.

Please give my best wishes to your dear uncle and aunt. I was very happy to hear that your dear ones did a lot for you. They'll have good luck from that in some other way.

I know that you have to work, that you may be tired, but how long does it take to write a letter? Do we have any other way until we meet again? We have to make our lives easier, so it won't seem like we are apart. But I'm sure you know best.

Today, I sold the living and bedroom furniture. Such is life. You, my dearest, have to buy things for a lot of money, while here, we have to sell practically everything. Even the down comforters are sold. The remaining pillows I'll bring when I come.

I still have big troubles about England, which I'd like to take care of before the long trip.

Please give my warm regards to your parents. First, a thank you to your mother for her little letter. I hope to be able to return the favor someday.

I'm happy that you, my dearest, like reading my letters. The same is true here, except that I get too few of them. I hope it won't take much longer until we change that. Please accept another thanks from me, and my warmest greetings and kisses.

I remain, your Chaskel Schlüsselberg, who loves you.

Clearly, she is not writing. Or rather, not writing *enough*. His life in Germany is ending, and hers in America is just beginning. Does she regret the whole business with this man? I have learned in this life, if you really want to do something, you do it. You make the time. If you want to write, you write.

By the end of October, between Yeva and Knud, only one-third of the fifty-six letters had been translated. It was still going to take months and months for me to get some semblance of a narrative about my parents' lives. Like my father, I, too, was now waiting for letters.

When a long-awaited translated letter would finally arrive by email, I was excited but read it quickly and then filed it away. Dribbling in, they didn't really make that much sense to me. I couldn't quite connect the dots. Perhaps once all the letters were translated, I thought, my parents' lives from another world and time would come into focus. Hopefully, they would explain the unexplainable.

I know now that I was able to read them perfunctorily and put them aside because I lacked a context for understanding them. But also, however unclear and disjointed, reading my father's words in black and white, their very existence, and hearing his voice, reminded me again and again of the depth of my parents' sorrows and struggles, of their miserable lives, so unenviable and tragic from beginning to end. In Yiddish, we say: "*Oyf mayne sonim gezogt.*" "Such a life you would wish on an enemy."

Theirs was such a life.

CHAPTER THREE

Berlin
(Early November 2017)

As luck would have it, I had a three-city European singing tour coming up that November with the band that I'd been working with: Frank London and the Klezmer Brass Allstars, a totally groovy bunch of freewheeling talented young musicians who, along with me, reconstituted Yiddish music and breathed new life into old tunes. Thanks to my refugee family, Yiddish was my first language, and I could authentically sink my teeth into the soul of that tongue, especially with Frank and the band. One of our concert destinations would be Berlin, the current home of my translator, Yeva.

I let Yeva know that I was coming. She had yet to give me some of the translated letters from that original batch of ten that had been due in October—and was now a month late. Also I still owed her money, since I had only paid her half the fee for the first five letters. Like a drug deal, we would exchange the stuff for cash when I arrived in Berlin.

We met for coffee in the lobby of my funky, formerly East Berlin hotel. It was the dead of winter, German style, which meant freezing cold and steel gray skies. Yeva walked into the lobby looking like she was straight out of *Doctor Zhivago*, with a rich dark-brown fur hat, embroidered overcoat, and soft, sturdy, femininely handsome leather boots. We embraced warmly even though we had only met briefly, once before, a few months earlier. The intimacies and details that we now shared from my father's letters gave us a kind of closeness and familiarity, as though we were old friends with a shared past. There was hardly a soul living who knew my parents, but now Yeva was one of them.

The lobby was furnished with soft, oversized, modern high-backed armchairs and small metal coffee tables, everything on casters, so you could roll around and arrange meetings into any configuration. We instinctively encircled ourselves like pioneers on a wagon train. Our cappuccinos came and we leaned in, speaking ever so softly. (In the future, I would often have to ask Yeva to speak up as her natural style was quiet, very unlike my own you-could-hear-me-in-the-last-row voice.) This meeting had an intimacy and reverence for our unique charge, breathing life into these letters so long buried.

As we sat with our coffees, I asked her about herself. She was originally from the former Soviet Union. Her parents were both Jewish, although her mother hadn't learned that about herself until later in life. (Secrets were a part of Yeva's family too.) They had immigrated to Germany as soon as they could, in the 1990s. Yeva, however, was not a fan. She seemed to hate Germany with a passion. She didn't trust the Germans, despising their rigid efficiency and their orderly aggressiveness. But it was still better than Russia, she said. Plus, this was where she and her Cleveland-born klezmer boyfriend were living, for now. Ironically, Berlin had become a major European hub of the revitalized klezmer world.

After she recounted her personal history, she leaned in closer and said, even more softly, "You know, my brother lives in Stuttgart."

"That's nice," I said.

"Yes, right around the corner from the address in your father's letters."

"What?"

"My brother and his wife just had a baby, and I am planning to visit them in January. But I could leave a little earlier and go there with you if you would like."

"What?"

"Yes," she said. "So, if you are free and you want to go...."

Wait. What? I thought. *Go? Where? To Stuttgart?*

"Yes, to Stuttgart. And to Ulm. It's nearby, just an hour or so away."

Ulm was the site of Donaubastion, the displaced persons camp, where my mother, her son, parents, and brothers went in 1945 after the war ended. When the Nazis invaded their town in Poland, the family fled east to Fergana, Uzbekistan, thousands of miles away, where they lived—if you call that living—for four years in a slave labor camp.

Ulm is where she and my father met and romanced. I had heard the name of the camp for as long as I can remember, but my family pronounced it "Donner Bastion," which was how I thought it was spelled. I had not been able to locate it, and at a certain point, I simply stopped trying.

Why they went to that particular camp in Ulm, I don't know. Perhaps they had heard that other living relatives were there, or perhaps it was because it was in the American sector of occupied Germany, which was where the best-of-the-worst conditions were available to the desperate refugees. Or maybe it was just where they were arbitrarily sent by whomever was in charge of refugees that week.

My family possessed a few small, scallop-edged, black-and-white photos from Ulm. In one photo, my father, in a bow tie and sport jacket, is clearly trying to kiss my young mother, who is wearing a worn, soft cotton print dress. She seems shy, coquettish really, trying to keep him at arm's length, on what appears to be a lovely spring day alongside a river. The picture doesn't let on that a few months earlier, their very existence was straddling between life and death.

There was another particular photo that I looked at so often that I could have painted it from memory. In it, my father holds his hand outstretched in the foreground while my mother stands on a pile of boulders in the background. The perspective makes my mother look like a tiny woman-doll standing in the palm of my father's hand. The photo is playful, and they look like they are actually having fun.

Clearly visible in that photo is a river with a bridge and a very high church steeple. The river and the steeple are the identifying location elements of that picture. I didn't know that the river running through Ulm was the Danube, pronounced *"Donow,"* and the steeple—the highest in Europe—belonged to the Ulm Münster, a Unitarian church.

Until that meeting with Yeva Lapsker, it had shockingly never occurred to me to go to Stuttgart or to Ulm. For what? I never imagined that there was anything to find there. Everyone was dead. The war was fifty years ago. What could possibly be left? I am embarrassed to say that I was content with my blurry impressions of the past. I thought I knew enough. As John used to say, "You don't know what you don't know."

Yeva was offering me some kind of once-in-a-lifetime experience to time-travel and open a door into the netherworld. I looked into her dark brown eyes and did not know what to say.

Frank London, my bandleader, knew everyone everywhere. His contacts worldwide were deep, but especially so in Berlin. The day before our concert in the restored Rykestrasse Synagogue—the largest synagogue in Germany—we were scheduled to do a sound check. Frank was having lunch with his friend and booking agent, Lutz Engelhardt, at the trendiest Vietnamese restaurant in town. For all of his Lower East Side proletarian ways, Frank is a devoted foodie and doesn't miss any opportunity for popular authentic dining anywhere. I was to pick him up there, and we would walk to the venue. When I arrived, he and Lutz were still seated, eating the last morsels of the many plates piled high on their overcrowded table. He introduced me rather perfunctorily since we were, as was often the case with Frank, late.

The next morning, as I walked through the hotel lobby for my coffee, I found Frank and Lutz already seated there. This time, Frank invited me to join them. In his gentle German-tinged English, Lutz said he was looking forward to our concert tonight. "Yes, me too," I said.

Lutz was probably somewhere in his fifties, with soft blonde hair and a fair complexion. Very satisfyingly German-looking and physically full—or as we say in Yiddish, *zaftig*.

Frank had told Lutz about my father's letters. I was surprised and moved that it had registered on Frank's radar.

Lutz seemed quite interested, and so I told him about the letters, as well as about Yeva's idea to go to Ulm and Stuttgart. In passing, I casually mentioned that in the letters, my father wrote of many visits to Ludwigsburg, a town I'd never heard of.

"Ludwigsburg?" says Lutz with raised eyebrows. "I know many people in Ludwigsburg—and in Stuttgart too, for that matter. Please, if you decide to make this trip, I hope you will let me know as perhaps I can be of some help to you."

Both Lutz' and Yeva's interest and enthusiasm were unexpected and somewhat baffling to me. It seemed almost greater than my own.

That meeting took place on Saturday, November 11, 2017. Our concert that evening had a lot of resonance for me. First of all, I would be singing Yiddish in this city where so many Jewish people had lived—and died. Yiddish was meant to die with them, but I was some kind of living proof that it hadn't.

Also, my half-nephew, Julian Titus Wrightson, born in 1959—six years younger than me—was coming to the concert with his newest wife, Nikki, born in the very late '70s (not that there's anything wrong with that). Julian prefers being called by his middle name, Titus. It's a more manly name than Julian, he thinks. I have mentioned to him, more than once, that it was the Roman Emperor Titus who sacked the city of Jerusalem in 70 AD and destroyed the most holy Jewish temple, murdering and enslaving its Jewish population. Undeterred, he calls himself Titus and, undeterred, I call him Julian. Julian was retired from the British Royal Air Force, and was enjoying life with his young wife in the south of Spain in a trailer community with other expats.

Julian was British because his father, Harry Wrightson, the son of my father and his first wife, Chana Schlüsselberg née Rubin, had been sent to England in 1938 on one of the *kindertransport* trains out of Germany shortly after the pogrom of Kristallnacht on 9 November 1938, one day after Harry's seventh birthday.

Harry Wrightson was born Heiner Schlüsselberg in Stuttgart on 8 November 1931. I didn't meet Harry or even learn of his existence until I was fourteen, in 1967, when my father told me during one of our weekly Sunday lunches that I had a brother. He told me that my brother lived in England. He told me that in 1953, the year that I was born, my brother married a non-Jewish woman and changed his name to Wrightson. My father stopped speaking to him after that. But now that my father was getting older—he was sixty-six and alone—he wanted for us to know each other. Those were his exact words to me that afternoon. "I want for you to know each other." And that was all he would say about that.

At the age of fourteen, I didn't know what to ask or how to ask it. What did I feel about that? Do I remember exactly? No. Shock? Anger? Betrayal? Put it on the list with all the other stuff that made my family weird and different. I always felt that they—we—were "Other." With all my heart, I wished that were not so. I wished that my world looked like Dick and Jane's—the children from those early schoolbook readers—with their dog and cat, Spot and Puff, and with their mother who stayed at home and wore a white apron, and their handsome father who sat in an armchair reading the newspaper and smoking a pipe. This new lunchtime information was just more of the same, although it did have an air of exotica to it since I now had a brother in England: the land of the Beatles and Terry-Thomas, that gap-toothed comic actor who personified Great Britain to me at the time.

My father and I went to visit Harry—the name he preferred to Heiner—that year at his home in East Anglia near Cambridge. Remarkably, Harry and I bonded quickly and easily, even though there was a twenty-year age gap between us. My father and he, on the other hand, were awkward with each other, and they would remain so for as long as my father lived.

Over the years, it was from Harry that I learned most of the few details about my father's life before the war in the 1930s and '40s—but naturally, only as they pertained to Harry. For example, it was Harry who told me that Charlie—as he called our father, whose actual name was Chaskel, the Yiddish derivative of the biblical Ezekiel—also had a daughter.

A daughter?

No one had *ever* mentioned that to me. Never.

I learned this from Harry only when it was too late, long after my father and mother were gone, when there was no one to ask.

Frida.

Harry said that his sister Frida was four years his junior. She had been too young to send on the *kindertransport* train with him, and she and their mother, Chana, had been killed in a concentration camp.

I also learned that it was Harry's wife, Joyce, who had convinced him, when they married in October 1953—I was born that May—to change his name from Schlüsselberg to Wrightson, the surname of the gentile British family who had cared for him during the war. I cannot throw stones at her for that since I, too, shoved the name Schlüsselberg off the train when I became a professional actress. (I took my middle name, Reissa, hoping business people would think I was Italian...) Unless you're living in Israel or Germany, "Schlüsselberg" is not a name that flows trippingly off the tongue, especially when you're trying to assimilate. But when Harry gave up my father's name, my father gave up Harry. That was it. The last straw on a tall stack of straws. Their communication all but stopped for the next fourteen years.

Julian and his wife, Nikki, had never been to Berlin and had never seen me perform, so this concert was an opportunity for them to kill two birds with one stone. Julian didn't seem to take much interest in anything Jewish or Yiddish, although when he was younger, I remember he had this fascination with the Star of David and collected them. He once proudly showed me a little wooden box that he kept in his bureau full of all sorts of Jewish star jewelry and memorabilia. Except for that box, he knew less than nothing about Jews, Judaism, or Jewish history. More than once, he asked me why Jews didn't celebrate Christmas. To him, it was just a fun national holiday and a chance to exchange gifts. Even though Harry was born Jewish, he did not identify with any religion. Except for my father, I believe that I was—and am—the *only* Jew that Julian, Harry, or Joyce have known.

Our concert that night was transcendent. The Rykestrasse Synagogue—an architectural jewel built in 1905, with a huge inner nave—was magical; lit in God's heavenly blue and packed to capacity. The reason the Nazis did not set fire to it on Kristallnacht was because they feared the fire would spread to the nearby non-Jewish German residences. They did, however, manage to destroy, desecrate, and wreck its interior. Singing there on that crisp winter night in 2017 in Yiddish, in that thick, expressive, poetic, earthy—and most importantly—living language of so many Jewish people, only sixty years after the devastation of the Holocaust, felt holy. Everything in my life had led me here, to exactly where I was meant to be, doing exactly what I was born to do.

After the concert, kudos from Julian and Nikki, although I don't know if they were moved one way or another. We said our goodbyes. The next morning, Frank and I would be off to perform in Vienna and then, Paris.

The remaining concerts went very well, and after Paris, I stopped off in England for a few days to see Harry and Joyce. I always tried to visit them when I could. From the time of our first meeting in 1967, it seemed that we had chosen each other, that we had deliberately and consciously decided to be related. We could have just as easily gone our separate ways, but instead, we held on to the thin thread that connected us—which was our father, Chaskel/Charlie. Harry and Joyce were now eighty-six years old (still more than twenty years older than me).

Each time I visited them, I feared it would be the last time. Someday, it would be.

Besides Julian/Titus, Harry and Joyce had had another child—a daughter, Johanna. Johanna died tragically when she was thirty. She had childhood diabetes, and it seems that while she was alone in her flat, she went into a fatal diabetic coma. They were—and still are—these twenty-five years later, shattered by her death.

A decade or so ago, I discovered a few photos of Harry's baby sister, Frida. In one of them, she's sitting in a baby carriage, with her older brother standing proudly behind her. His hair is cut short, like the bristles of a brush, and he is wearing actual lederhosen.

There is another photo of her sitting in a garden, grinning from ear to ear.

And there is even one of my father with his first wife, and Frida.

How they are in my possession, I do not know. Obviously they're from my father, but how did he get them? He didn't have them in Auschwitz. How did any of my family get pictures from Europe, from before the destruction and death? From a relative who fled to Israel or Canada? Sewed into the lining of a coat?

Harry's daughter Johanna very much resembled his sister Frida. Both had a shock of fire-red hair and the round Schlüsselberg face with the smiling oval green eyes. She was, after all, Frida's niece. Or would have been.

And yes, I have those eyes and that face as well.

Harry told me that although they named their daughter Johanna, they had originally intended to name her after his mother, Chana. When he said his mother's name, he pronounced it "*Ch*ana"—with the "CH" as in "chapel." I was flabbergasted. Of all the bizarre and tragic things that had happened to Harry, the fact that he did not know how to pronounce his mother's name saddened me enormously. To know so little about one's family, one's culture, one's own mother, and consequently, oneself.

When I told Harry that "Chana" was actually pronounced with the Middle Eastern guttural sound "KH," he was surprised and looked confused. He took a breath and then, a moment later said, "Oh well, I prefer it my way." "*Ch*ana" as in "*ch*apel." If anyone was ever going to turn over in their graves, that might have been a good time.

Visiting Harry and Joyce that November, we spoke about my concerts on the Continent, life in general, and a bit about my boyfriend John, whom they had met and liked very much. Then I brought up the subject of the letters.

"Don't you think those letters are rather private?" Harry asked in his proper Queen's English. "They're not actually addressed to you, you know."

"Well, yes, I know, but they are addressed to my mother and were written by my father."

"But why do you want to know what's in them?"

"Don't you want to know what's in them, Harry?"

"Well, no, I don't," he answered. "I don't like to look back."

"And I can't seem to stop looking back," I said.

He paused. "Well, I wish you good luck with them," he said supportively.

And that subject was closed.

Yet it was primarily from Harry's recounting of his childhood experiences and memories that I learned most of what I knew up until that point about my father: the details of Harry's trip on the *kindertransport*; the time he stopped receiving letters immediately after the war from our father, leading him to believe that he had been killed along with his mother and sister; and then his shock years later when he learned that his father was actually alive. It so frightened him to think that he might be forced to leave his home again—this time, England—with a man who was practically a stranger. It was nearly paralyzing for him, he'd said. Harry told me these stories over and over again. He seemed hungry to talk about it whenever I was visiting. I don't know if anyone else in his life wanted to know.

Harry was a natural storyteller, and so I was able to imagine and internalize his recollections, especially his description of the tragic meeting at HIAS (Hebrew Immigrant Aid Society) when Chaskel came to fetch him in 1949. They had to communicate through a translator because Harry no longer spoke German or Yiddish, and our father spoke no English. Thanks to Harry, I could imagine their fears and conflicts, as well as their many tears.

Chaskel/Charlie, so recently revived from the horrors of the camps, was losing his son again, his only living child—whose life he had saved—because Harry didn't want to go with his foreign/Jewish father to America. I try not judge Harry. I am certain he carries his own heavy burden of guilt for this. He was young, and war makes every damn thing complicated. Every choice, every move is impossible—and excusable. But giving up the name of the man who bore him and saved his life? How much did that hurt my father? Just add it to the list.

Harry remembered little of his life in Stuttgart from before the war: a bit about Kristallnacht and a few details about his baby sister, Frida, whom he adored. The only time I ever really saw Harry weep— and that includes the cremation of his daughter—was when he spoke of Frida. Speaking of her would always choke him up. He would say that he couldn't understand how the Nazis could kill such a lovely young girl, a child. "What had she ever done to them?" he would ask innocently, his blue eyes brimming.

When he said such things to me, I would just look at him and nod, but inside I thought: *Are you nuts, Harry? They were Nazis! That's what Nazis did!*

CHAPTER FOUR

New York
(Late November 2017)

I was back in New York after the European concerts. Both of the translators were moving at a snail's pace. Letters were trickling in from Yeva and Knud, and it was maddening. I am not a patient person even on a good day.

One afternoon, while complaining about the translations to my therapist—not that I needed one—she mentioned that she knew someone who might be able to help: a German woman in her book club, Daniela Schult. Daniela was a hairdresser living and working in New York who had done some translating. A German hairdresser-translator? Sure, why not. We met that week for tea. She was definitely nice enough and very game, happy for the extra cash. A deal was struck.

There were a lot of moving pieces, and it was becoming difficult for me to keep track of which letters went to whom and which had or had not been translated. This whole project was becoming a disorganized mess. Chicken bones scattered everywhere.

January was just a month away and I needed to decide if I was going to join Yeva in Germany or not. There were so many considerations: the money, the value of the idea itself, and, of course, the worthiness of the person who had the idea. (No, not Yeva.)

Then fate intervened again. In early December, I got a phone call from a friend in Israel, an American expat, Evan Fallenberg. Evan was originally from Ohio, and currently a professor of English literature at Bar-Ilan University near Tel Aviv, as well as a translator of books from Hebrew to English, and a published novelist in his own right. He was also very successful on the artist residence circuit. He managed to spend time at some of the most prestigious and delicious writing colonies in the world. Once you're on that exclusive track, you could ride that gravy train for a long time. (Not that I begrudge him.)

Evan and I met by chance one evening when we were both attending *La Bohéme* at the Israel Opera. We sat next to each other in what were thankfully house seats. That was in 2014, when I was in Israel directing a play, just as my second marriage was ending. (I never dreamed I would speak of my second marriage in the past tense. We were extremely happy for the first few years and extremely unhappy for the last few. As it happened, he was a Jewish doctor, which would have finally brought some joy into my mother's life if she hadn't already been dead.)

It was just "one of those things" with Evan. We bonded instantly and easily, and have maintained a rich, intimate friendship. Just before we met, Evan had purchased and renovated an ancient building in Acre/Akko, a historic port city in northern Israel. He envisioned it as a unique boutique hotel, but more importantly, as a place that, if the finances were right, could be turned into artists' residencies for a few weeks a year. A way for him to give back, he said.

Evan was calling that December day to tell me that his hotel, Arabesque, had indeed been doing well enough to close down for two weeks, and he was planning his first artists' residency.

"So, are you working on anything?" he asked.

You've got to be kidding, I whispered to myself.

"What are the dates, Evan?" I asked softly.

"January 20th, 2018 until February 4th, 2018."

Yeva's availability to travel with me in Germany was from January 14th until January 18th. This would begin two days later.

The deal? All expenses paid except for the airfare. I just had to get myself to Israel.

Dearest Jesus, Moses, Allah, and Krishna, I thought, *what an antidote to whatever darkness I might find in Germany.* (I had no idea, in fact, what an enormous antidote I would need.)

"Thank you very much, Evan."

And that was it. My decision was made.

CHAPTER FIVE

Logistics
(Early December 2017)

I had a month to get it all together. I needed to book flights, hotels. How long would I stay where? When would I leave, when would I return? What did I need to bring/think/know before I left? It was a lot of heavy head-in-hand time for me. There was no playbook. There was no one in charge, no one paying the bills. (Well, yes, someone *was* paying the bills.)

Why was I doing any of this? Translating the nearly sixty letters, spending all this money? What in the world did I think I would accomplish by going to Germany?

It was all just instinct, the way I did almost everything. It didn't seem to interest Harry, whose history it actually was, nor did it interest my other half-brother Seymour, to whom all of the letters are co-addressed, as in *Dear Ruchale and Shamale*. (At the age of eight, when Shamale came to America, he was given what some assimilated Jews thought was a new sophisticated American name: Seymour.)

I had grown up with Seymour. He was there from the very beginning, *my* very beginning—literally, from the day I was born.

I never thought twice about whether or not he was my real brother. I didn't even think of it as a question to ask. He obviously was. No one said otherwise. Only later, when I learned that I had one half-brother, did I also understand that I had another half-brother, but on my mother's side.

Seymour/Shamale was born in Bilgoraj, Poland on 7 April 1941. If you do that math, you may wonder how in the world such a baby managed to live through the Holocaust and its aftermath. Not many children did.

Seymour is twelve years older than me and eighteen years younger than my mother. We both relied on him in more ways than he probably bargained for when my parents' marriage dissolved.

My mother's first marriage to someone named Zilberschmidt happened early in her life and did not last long. I once saw a photo of

Zilberschmidt, and Seymour looks exactly like him—tall and angular, no resemblance to me at all.

Seymour says Zilberschmidt abandoned them when he was just a baby, and he, Seymour, didn't want to ever know anything about him. As far as Seymour was concerned, he had no father. (Can a person decide that?)

In September of 1939, Germany and Russia, who were allies at the time, invaded Poland in what basically began World War II. They signed a non-aggression pact that would keep the peace while they divided up the spoils of Poland between themselves, with Germany getting all of western and central Poland, and Russia getting eastern Poland. Bilgoraj was on the border of eastern Poland.

As it turned out, the German/Russian non-aggression pact was merely a sneaky little trick by the Nazis (can you imagine?), who, according to secret documents (not anymore), had planned to break the pact with Russia as soon as it was convenient for them, which turned out to be two years later, in 1941, the year Shamale was born.

My mother didn't talk much about the war, but she did say that having first experienced the German invasion followed by the Russian occupation, she preferred the Russians, who were plenty vicious but not quite as calculating and brutal as the Germans. What a great choice: Hitler or Stalin. So, as Germany marched on Russia, and the Russians fled Poland, my mother and her family exited with the Russians to the East.

That meant that when Shamale was less than a year old, they—my mother (and possibly her husband); her parents, Leah and Isak Hoff; and her three younger brothers, Leibel, Henyu, and Moishale—went East. "East" meant Fergana, Uzbekistan, 420 kilometers southeast of the capital city, Tashkent, in the center of a triangle between Kyrgyzstan and Tajikistan in Central Asia. It was so far to the east, they were practically in China! From Poland to Uzbekistan? 4,700 kilometers or 2,920 miles. Like traveling from New York to California. Except in 1941. And during a world war. How? Too late to ask and no one left to answer. But they got there and fought like hell to stay alive.

Shamale spent the first four years of his life in Uzbekistan. All he remembers from that time is feeling hungry, and the smell of *shashlik*—grilled meat—wafting through the air. When the war ended, they got to Germany, somehow. Like wildebeests in Africa, they must have sensed that was where the food was, or maybe where other family, friends—somebody—might still be alive. They did not know it then, but most of their relatives were no more.

Ironically, according to the map, the most direct route to Ulm was not only through Poland but through their hometown of Bilgoraj. Did they dare to go back to their town? I wouldn't have thought so, but I learned recently that they did stop in Poland on their way to Germany. My mother, always thinking ahead, was trying to officially declare herself a widow. (In the Jewish religion, a woman who is abandoned by her husband can never remarry. She must provide proof that her spouse is deceased. The mass murders of the Holocaust made that impossible, so exceptions were made.)

That they made this arduous journey twice, once each way—more than 6,200 miles, or 10,000 kilometers, total—is astounding. And that was *after* the horrors and hardships of the war. What time of year, I wonder? There is no good time for such a trek, but based on Germany's surrender in May, I hope they traveled that summer or early fall.

For the next five years, from 1945–1949, my family would be in Ulm, Germany, in Donaubastion, the displaced persons camp. In 1949, they would get their visas and go to a different *shtetl*—Brooklyn, where I was born.

That was all I knew. Before.

Seymour currently lives in San Jose, California, with his first and only wife of over fifty years, Lorraine: American-born, tall, beautiful, a former elementary school teacher with excellent diction—which was very impressive and important to me at the time—as compared to my embarrassing family of greenhorns with their broken English and Yiddish accents. When I was a young girl, Lorraine's American accent and long straight blond hair were characteristics I could only dream about. They would remain out of my reach, although I did learn later that being blond was within everyone's reach—even mine.

In 1965, with Lorraine's urging, Seymour heeded the words of Horace Greeley and went West, 3000 miles—about as far west as you can go without swimming. Seymour had been the man of our family, and his absence was felt very deeply for the longest time. But I am often reminded that everything happens for the best (which I know is not always true, but it is sometimes).

When I told Seymour that I was trying to have the letters translated, he asked why.

"Don't you want to know?" I said. "You know, Seymour, the letters are actually addressed to you—to you and Mommy. In fact, they're *your* letters, not mine."

"Let me know if you find out anything interesting."

Okay.

So I was totally on my own. Neither of my half-brothers seemed to care one fig about this. And even my beloved John was distancing himself.

"No need to be in touch with me while you're away," he said. "This is your journey, and I don't want to be a distraction."

I should have understood what that meant at the time, but I missed it. I would understand soon enough. What a chicken-shit. (Him.) And what a fool. (Me.)

Then there was the elephant in the room—the letters. By this time, more than half of them had been translated, although not chronologically. The narratives were inconsistent and the letters varied in tone. Some sounded awkward and jagged; some had sections that made no sense. Others seemed angry; others casual. But all of them sounded desperate, filled with longing, pain, and anguish.

In a portion of the letter dated 24 August 1949, one month after my mother and Shamale had left for America, my father—not yet her husband—still in Stuttgart, waiting for his visa for England to retrieve his son before going to America, writes:

39

After the rain comes the sunshine. May we all do well, with God's help, and we won't be separated from anybody anymore, or from each other; we will simply live like human beings.

Unfortunately, there is something else I have to point out to you, my Ruchale, that you won't like; either you are not reading my letters correctly, or you are forgetting to answer them adequately when you write me back. I beg you, don't underestimate me, I beg you...

Also, you know my situation. Please write me whether I should sell everything or bring it along; even the earrings and so on.

Finally, I want to ask you, my loving Ruchale, not to get upset; everything will work out fine. I'm greeting you and kissing you a thousand times.

Your loving Chaskel Schlüsselberg

One of the many unfortunate things about these letters is that they only go one way, from my father to my mother. He did not have the luxury of saving them because his luggage would have been filled with life's necessities: items my mother had asked him to bring for their new life in the New World. Why she saved his letters for thirty-five years—including the twenty years after their divorce and then the ten years after his death—*and* never mentioned their existence to me or Seymour, is a mystery.

As their time apart grew longer, my father's letters became more skittish and insecure. From what he writes, it's very clear that her letters are not what he was hoping for; not frequent enough, not long enough, not loving enough. This one is translated by Knud from Colorado, dated 16 November 1949, a month later:

My beloved Ruchale and Shamale!

I'm coming with another letter today, although I see that you are not too fond of them anymore. You seem already have enough of my letters. You're barely home from work and already there is a letter waiting from me; some days heavy with information, some days light. One thing is for certain—one almost cannot call them love letters anymore. At most, it's a friendship without any footing, right? I, for my part, have always been proud of us and was longing for your letters, except for the past fourteen days, when the dark cloud descended on us. Why? Could you erase all the trust we have built over the years in one day? What happened to this sincere friendship? We never gave up; even when one of us thought it was over, it always turned out to be impossible to break up, and we always reached an agreement. One time I would take the blame, another time maybe even you would take the blame. Please think about this and let's fix it, and write me at your next opportunity. We can't do without our written communication. How happy we were to receive a letter not too long ago. There is a German proverb: "Better to have a louse in your salad than no meat at all."

"Better to have a louse in your salad than no meat at all!" Cynical *and* sarcastic? I always believed that my sharp tongue came from my mother. I was definitely not familiar with this side of my father.

What do we know about our own parents? Very little.

Until we do...

And even then, the gaps are enormous.

Still, I was not paying that much attention to the letters. Too much to do. I had to solve the logistical details of my trip—first collect the chicken bones and then figure out what to do with them.

I contact Frank's friend, Lutz, and tell him that I will indeed be going to Germany, and I remind him of his generous offer to connect me with some people there who he thought could be helpful. I didn't need to remind him. Lutz remembered and was happy and quick to help me. He cc'd me on emails, introducing me to a few people in Stuttgart and Ludwigsburg. His primary contact was with a fellow named Hans-Dieter Huober, who said I should call him "Hardy." I could only think of "Hardy Hands Huober," which made me laugh. I called him Hans.

Hans seemed very proud of his English. Years ago, he had worked in public relations for IBM in Texas. Now he was back in Ludwigsburg, where he was born. Hans asked me for my parents' names and

41

their birthdates and places of birth. He would see what he could find out in advance of my trip. I gave him the information he asked for, but I expected nothing from it.

He asked if there was anything else I might want to do in Stuttgart. I thought about it. Yes, what else might I want?

I had some photos of my father from before the war. They were studio shots, portraits of him rather smartly dressed. In an email, I asked Hans if he could introduce me to a costume designer, either from the theatre or film world. My work in the theatre taught me that costume designers did enormous amounts of research and are fastidious, curious, and insightful artists when designing clothes for characters. They know history, what kind of person would wear what type of clothing, and why. They know how clothes reflect class and character. I knew nothing about my father's pre-war life. I suspected that those photos could provide clues as to who he was as a young man, when life was perhaps more normal, before the unimaginable.

Other than that, I told Hans, I was putting myself in his hands and would be most appreciative for whatever he could put together for me.

It took only a few days before I received his email response. Hans had made some inquiries and had found some information about my father. He discovered sworn testimony that my father gave in 1947 to what he called "the Ministry of Justice" in Ludwigsburg. He would arrange a meeting for us with the head archivist, who would give me that actual document. Hans said there was also some information about my father in the Staatsarchiv (the state archive) in Ludwigsburg, and we had an appointment with that archivist to show me her findings.

To say that I am shocked is an understatement. I had expected nothing.

"Does that sound all right?" Hans asks in his letter. "Here are some other things I could arrange too," he says:

Would I like to visit the memorial for the transport victims of Stuttgart?

Would I like to speak to someone at the Jewish Community Center in Stuttgart who has some knowledge of the Jews before, during, and after the war?

Would I like to meet with the leading costume designer at the Theatre Haus in Stuttgart and show her my photos?

Would I like to meet the man responsible for another Holocaust memorial in Ludwigsburg called "Stumbling Stones?"

Would I like to have a classic Swabish dinner with him and his wife on one of my nights in Stuttgart? Did I only eat kosher? (No.)

Would I like to hear a Leonard Cohen cover band? (You can't make this stuff up.)

And finally, would I be willing to allow a reporter from the *Stuttgart Zeitung*, their daily newspaper, to join me on my journey? She had gotten wind of my visit and was writing an article for Holocaust Remembrance Day, which was coming up.

Holy cannoli. I gratefully—and quickly—agree to all of it, including the journalist. As a freelance theatre artist, I am always happy for publicity and attention, thinking it might lead to work, believing that there is no such thing as bad press. As usual, I didn't really think this through; what it would mean to have a reporter follow me around during this unknown and unknowable exploration. I definitely confused publicity with reporting. No, Virginia, they are not the same. Careful what you wish for.

Hans' agenda was more detailed and specific than anything I could have conjured up in my wildest dreams. My own imagination was limited to a childish kind of sense-memory experience: seeing the river and the church steeple in Ulm; getting a general feel for Stuttgart and maybe Ludwigsburg; seeing if my father's address in Stuttgart was still there. As they say on Passover, "*Dayenu*"—that would have been enough. This was so much more.

I thank Hans profusely and say yes to everything. I thanked him many more times over the course of the days, both before and after the trip. I also thanked Lutz and Yeva. It was staggering to me, the level and depth of interest and kindness that these strangers were offering me.

Now there was some kind of plan—a substantial plan, in fact. The knee bone was definitely connecting to the thighbone.

CHAPTER SIX

Decisions
(Late December 2017/Early January 2018)

How to book flights for such an unknown adventure? Yeva is sched-uled to leave me in Stuttgart on Wednesday, 18 January 2018. My residency in Israel miraculously begins three days later on Saturday, 21 January, and concludes two weeks after that. There are boatloads of choices to make about each leg of the trip. Decision-making is not my forte.

Yeva offers to advise me about hotels in Germany. She will be staying in the room with me, and she knows it's all coming out of my pocket, so she is being financially considerate, a.k.a. cheap. The hotels she recommends are one step above youth hostels. The plus side of getting older is that I absolutely know that even though this will save me money, it will also make me miserable. Although I appreciate her input, I go on my own exhaustive search, reading and rereading hotel reviews. Choosing makes me anxious. Often, simple decisions have the weight of life-and-death to me. I believe this is Holocaust related; any small choice or decision could be arbitrarily life-saving or life-ending.

For the Ulm portion of the trip, the decision is relatively easy. Ulm is a small town, and, thankfully, there are not many choices. I pick a clean, modern hotel, right in the middle of the town, near the church.

Booking the hotel in Stuttgart, however, is a different matter. It is a major city, and I get overwhelmed in my search. Too many options. In an email, I appeal to Hans for suggestions and he recommends a few places. They are not cheap, but they are not exorbitant either and I find a decent deal on a hotel within walking distance of the Hauptbahnhof, which I can recognize from my Yiddish as the "major train station." This hotel also has bathtubs, which I know will be a sweet comfort to me in January.

Okay, logistics are done and a kind of plan is in place. I feel enormous relief and can now stop thinking about all of that.

Last Licks

The days fly by. Thanksgiving, Christmas—I mean, Chanukah—and New Year's. How can I be as ready for this trip as possible? What can I do during these last few weeks to prepare myself for the unknown? Is there anyone I should speak to before I leave?

I think about it. The answer is definitely yes.

Seymour

I decide to speak to my brother Seymour again. He is going to be seventy-seven this year. If I don't ask him now.... And after all, he *was* there, even though he was only five years old when they got to Ulm, and eight in 1949 when the letters began, when he and my mother left for America. Maybe he remembers something, some small details.

I phone him.

"Hey, Seymour. You know I'm going to Germany—to Ulm and Stuttgart—and I was wondering if you could think about it and maybe tell me things you remember."

"Sure. What do you want to know?"

"Whatever you remember about that time. About coming to America, about being in Ulm. About my father. About Stuttgart. Do you have any memory of Mommy getting letters from my father?"

"No, I have no memory of letters. I can tell you that when we got to Brooklyn, we lived with Uncle Charles for about a year." (Charles Hoff, my grandfather's older brother.) "We went straight to his house from the boat. I definitely remember the boat to America. I loved that boat. Everyone else was sick but me."

To this day, one of Seymour's greatest pleasures is being on the water, fishing. All kinds of fishing, especially deep sea fishing. No matter how rough the seas, he is always the one who never gets sick.

"Anything about Ulm?" I ask.

"Ulm? Well, in Donaubastion, we all lived in one room—me, Mommy, Leibel, Henyu, and Baba and Zeyde." Leibel and Henyu were two of my mother's three younger brothers.

Baba and *zeyde* are Yiddish for "grandmother" and "grandfather." They were my mother's parents, Isak and Leah Hoff—my only grandparents who were not killed during wartime. They had four children, my mother being the oldest, followed by three boys. My mother's youngest brother, Moishale, who fled with them from Poland in 1941, died in Uzbekistan. I remember a photo of him, now long gone. I never knew the circumstances of his death, only that he died as a young boy. Baba would weep for him each holiday and over candle-lighting on the Sabbath. In one of the many upcoming surprises of this journey, I would learn more about my deceased young Uncle Moishale.

Seymour goes on:

"Baba and Zeyde, I remember, had a curtain in that one room that hid their bed—for some privacy. Uncle Henyu, who was seven years younger than Mommy, was a teenager then and was my playmate. There was a community-like kitchen where all the families of the camp cooked. I went to Jewish school there, a *kheyder*. We had to wear a uniform, a kind of military-style outfit. I still have my report cards somewhere."

"Really?"

"Yeah, I have them somewhere. If you're interested, I'll look for them."

"Yes, please."

"I remember there was a fence around the camp, with openings that we could sneak through, and we used to play in the bombed-out buildings all around. Also, down by the river. You know, I almost drowned in that river, the Danube."

No, I didn't know. I also didn't know that the river in all of the photos was the Danube. I didn't know anything, and what's worse is that *I didn't know* that I didn't know anything. All this time, I thought that I knew enough. (Isn't that how it is with people who don't know anything? It's the people who do know something who know that they still know nothing.)

"Anything about my father?" I ask.

"Well, he lived in Stuttgart, which was about an hour or so away by train. He had a motorcycle with a—what do you call it—a sidecar. Yeah. He would let me ride in that. It was a lot of fun. I remember he was religious and active in the *shul* there, and I would spend *Shabbes* with him in his apartment in Stuttgart. I remember we would sleep together in one bed—me, your father, and Uncle Hershel."

Hershel was my grandmother's brother. My parents were related, so not only was Hershel the uncle of my mother, but he was also the first cousin of my father. Complicated.

Hershel made it to the United States, and I knew him when I was a little girl. He and his "wife" Peppi had a chicken farm in Millville, New Jersey. After my parents' divorce, we visited there yearly—my mother, grandparents, and Uncle Henyu, still a bachelor and the only family member with a car at the time. I say "wife" because it's hard to believe they were married. Hershel was a short shy little fellow with a soft melancholy face and a kind heart, while Peppi was an Austrian Jewess: tall, exotic, elegantly dressed—even on their chicken farm—smoking Pall Malls out of a tortoise shell cigarette holder, with polished red fingernails, and rhinestone glasses. She was a brunette version of Eva Gabor in that TV show, *Green Acres*. She definitely didn't belong on that farm. She had a son, Julius, who, I understood from overhearing family talk, was not Hershel's. They also had a big friendly dopey dog, Butchy, even though my mother said Jews don't have dogs. (She never did say why.) We'd bring him presents—huge cow bones from Zeyde's butcher shop to gnaw on. Butchy and the chickens made those visits to Hershel a lot of fun for me, even though it was a long trek to go there and back in a day.

Recently, I learned that the Jewish Agricultural Society (who knew there was such an organization?), as well as the Hebrew Immigrant Aid Society (HIAS)—the same group that oversaw the disastrous meeting between my father and Harry in 1949—gave many Jewish refugees and former displaced persons an opportunity to go into business for themselves by owning chicken farms in New Jersey. It seemed weird to me at first, but in retrospect, what a blessing: providing food, income, and country living to those who had been starved and forced into work prisons and concentration camps. It spared them the drudgery of oppressive factory sweatshop life, which was what my parents experienced.

"You know, speaking of Hershel," Seymour continues, "at that time, no one knew yet if he was dead or alive. Everyone had been separated during the war. I remember this: during one of the first Passover Seders that we had while we were at Donaubastion, in the part of the Haggadah where you are supposed to open the door to welcome the prophet *Eliahu* [Elijah], they sent me to open the door, and when I did, Hershel was standing there! Standing there at the door! Oh my God, you can't imagine. The crying, the hugging." He pauses. "Yes, I definitely remember that."

Then Seymour says, "I'm sorry. I don't remember much more. I think if things didn't involve me directly, I didn't really pay attention to what was going on around me."

Sometimes Seymour surprises me. He is more self-aware than I give him credit for.

We spoke a little more, and then I asked about his birth father, Zilberschmidt. (No one, including my brother, is certain of his first name.) Seymour has carried a hatred of him his whole life. He would not and did not forgive him for abandoning them. Perhaps he simply could not.

"What actually happened to him, Seymour? Do you know?"

"I remember when I was little, I'm not sure if we were in Uzbekistan or Ulm," he said. "I asked Mommy where he was, I was crying because I missed him. I remember soon after that, he showed up and took me to spend a day or two. But he was with some woman—his girlfriend, I think. I couldn't be with him anymore and wanted to go back to Mommy. I never saw him again. To me, he was dead."

"Did you ever learn what happened to him?"

"I found out later that he managed to get to Israel, and I guess he died there. Who knows, I could have half-brothers and sisters."

"Don't you want to know?"

"No."

I am sad for him sometimes, my brother. I believe there is much unexamined in his heart and soul; the many ways that this nightmare affected him. He lived through so much as a young boy—such darkness and fear, hunger and cold and loss. The complete opposite of a safe, sated childhood. Maybe it hurts too much to shine a light on those black days. Maybe once you give them currency, they will never leave you. Maybe it was enough just to manage to live through them. To him and Harry both, I need to be more forgiving.

"Hey, Seymour, you know, all of these letters, fifty-six of them, they are all addressed to Mommy and to you. They are yours, Seymour."

"Yeah, ok. Let me know if you find anything interesting in them," he says again.

"Okay. Thanks, Seymour. Thanks for helping me."

Yes, I have to be more forgiving...

Sam Norich

I think: *Who else? Who else should I talk to before I go?*

I remember that Sam Norich—a friend, Yiddishist, and former publisher of *The Forward* newspaper—was born in a displaced persons camp. He is a man who shoulders a wealth of facts, as well as memory and heart. I drop him an email explaining my trip and invite him to lunch or dinner.

It takes us a few tries, but finally we will meet at that hip yet expensive (I learn later) bar/restaurant/coffee house in the Village, Joseph Leonard. It's way too cool to be cheap. The hour of our meeting is neither lunchtime nor dinnertime, but four in the afternoon, a few days shy of Christmas.

He orders a scotch and I get a glass of red wine even though I am not really drinking these days.

"What do you want to know?" Sam asks.

At that moment, I realize I have no idea what I want to know. I realize that yet again, I am just flying by the seat of my pants. I don't even know where to begin. Fortunately for me, Sam can begin all by himself. I take notes.

"At the end of the war, ninety thousand inmates were found barely alive in the camps," Sam says, "all in severe stages of starvation, which was called 'the hunger disease.' Prolonged starvation causes profound physiological changes. Those wracked bodies could not digest easily, especially the fatty foods that they were given after the war. Within three weeks of liberation, thirty thousand survivors were dead from overeating.

There were about ten million refugees after the war, Jewish and Gentile. People didn't know where to go. Refugees were pouring into Germany from all over Europe because that's where the American, British, and French were. Their saviors. Displaced persons camps were meant to be temporary. There, the refugees hoped they would find food and protection. The Allies believed that the refugees, after recovering briefly in these camps, would return to their homes in their countries of origin. Well, that's not exactly what happened. The Gentiles did go back to their homes. But the Jews, about a million of them, did not. Their homes were either destroyed or were now occupied by their Christian neighbors. Their towns were indelibly associated with the murders of family and friends, with lives that were obliterated—often with the deadly collaborations of their very own neighbors."

He pauses.

"What else do you want to know?" he asks.

I just look at him. I apologize for my lack of preparation. I tell Sam that I don't know what to ask him and would he be kind enough to free-associate for me. I tell him that I know no facts, no history. What little I do know, I learned from my own eyes and ears, overhearing family conversations or looking at photos. Up until then, I had been a believer in Holocaust osmosis.

Luckily for me, Sam had plenty to say.

"There was a Jewish organization called *Bricha* that was trying to get Jews out of Europe and into Israel, which at that time was illegal. They created underground railroads, bribed officials, and counted on the kind hearts of many American Army personnel, who would look the other way, defying orders and allowing Jews to do what they needed to. Then, in June of 1946, Stalin allowed the Poles—Jewish and Gentile—out of the Soviet Union. Many of them tried going home, back to Poland. Three weeks later, the Kielce pogrom."

I am listening to Sam, writing feverishly. I am amazed by his ability to rattle off dates and make chronological sense out of the insanity and chaos of seventy years ago. I never for a moment imagine that after my upcoming trip, I too would be able to rattle off dates and make some kind of sense out of that senselessness.

I had heard of the Kielce pogrom but, once again, had only a vague, uninformed notion of it. What I learned from Sam that afternoon was that on the fourth of July in 1946, the Poles (Gentiles) in the town of Kielce attacked the housing facility where the Jews (Poles), who had returned to their *own* town, were being temporarily housed. Using the false yet historically common pretext of Jews kidnapping Christian children, the townspeople (neighbors), aided by the police (Poles), murdered more than forty-six Jews. This event had the distinction of being the deadliest pogrom against Jews since the end of the Second World War. This was a major catalyst for the Jewish flight from Poland. (Later that day, when I get home, I look up the Kielce pogrom on Wikipedia. It asks me *which* of the pogroms I want information about: the pogrom of 1918 or the pogrom of 1946.)

The clarity of Sam's knowledge flows freely. He continues. "By the summer of '48, the population in the DP camps grows to two hundred and fifty thousand. Former army bases, ancient fortresses, or bastions are enlisted to house these huddled masses. All of the refugees in the camps were on ice, waiting to get out. Look, no one survived the war in order to find themselves back in a camp again."

There is a short pause. Sam was born in the DP camp, Feldafing, not far from Ulm, where my mother and her family were housed.

"Here's a unique fact," Sam continues, as though every word he has uttered up until now had not been a unique fact. "In 1946 and 1947, the birth rate in the DP camps was the highest of anywhere in the world. Why? Because practically *every person* in those camps was of child-bearing age. Think about it," he says. "Of course, there were exceptions, but—of all of the refugees, the only ones who could have survived the deadly conditions of the Holocaust would be neither too old nor too young. They would mostly range in age from their late teens to their late forties. Child-bearing age. Those were the only people who would have had the unimaginable strength to possibly survive the war."

This had never occurred to me before, but now that he says it—well, yes, of course, it must have been so. The children were murdered outright or slowly starved to death since they could provide no labor for the Nazis. And the same was true for those who were in their fifties or sixties—the age that I am now. Too old. Useless as workers/slaves, and therefore, killed.

"There was," he continues, "a famous story that I remember my father told me about a woman who had a baby in a DP camp late in '45. So soon after the war. Think about it. This was like a miracle. Birth was possible after all the death. This was proof; a testament to the determination and will to survive. New residents were taken to see that woman and her baby. She was an inspiration. See? Life was an option."

There was much more he talked about: other organizations that had helped the refugees—especially the Joint (the American Jewish Joint Distribution Committee)—and the brave, singular humans who put themselves and their lives on the line for these exiles. We sat there for more than two hours. Eventually, even Sam ran out of steam. He had to go.

I was ashamed of my inexcusable ignorance. I asked him if there was anything I should read or do before I left for Germany. He said the best book on this subject was *The Saving Remnant* by Herbert Agar. If I couldn't find it, he said, he would give me his copy.

He stood up to leave. I told him I would stay a bit longer, just to finish up my notes. I thanked him profusely. We hugged, and he wished me safety and good health on my upcoming journey. I promised him a lunch or dinner when I returned. I sat in the restaurant a while longer, pained by the enormity of my stupidity and the specificity of the horror.

I now believe that I didn't know anything because I didn't *want* to know anything. I instinctively understood that it would be too much for me to bear, too much for me to incorporate those nightmarish details into my own daily life. The vein was too deep. How can you go on when you know all that?

When I got home, I looked for *The Surviving Remnant* and found it on Amazon. It would become my bible during the three weeks of my trip.

CHAPTER SEVEN

My Itinerary: One Week Before My Trip
(7 January 2018)

I receive an email from Hans:

Dear Eleanor,

In contrast to New York, we have spring temperature in the southern part of Germany at this time—of course, that's not usual and could be it will change when you will arrive in Munich at 13 January.

We understand you will have your own plan from 13 January until 15 January.

We will focus on your activities after that and assist you in Stuttgart and Ludwigsburg. Please let me know if the dates are o.k. to make sure that we have planned our time correctly.

His next email contained the exact plan:

Dear Eleanor,

These are only suggestions and feel free to change or add—whatever you like.

We would like to suggest you the following agenda:

Wednesday, 17 January
  Morning:
  9:30—Visit to the Jewish Community Center, Stuttgart, Hospitalstraße 36

Afternoon:

14:30—Visit to the Zentrale Stelle zur Verfolgung von NS Verbrechen, Ludwigsburg. There we meet with Dr. Gohle, Public Prosecutor Office For NS Cases. [*NS is the abbreviation for Nazi/National Socialism]

They have testimony from your father.

Evening:

Dinner and Meeting with Gudrun Schretzmeier: Stage & Costumes Designer at Theatre Haus, Stuttgart. She is a leading German costume designer working for TV, film, and theatre, and lives in Stuttgart.

Please bring your photos.

Thursday, 18 January

Morning:

9:30—Visit of the Staatsarchiv Ludwigsburg with Elke Martin, archivist.

They have records about your father.

Afternoon:

14:30—Meeting with Jochen Faber, the creator of the Holocaust memorial Stolpersteine Ludwigsburg at the Synagogen Place, Ludwigsburg.

"Stolpersteine" means "pitfalls" and are special stones on the ground or walls in the city with names of murdered Jews which lived there.

Later: Visit to another memorial for the transport victims from Stuttgart at the Transport Station.

Evening:

Traditional Swabian Dinner

Also—Special question:

Do you like Leonard Cohen? If yes: friends of us have a band called "The Leonard Cohen Project" and would like to meet you too.

Let me know if this agenda is o.k. for you, and feel free for any additional suggestions. We are all looking forward to meet you. Have a good and safe trip to Stuttgart,

Warm regards, Hardy

Well, now *that's* a plan! Light years beyond my own tiny imagination.

I write him back. I tell him that his plan looks incredible. I tell him that I am not religious and that I eat everything. And yes, I do like Leonard Cohen.

And from now on, I call him Hardy.

Time to Leave

What to bring on such a trip? I decide to travel with carry-on luggage only. (Really? For three weeks?) I tell myself that I want to do as little *schlepping* as possible. I remind myself over and over that people do wash clothes in their hotel rooms, plus I usually wear the same *shmatas* every day anyway.

Please let me pack light, I say to myself as though there are two of us traveling.

But I don't.

In my defense, I am going to two different continents with entirely different climates. Still, there must be some way to do it, I tell myself. What's the word I'm looking for? Oh yeah, layering.

I also need to think about what to bring document-wise. The letters? Goodness gracious, the letters alone; there are fifty-six of them. Plus they exist in three forms: as Xeroxed copies of the original longhand German letters, as the more legible typed letters in German, and as the translations in English. Do I bring all of them? If so, that's over a hundred and fifty pages of paper.

I try to remind myself of the point of this trip. Why in the world am I going? Another un-researched science project?

I stop and think.

What are you doing, Eleanor?

Here's what I come up with, time and time again: My parents have been dead for more than half of my life, more than thirty-five years. That's a long time to be without parents, without people who know you and know where you come from. And without the unconditional love that only they could give. I miss them. I want to see them, be with them. That's why I'm going. I'm going to be where they were, where they lived, worked, made love. Where they walked and wept and starved and froze. Maybe somehow, I will see them, meet them there; find clues, even after sixty-five years. Maybe…

These letters are my treasure map. The "X" must mark the spot to somewhere, no? My mother kept these fifty-six letters written by my father for over forty years for some damn reason, no? After their divorce. After his death. Why? What did they mean? What was in them that was worth saving? And like her, I kept them too—for more than twenty years, untranslated, just lying in their baggie in my sloppy underwear drawer. For what? What should I do with them, with my inheritance? Nothing?

No. These letters are a message to me from beyond. From my father who wrote them and from my mother who kept them and now for me, who will follow them.

I tell stories for a living, as an actress, writer, singer, director. That's what I have spent my life doing—albeit in my own helter-skelter fashion. My work is an enormous part of who I am. And I am my parents' daughter. So, if I don't find out who they are/were, how the hell will I know who I am? I'm going to pull on this thread for as long as it's got give and see where it takes me. My own DNA strand.

I identify—and always have—as the daughter of Holocaust survivors. That is my gender. My invisible birthmark. This trip is about not letting the dead go gentle into that good night; about giving voice and life to those people, my parents, who had neither a voice nor a life, yet lived on this Earth during such a dark deadly time, and struggled and cobbled together a daughter, like a dinosaur made of chicken bones, whose own story and life is inexorably bound up in theirs. And theirs is still so unknown.

Sometimes I wish I could forget about the Holocaust and just move on, like everyone else. But I cannot. It's attached to me like my skin, and I would be formless without it. I am glued to the dark truth about the world that I cannot escape—its humanity as well as its cruelest inhumanity.

Carry-on luggage? Forget it.

I decide to bring all of the letters in all of their various forms. Just in case. (The same reason my closet is filled with clothes that I haven't worn in years.) Just in case someone somewhere might want to see them, either in German or English or whatever. I will certainly want to work with them in Israel. I imagine my room at the residency in Acre. I imagine taping all the letters up on the wall so that I am surrounded by them—like laundry, like a cave of hieroglyphics, like a whiteboard at a crime scene—so that I can go from letter to letter, look at them, touch them, see them all separately and yet together, surrounded by the greater story. I imagine a play, a story told in the only way I know how—theatrically.

That's my plan—a project, a play called *The Letters*. I imagine it with three characters: A Him, a Her, and a Me. That's what I'm thinking.

Chicken bones, anyone?

I also want to bring some of the photos from that period, pictures that I've been staring at my whole life. There are maybe twenty, mostly black and white, some sepia. Some of my father from before the war, some of my mother before the war, separately and together. Other photos from after the war. A few of them have Yiddish or Polish or German writing on the back, identifying the people, some with a date and place. I have lugged these photos around, from apartment to apartment, from husband to husband, year after year. Now I will finally bring them home, to where they were created, where the moments were captured. I want to find the exact places where the pictures were taken. That's one of the few things I know with certainty that I'd like to accomplish.

I will bring that book with me too, the one Sam Norich recommended, *The Saving Remnant*. I have begun reading it, and it is a direct, unsentimental, passionate account of what happened to the nation of Jews, mostly after the war. I am not usually a reader of nonfiction, but this is different, even though is filled with information I always thought unnecessary to concern myself with—you know, facts. But the book grabs me right away on the very first page, in its introduction:

In Warsaw, on 16 October 1940, a decree establishing the Ghetto was placarded in German and Yiddish. This had long been feared and predicted by a few; but most people are able to believe that the worst things in the world will not happen, at least not to them.

Yes. That is the truth, even today. We are no different. The worst will not happen—at least not to us.

Until it does.

One morning, while still in New York, eating a lush, privileged breakfast of three-grain toast, organic eggs, and freshly ground coffee, I'm reading about what was happening in Warsaw in 1942. While the ghetto was being starved to death, the Jewish doctors in the ghetto—who were also being starved to death—used their fleeting time to do a scientific study on death and starvation. They were scientists after all, and that is what scientists do. Work with what you've got, they decided. (*Yes,* I thought, *me, too.*)

Agar writes about their study which they called "*non omnis moriar,*" meaning "not everyone dies." I stop. "Not everyone dies." Those were words of optimism in the ghetto. Not *everyone* will die. And so it was—not everyone would die, which is the basis of *The Saving Remnant.* I realize that I am a by-product of that study. I am alive precisely because *non omnis moriar*—not everyone died.

I decide to also pack a few copies of my own book, an anthology of my plays *The Last Survivor and Other Modern Jewish Plays* as perhaps gifts or whatever. The book contains five plays that I wrote about my family and myself over the past twenty years. Last year, when I was organizing the plays for the anthology, it was the first time I had seen them all together as a single body of work. I recognized then that each of my plays ended in the same way—the dead would somehow come back to life and make the family whole again. That was what I unconsciously yearned for. Always. Still. My version of Monet's lilies, painted over and over again.

I will also bring some of my musical CDs, some with Frank London, some with other musicians. It's never the wrong time to do business. Is it? A constant dilemma for me: When is it too much, when is it time to stop selling, stop attempting to advance myself—I mean, my work. I tell myself that bringing Yiddish to Germany is more than just promoting myself. And besides, CDs weigh hardly anything. And if not me, who?

Okay. I'm packed.

Carry-on? What a joke. Even my checked luggage is bursting and will surely be overweight. And I can barely zip up the former carry-on little wheelie bag. Plus there's a backpack? Damn. I pack and repack and find nothing more to remove. Clothes for the frigid winters of Germany and for the balmy days of Israel. Layers? Yeah, fuck layers.

Everything seems to be in place. Finally.

John, my equivocal boyfriend, has decided not to drive me to the airport, a decision that I'm secretly relieved about, as I don't really want to deal with that or him on this last day. Nonetheless, of course, it hurts my feelings. It's another sign of his one-foot-in/one-foot-out relationship with me. But that's not for now.

I water my roommates—two orchids—lock up my sweet apartment, and whistle for a yellow cab, which I prefer to Uber or a car service. Those yellow cab drivers are hard-working immigrant guys whose work has been whittled down by all these new phone-app alternatives. Also, my Uncle Henyu, my mother's brother, was a Yellow cabbie.

My whistle hails a cab driven by a man from Ghana. He's in a talkative mood, which surprisingly I don't mind today. He preaches about not getting upset by the little things, about trusting his path even though he doesn't know where it will lead. He makes me feel like I am in the right place at the right time. I feel optimistic and positive. The beginning of a real adventure.

"*Good for you, Eleanor,*" I say to myself.

CHAPTER EIGHT

Departure: New York City to Germany
(13 January 2018)

The first letter from my father to my mother was dated 24 July 1949. The last letter was dated 12 January 1950. It was his last letter because on the following day, the thirteenth, he was scheduled to leave for America.

Today, sixty-eight years later, I leave for Germany.

His last letter was not on his usual business stationery but on one of those airmail all-in-one, self-folding, thin, sky-blue *par avion* papers; the kind where you write on the inside, fold it up, and it becomes its own envelope. I don't know if they exist anymore. That airmail paper was a delicate and exotic symbol of the effort to connect in this vast world. At that time, "the other side of the world" really felt like it was on the other side.

In this last letter, my father notes his whereabouts. No longer in Stuttgart, he is now in Bremerhaven, the German port city, anxiously awaiting passage on the ship that would carry him to Brooklyn; to his beloved and to his new life, filled with fear and dread and hope and possibility. In that very last letter, my father, for the first and only time in any of his previous fifty-five letters, mentions Auschwitz. He describes one tiny detail of his life there.

People often ask me if my father spoke much about the Holocaust and his time in Auschwitz. He never said anything about it except for three seemingly small details that he did share with me: that he slept on his shoes so that no one would steal them, that someone once gave him extra bread through a fence, and that he cut hair in Auschwitz. Nothing more. No other details—oh, except once when I was visiting him in the nursing home and trying to get him to cut down on his cigarette smoking, I brought him a brand of cigarettes called True Blue, which, in those days, was advertised as a "healthy" cigarette because it had a kind of recessed filter. One of my father's very few pleasures, when I knew him, was smoking cigarettes. But as a watchful daughter, I did my best to limit his cigarette intake (even though I, too, was a smoker at that time!). I doled them out parsimoniously when I visited. He waited hungrily for those visits when he could smoke, when I would finally acquiesce and deign to give him a cigarette. I did not understand the risk/reward aspect of those smokes then, that this unhealthy treat was worth any amount of damage it might cause him. I did not understand how entitled he was to have whatever the hell he wanted. Yes, I regret that.

Anyway, on that day, my father took a puff of that True Blue. And then another. He inhaled that cigarette with all his might, nearly sucking the whole thing down his throat. Then he looked at me with such disgust—bordering on hatred—and said, "In Auschwitz, I smoked dirt rolled in newspaper and it tasted better than this. Tomorrow, you better bring me a real cigarette."

And that was it. That was all he ever said to me about Auschwitz. In part of his last letter, he writes:

You know very well, my dear Ruchale, how life was for me in the camp. I slept in the second row on top. One morning, I wanted to step down, and I put my feet onto a broken little step, so that it fell over and onto my foot, and I was a little injured by this accident.

I read that sentence several times: "*I slept in the second row on top.*" Over the years, like everyone else, I've examined those photographs in magazines, books, and archives of the starving skeleton men in the striped pajamas, staring with their sunken eyes and hollow cheeks from the overcrowded wooden shelves where they allegedly slept, like inventory in a warehouse. Did I ever think of my father on one of those shelves, as one of those huddled, starving, frozen men? Yes, I did. It was unimaginable and yet I tried to imagine it. For as long as I can remember. Peering into the faces of each of those men, searching for my father's face, which I never found. At some point, I stopped looking for him, as if perhaps he wasn't really there. But now, I know. Now, I will always see him. My starving bag of skin-and-bones, head-shaved, lice-infested father—who would somehow live long enough to give me life—was in *the second row on top.*

I get to Kennedy Airport early. In my dotage, I have given up rushing. I go to the airline desk for my boarding pass and to check my luggage. As suspected, my check-in suitcase is overweight—by a lot. The airline attendant wants to weigh my carry-on bag as well. And she does. "Too heavy to carry-on," she says. I am about to argue but then decide against it. Screw it. My mighty attempts to underpack are for naught. The attendant checks *both* of my bags, *plus* charges me the additional fee! I concede. It's a good thing, I decide: one less bag for me to *schlep.*

Two hours later, I get on the plane to Munich, take my window seat, swallow a half of a Klonopin, and hope for a few hours of sleep.

Sixty-eight years ago, my father left for the New World. Today, I leave for the Old World. He was trying to move forward and forget the past, and I am traveling backward to find the past. I have my own date with destiny. For me, as for him, the journey holds some small hope of reunification—to be with my parents and my family again, whom I have not seen for such a long time.

CHAPTER NINE

Germany: Munich to Ulm
(Sunday, 14 January 2018)

I had been to Munich once before, decades ago in the 1980s, as a performer in a Yiddish play at a Jewish theatre festival there. That experience was an uncomfortable one for me. The city was Aryan—all white and mostly blond. Since it was only thirty years after the war, I looked at every middle-aged and older person with mistrust. *Were they now or had they ever been…?* I wondered. It was wrong to assume anything, but still I imagined. They were decidedly members of the suspiciously complicit generation.

To add insult to injury, the city itself is a mere twenty-minute ride by commuter train to the concentration camp—and city—Dachau, which I managed to visit then. That day, thirty years ago, like this day in 2018, was bitter cold and especially bleak. At that time, I went to Dachau with another Jewish performer, Rosalie Gerut, whose mother was also a slave in Auschwitz. Getting off the train at a station called "Dachau" felt surreal and impossible and too close to the bone for both of us.

It was a short walk to the camp.

We went, we saw, we wept, we were enraged, and we left.

After that, I decided I had no further need or obligation to go to any other concentration camp. Ever. Having a father who lived through that horror gave me the right to use my

Get-Out-Of-Concentration-Camp-Free card. I liked to tell people, when they would ask if I'd ever been to Auschwitz or some other camp, that "I gave at the office." A few people understood what I meant, but most had no idea of what the heck I was talking about. I felt like I was entitled to make humorous, contemptuous, inappropriate cracks about Auschwitz and the Holocaust. That was *my* version of entitlement.

I don't speak about it so recklessly or sarcastically anymore. (Only sometimes.) Our world has come precariously close to repeating those cruelties, and so I have become more careful with my speech.

At the Munich airport on this Sunday in 2018, I collected my checked bags and found the train that would take me directly to Ulm, where Yeva would meet me that evening.

Ulm

Ulm was where the DP camp was located that my family lived in from 1945–1949, and where my parents met. That's all I had on Ulm. Oh— and that Einstein was born there.

I arrived in Ulm at around 2 p.m. The town was awash in construction: road barriers, earth-movers, and steel cranes everywhere. The GPS on my iPhone 5 seemed confused and kept changing its mind about which way I should go. Maybe it was time for that upgrade. Or maybe it was me. I only slept three hours, and that was thanks to a sleeping pill. I was the poster child for groggy, harried, and disoriented. Plus, I had the overstuffed backpack and my two suitcases, one of them very large, and both of them very heavy. Yes, they did roll, but on the cobblestone streets of this old city, the wheels were merely one of God's spiteful jokes. "Hahaha," said God.

I managed to get to a central square but couldn't figure out the way to the hotel. Hardly anyone was in the streets since it was freezing, and it was Sunday. After an hour of dragging my luggage in circles, I looked up and saw a small sign for the hotel, easy to miss.

I went up to the room. It was clean and minimalist; modern yet homey enough. I was plenty relieved. Yeva would be arriving on her train from Berlin at about 6 p.m., in time for dinner. I decide to head out and have a look around.

The receptionist, who is not German (I'm just saying), is helpful and offers me the one-page map of Ulm. Easily, I find a wide street that leads to a modern bridge that spans the river. It's the Danube! Not exactly blue but close enough.

I walk onto the bridge and stop midway, watching the rushing waters, looking up and down the river, trying to get my bearings. There is another bridge farther upstream, older, clearly from another time. In my head, I try to conjure up those photos I'd seen so many times of my mother and father romancing on the banks of this river with the church steeple in the background. Where was that spot? Where am I in relation to that?

I continue walking across the bridge. According to the map, I am now standing in Neu-Ulm (New Ulm). I find a paved walking path along that side of the river. Young couples bundled up pushing their baby carriages, runners jogging, smartly dressed older people in

overcoats and fedoras. Like Sondheim's *Sunday in the Park with George*, but with Eleanor—and in Germany.

Me? I am wearing my nondescript infamously unfashionable winter layers, including a hoodie and an old down jacket. Who in this picture does not belong?

I look across the Danube and see the old town; that spire of the Münster rising up high in the sky, just like in the photos. I hear ducks quacking and see them paddling upstream like mad, furiously fighting the fierce current just to stay in place. I remember Seymour telling me that he had almost drowned here, and I see now that he wasn't being hyperbolic. That river is strong and moves fast. I picture him, my skinny little seven-year-old brother, scared to death that he was going to die by water.

I record my thoughts on my iPhone Memo app:

At the Danube—the Donau, as it's called here. This current is moving fa-a-a-ast. I imagine I see the spot where my parents took those photos, but now ducks and their partners are romancing in their stead. Unlike people, ducks mate for life.

What did I think I was going to find here? What did I want? To re-create the past? To see it for myself? *Okay, Eleanor, well now you see it for yourself.* "And what do you see for yourself?" I ask myself out loud, as though I am playing that children's game, "I spy with my little eye." My response? "I see a German town seventy years after the war and everyone who lived here is dead." Tears start sliding down my face and drying icily on my cheeks. This trip has officially begun.

I continue walking upstream, towards the older bridge in the distance. I recall one of Einstein's theories, something about time flowing like a river, and if you want to return to the past and go back in time, all you have to do is walk upstream to where the past still exists. That's what I want to do. I want to lift up that shroud covering the past and shine a light into the crypt where my family is still alive. I want to see them again. More than anything in the world. That is what I am looking for here. Them.

Well, if that is what's true, this trip will be an abject failure. I am not a fool. I understand that they are dead and that I will not find them here—or anywhere else.

I look across the river. Every few steps, I examine a new angle, looking for the spot where my mother and father and Uncle Hershel took those photos. *Is it here? Or here?* No, I have not found that exact spot. *Is that so important, Eleanor?* I keep walking, talking to myself out loud, encouraging myself, trying to pour kindness and love into myself, reminding myself to be patient and quiet; that I need only to be open-hearted and walk gently. There is no agenda; no goal, except to take this journey.

I reach the older bridge and walk back across the river into Ulm. I find a path into the town. It is pretty darn quaint. Crooked houses, centuries old, with exposed wooden beams that could not hold a plumb line even close to straight. Time has shifted their center, but still, they seem sturdy.

By now, I am colder and hungrier. I pass a pub that advertises pancake-like dishes, similar to Ethiopian food, with soft flatbread lining the plates that hold the curry or goulash or whatever. I go inside.

It looks warm and inviting, but it is not. I mean, the room temperature is warm, but not one face greets me with any kind of curiosity or smile or acknowledgement. I decide I will wait for Yeva, and I head back to the hotel.

The minute I get into the room, I receive a text from Yeva that her trains are all mismatched, and she will arrive closer to 9 p.m. Okay. I put my coat back on and try to find that pub again. I had my culinary heart set on that place, but now it's getting dark and I can't seem to find my way. The town is so small, I thought it would have been simpler.

After what feels like too long, I find it. I sit alone at the bar. A bunch of other patrons sit at surrounding tables. The barmaid doesn't pay the slightest attention to me until finally, she does. Not friendly at all. Barely polite, in fact.

The menu has pictures because Ulm is now a tourist destination. Yay. I point to the good-looking photo of spicy pork with beans and vegetables. I also order a half pint of a local beer, which I accept as a reward to myself. I hardly drink any more these last few years, thanks to John. His abstention, plus my desire to please him and support him, have kept me mostly dry, both in and out of his company. I'm grateful to him for that. I hadn't noticed until I stopped drinking how much I actually drank; for more than thirty years, I had not eaten a dinner without a minimum of two glasses of wine. Every night. That's sixty glasses of wine a month. Minimum. What happens to a person who drinks that much for that long? Who can say exactly? But I *can* say what happens to a person when they *stop* drinking. Right off the bat, I lost ten pounds. Bang! They just fell off me. More importantly, I became more clear-headed. Much more. My memory improved. Enormously. I was less depressed and angry. More patient and productive. Secretly, I wonder if my marriage/career/life might have been different had I been more sober. Too late. Those cows have already left the barn with the spilt milk.

The local beer is delicious—crisp, clean, and refreshing. Gold Ochsen, it's called, which means—as it sounds—gold oxen. I feel entitled to enjoy it and I do.

No one at the bar or restaurant cares to speak to me or look at me. No one is curious about what this Jew is doing there. Yes, I do feel like a Jew there. An "Other."

At the bar, I write in my journal, my constant and faithful companion, and enjoy the meal, which is huge. I will take half of it to go. Perhaps Yeva will be hungry.

I pay the check and find my way back to the hotel to wait for Yeva. Finally, she arrives a little before 10 p.m. We speak a bit about how we are and talk about tomorrow—our first day—and try to paint a general picture of the upcoming week.

We are both exhausted and so we say goodnight.

CHAPTER TEN

Day One: Morning
(Monday, 15 January 2018)

We sleep for eight hours and wake up at 11 a.m. That is definitely not what either of us planned, but definitely what both of us needed.

Before she left Berlin, Yeva made an appointment for us to visit the Ulm Archive this morning, which might have some information about my mother's family, since they had been in the DP camp here. I want to find the camp itself and see what's left of it. That place has been a vague, imaginary notion to me all my life. I had no idea what it was or what it looked like. I also want to go to the synagogue here, even though Yeva had done some research and learned from its young rabbi, via email, that he knows nothing about what happened in Ulm in the 1940s. Still, I want to see it and meet him.

The thought of visiting archive offices was nowhere on my radar when I first planned this trip. I was not a researcher, neither by nature nor by nurture.

First, though, coffee and something to eat.

There are so many coffee shops in Ulm, but we walk past one after another. Yeva is very particular about her coffee, she says, and has been told about this great Italian coffeehouse, which we simply must find.

Yeva dislikes Germany and everything German. Her negativity is pervasive and I make a note to myself not to fall into her pool of darkness. I have my own pool and I don't need to add hers to the mix. I am not here to condemn Germany or Germans. To me, of all the countries that were and are anti-Semitic, only Germany has attempted to look into its ugly face and admit what they did to themselves, to the Jews, and to the world. I don't blame people living here (unless they're over eighty) or unless I sense their bigotry directly. Yeva, however, does live here and says she feels it directly—the racism and close-mindedness. So far, no one has been unkind to me (except at the pub last night.)

We finally find the Italian coffee shop, and of course, they're out of everything except for cream-filled pastries, which satisfies me not at all.

Sitting in that coffee shop, I decide that even though Yeva speaks German and is my translator, I do not want her to be my guide. She and I have different tastes and slants on life and the world. I want to lead this journey with my own impulses and instincts. I need to encourage and trust myself in this, which is not easy for me. I must hold on to myself here, even though my lack of German is a disadvantage.

We walk a few blocks and locate the Dokumentar Archiv of Ulm. It is a small, narrow, nondescript, utilitarian, three-story building. The two archivists, a twenty-something man and a middle-aged woman, greet us when we enter. Both speak good English and invite us upstairs to a sitting room.

They ask about my family's relationship to this town. I describe what little I know about my mother's family: their Polish origin and

where they were during the '40s. I mention that I brought photos and ask if they'd like to see them. Excitedly, they say yes.

I show them the eight or so photos I'd brought of Ulm: some from along the river, and others in front of a massive tower. Based on what my future parents were wearing, you could identify the time of year, that it was either springtime or winter.

My parents look enamored with each other. Intimate. Comfortable. Hugging and kissing by the river, as well as that perspective photo where my father appears to be holding my little mother in the palm of his hand. Josef, the young archivist, is especially excited about that photo; he has never seen any photos like it, he says. Could I please leave that one and perhaps another with them overnight so that he could scan it for their archives? He promises to take good care of it. Yes, of course.

"Could you be of any assistance to me in my journey?" I ask. They would certainly try. They would need my family's names and dates of birth, which I give them. Josef says that they will search for information as well as inquire with the more substantial archive across the river in Neu-Ulm. Hopefully, they will have something for me tomorrow morning when we return to pick up the photos. We thank them and leave.

Our plan now is to try to find the displaced persons camp of Donaubastion, which I had always mispronounced and never realized meant "Danube fortress." (How could I have known so little?)

We find the riverwalk and take it upstream. Is this our opportunity, as Einstein had suggested, to walk back into the past?

The current of the Danube was still fierce and fast. The day was still bitter cold and gray. Yeva wore her faux fur Dr. Zhivago hat, which suited her so well. She was a fashionable beauty and paid attention to herself, with her kohl-outlined eyes and wine-colored lips. I, on the other hand, was without a stitch of makeup, thoughtlessly layered, nothing matching anything else: a Uniqlo down jacket (baby-blue but dirty), a hand-me-down shearling vest, and a Seven Dwarfs-style fuzzy black hat with a fake leopard neck warmer. We were Beauty and the Beast. No need to guess who was who.

With some uncertainty, we walked north and then inland, east. Not far. About a half a mile.

There it was. A fortress. An actual fortress.

Was that it? The DP camp? That?

Even though I had seen my family's photos all my life, I never really understood what I had been looking at. I believed Donaubastion was like an actual camp, with bunkhouses or cabins. My impressions were based on nothing but a kind of lie I told myself, where my imagination replaced the need for knowledge and where my ignorance was acceptable. Until now. At the rapidly ripening age of sixty-four, I would finally learn the truth; see the real place where my family lived for more than four years after the war.

So no, Eleanor, this displaced persons camp was not an actual camp. It was a massive building. A stone fortress. A fucking prison. We just stopped and stared at it. It was enormous. From another time.

After the trip, when I returned to New York, I looked for information about the fortress. (Better late than never.) There was nothing about it in the Wikipedia entry for "Ulm." One might have thought that the history of Ulm would have included information about the post-war years and its importance to the tens of thousands of people—refugees—who lived there. No. Not worth mentioning, I guess. There was plenty of other information, though: photos taken from every angle of the church with the highest spire in Europe, plus what a nice town Ulm is for bicycle riding.

Finally, I found something:

The Upper Donaubastion was built between 1843 and 1855 and could hold up to 2,253 men. The largest and still preserved building of the bastion is the four-story fortress structure which was used as defensive barracks. It has a stair tower in the front and two flank towers.

Yes, that was exactly where we were. But nowhere did it mention what function this place served for thousands of people from 1945–1950.

Further searches revealed that little was known about displaced persons in Ulm until the year 2000, when a batch of Yiddish documents were discovered in a decaying house. Hundreds of thousands of refugees went through these camps, and yet information about them was virtually nonexistent. I guess no one wanted to document that time, hoping that the people and their suffering—*and* German complicity—would just decompose with the rest of unwanted history.

After World War II, more than ten million people had been displaced from their home countries, with about seven million in Allied-occupied Germany alone. Jewish refugees could not return to their former homes because these no longer existed or had been expropriated by their friendly neighbors. In 1945, most Jewish survivors could not leave Europe and had little choice but to stay in the DP camps. Britain had curtailed legal Jewish immigration to Palestine, although bold underground movements carved out narrow, impossible pathways. Jewish refugees hoping to reach other countries, especially the United States, were met with prohibitive restrictions and quotas. As I write this, the past and the present are colliding in the United States as we stand by, watching history repeat itself. Again, the suffering of hundreds of thousands of refugees: Mexicans, Colombians, Hondurans, Syrians, Palestinians, and others. Children living in cages separated from their parents. Restrictions and quotas. Again. To be the daughter of Holocaust survivors, and merely observe and bemoan this inhumanity feels shameful.

The massive fortress, Donaubastion, stands directly in front of us. Yeva and I walk around the structure to get some sense of it, and before long, we are facing the rounded white stone tower familiar from the photos. From my backpack, I take out the FedEx envelope that holds the pictures of my family and find the photo I am looking for. Here. They are here. Standing exactly where I am standing now.

My mother, brother, uncle, and grandfather, staring grimly into the camera.

Yeva and I stand on the same spot looking nearly as grim. My heart is pounding; water collects in my eyes and spills down my face. I remind myself to breathe. Had I actually expected to find this place?

Yeva looks moved as well. She has a caring, empathetic nature with the soul of an artist. She was associating the cruelties suffered by my family onto her own family's indignities in the Soviet Union. For her, this was more evidence of the evil that men do—especially German men.

By translating the letters, she came to know my family's cast of characters. At the end of each letter, my father would send his regards to my mother's parents, Isak and Leah, and to her brothers—Henyu and Leibel. Here, for the first time, Yeva is looking at them; connecting the names from the letters to the faces in the photos. That face is Henyu, that one Leibel, and so on. My mother, my father. Now she sees them too.

We just stand there in the cold. The frozen vapor of our breath forms a misty curtain between us and the fortress, between us and the past, like a dream. I look and imagine. Them. My mother. My brother. My uncles, who were still teenagers at the time. My grandparents, who were such gentle, pious people. Later, during this trip, I will find documents about them too, about my grandparents, born in 1892. Doing the math, my grandparents in these photos, in 1948, were in their late fifties. Years younger than I am now. They look into the camera. Their faces register a life hard-lived, a pallor of misery and despair, cold and hidden. Their eyes look empty and numb from their days, their nights, their lives. Their sufferings. All of those things and more are captured in these small photos. My eyes are dripping and will remain in this state for most of the week.

I ask Yeva to take a picture of me in this spot.

Like the photographer who must have directed my parents at the river, Yeva directs me where to stand. She holds the photo of my family in her left hand and is trying to line me up to look exactly like the photo she is holding. With her right hand, she presses the button on my iPhone. I do not realize until she shows me the picture that she has included the photo from the past and juxtaposed it together with me in the present, so that my family and I are here in the same picture.

For this one moment, we are together.

We just stand there. I am in no hurry to move or leave or do anything other than what we are doing. I look around from where we are standing to get a sense of where this is, where we are, what's around here.

I'm looking, looking…

It takes a minute, but then I see these buildings across the street. A row of houses. Do they look familiar? Yes, they do. I reach again into that envelope and find two other photos: one with my mother and her two brothers, and another with my father and Hershel. In both photos, it's clearly wintertime, very much like today. In the background, there is laundry drying, draped on bushes.

I look from the photo in my hand, to the houses across the street from where we are standing. The laundry is gone and some of the trees are missing, but there is absolutely no mistaking this for the place where the pictures were taken. Where I am standing right now, my father stood then. In his winter overcoat and hat, holding his leather gloves. With Uncle Hershel, a smaller, more delicate man, with his sad, sweet smile and his own overcoat and hat. You would never know by looking at them that they had just escaped from Hell.

Again, Yeva holds the photo in one hand and takes the picture— me standing alongside the old photo of my father, in the same spot,

just across from the houses. Time frozen. Past and present merge into one. I feel such sadness and longing and yet an odd kind of delight and relief.

Einstein was right. You could walk upstream and find the past.

We are ready to see what this fortress looks like from the inside. There are some colorful banners flying on one side of the fortress, signage saying something about a museum. We walk up to the modern glass doors and try to get in. Locked. It's Monday. Damn. The museum is closed.

Well, we did not come all this way to be summarily dismissed. We would break into that fortress if we had to.

We walk around the building. In the back, in the parking area, we find a door. Unlocked. Fortunately, no break-in necessary.

We head up a wide flight of stairs to another door. That opens too. Good luck is with us today.

We are in a vast dark hallway. We can't see anything but I can feel the wide girth of the space, like Jonah in the belly of the whale.

I have lived all of my days to get here, to this very moment, to this building, to this place. Whatever I was looking for, I had found it. This imagined yet unimaginable place. My mother and grandparents and brother had lived here. This was their home. For more than four years. In this nineteenth-century fortress.

Just then, the overhead lights come on. We are slapped back into the present. A couple of young men in their twenties walk out of one of the many iron-bolted doors that I can now see along the mighty hallway.

"*Sprechen zi English?*" That was the best of my German, right there.

"Yes, we speak English," they say confidently.

"What is this place now?" I ask.

"Oh, we are a theatre company and these are our offices. The building contains artists' offices."

A gentrified fortress! You don't see *that* every day. My brain rattles in disbelief. It's like the 1960s and 1970s of the avant-garde theatre scene in New York City, when poor young acting companies would occupy vacant factories and abandoned lofts. That was where and how my own acting history began.

"Do you know what this place was?" I ask.

No. They do not know. (How will we ever stop repeating history if we don't learn it?)

They are in a hurry and must go. We thank them and they move on.

I stand still. I wait. Again, I do not want to move. I just want to fill my lungs with the air of then and them.

I begin to walk down the very long hallway, slowly and deliberately, looking at those mighty iron doors on each side. Left foot, right foot. It is an effort to move my legs.

I stop. I look. I listen. I am like Superman. I have x-ray vision.

I see them. My family. I feel their lives here. Their breathing. From behind the doors and in the halls. They are flying all around, phantom shadows in the gray air. I hear babies crying and Yiddish and Polish and shouting and occasional laughter and the footsteps of the children, clopping, running, shrieking as children do, and fathers' yelling and women weeping. A dream within a dream. I inhale them into the center of my soul. I swallow this fortress and I become the whale.

Then I see my grandparents, my beloved grandparents, of blessed memory; the mourning in their eyes, so evident in the photos. And my mother, so young and beautiful. And my brother, such a skinny knob-by-kneed little boy who had travelled hither and yon, from pillar to post, knowing more hardship than any young boy should ever know. I hear them and I see them all around me. I want to touch them. Maybe if I stand here a bit longer, they will materialize and come to me. That is my wish. And I am certain that they would be happy to see me too. I have never been more certain of anything in my life. I do not move. I will not leave. Oh my God, why would I ever leave this place? I want to be preserved here, happy to be like Lot's wife. Frozen in time. I want to wait for them. I know they are here. I am submerged with the ghosts, and I want to swim with them forever.

Yeva looks at me sadly but knows me well enough by now to leave me be. I don't know how long I stood there.

Eventually, we leave, although not before we try to open a few of the steel doors to see if we can get inside whatever space lay beyond them. One of the doors opens. We enter. It's the size of a small storage space, but I'm sure it housed families. How many people would have lived in here? The walls have been whitewashed and all its secrets smoothed away, hidden under the layers of paint and plaster.

We go back into the hall. That's where the spirits walk. And run. And shout. And cry. (Or maybe that's just me.)

We finally go outside. The air is damp and brisk and brings our blood back into the present. We walk around and find a doorway leading to another kind of storage area. It's a store! On the street level of the fortress. We get closer. What kind of store? Wait for it....

Fortress Liquors! Perfect. If I was still drinking, it would be a great time to crack open a bottle of something.

We are ready to move on. We take the walkway back down toward the beautiful Danube. I still want to find the exact spot along the river where those photos were taken of my parents wooing, but by now we are plenty spent. We'll save that location shoot for tomorrow afternoon, before we leave for Stuttgart.

We are free until 6 p.m., at which time we have our appointment with the local rabbi at the new synagogue in Ulm. We decide to become tourists and check out Ulm's most famous attraction, the Ulmer Münster. Yes, with the world's tallest steeple.

It's late afternoon, so Yeva and I have the church all to ourselves. It is, as the guidebook promises, an impressive church in the Gothic style. Buttresses flying all over the place. Enormous arches, beautiful stained glass, a glorious ceiling, an intricately carved choir section. I walk past the altar and into a small room off to the side. Hanging catty-corner on the wall are two sculptures of Jesus on the cross. In both sculptures, he is emaciated and in obvious agony. I stand in front of them for a while and look from one to the other.

Yeva comes into the room. "Can you imagine?" I say. "That people who worship this man and elevate his suffering to a religion are able to do these same horrible things to other people? Starve them and torment them and murder them, like their own savior, the Son of God? How could they do that?" (And with that rhetorical question, I sound as naïve as my half-brother Harry.) Yeva nods and raises her eyebrows knowingly.

It is, in fact, impossible to understand. How can any people who follow Jesus, the Prince of Peace, the man who died on the cross and suffered for us all, how could his followers treat other people as the Romans treated him? Where is the disconnect? Even beasts are fed and not slaughtered randomly. Plus, if you factor in the elephant in the room—that Jesus himself was a Jew—it's all even more dumbfounding. Today, countless acts of cruelty and injustice continue, often in the name of God—always against our weakest and most vulnerable. Where is the "never again"? Did that just mean "never again" for us?

It was time to exit the church and head over to the synagogue to meet the rabbi. We were nothing if not inclusive and ecumenical.

On our way out, Yeva spots a laminated sign on a charity box. I would have missed it. It says: "*Wir unterstutzen die judische Gemeinded in Ulm bei der Anschaffung einer Thorarolle.*" Underneath was the English translation: "*Donations for a new Torah Scroll for the Jewish Congregation.*"

We didn't make a donation, but we did take photos of it and laughed our asses off. We come by our cynicism honestly.

CHAPTER ELEVEN

Day One: Evening
(Monday, 15 January 2018)

The synagogue was not far from the church. Ulm is a small town. According to the city map, the synagogue is marked on a street in the "Jewish area." The "Jewish area" is one block long.

The synagogue is a modern building, cube-like, with an outer wall comprised of Stars of David carved into its pale stones. By day, it lets light into the sanctuary, and by night, its light shines outward. It was built on the exact spot of the original synagogue, which was burned to the ground on Kristallnacht in November 1938. My brother Seymour had told me that when they were in Ulm, he used to go to the synagogue in Stuttgart where my father lived. I just assumed that it was a choice, as in, "I'll visit Chaskel and go to the synagogue in Stuttgart *rather* than to the one in Ulm." But it wasn't a choice. There *was* no synagogue in Ulm after the war because it was destroyed in '38.

The outer doorway of the synagogue is nondescript. Opaque, smoky glass doors, thick and impossible to see through. Yeva rings the bell. We stand and wait. Finally, the heavy glass door opens. A man, looking like a thug in a black leather jacket and jeans, asks us what we want in German. Yeva answers him, that we have an appointment with the rabbi. He asks our names, and then lets us in through the first door. When that door clicks shut, a buzzer sounds and the second door clicks open into the lobby of the synagogue. Nowadays in synagogues, Jewish museums, Jewish concert halls, and Jewish community centers throughout Europe, rigorous Israeli-style security systems are in place. They've seen the nightmare before, and they don't mean to see it again.

"The Rabbi is still in prayer service and will be out shortly. Please to wait in lobby," he says in his thick Russian-English accent. (He is not German.)

"If there are services now," I reply, "I would like to go into the sanctuary and see them."

The man is emphatic that I cannot go into the sanctuary and that the Rabbi had specified that we were to wait out here. Just as I am about to argue with him, the doors to the sanctuary open and men start coming out. "Ah, service over," he says victoriously.

We wait as an assortment of middle-aged men put on their coats and leave. I walk to the open door of the sanctuary. There is one man inside, the only candidate we could cast as The Rabbi. He wears a black suit, white shirt, black fedora. An obvious *Chabadnik*, meaning a follower of the late Rabbi Menachem Mendel Schneerson, leader of the Lubavitch sect of Hasidic Judaism, known for its interest in outreach.

The Rabbi was texting on his cell phone but stopped when he saw me. I introduced myself and Yeva, but did not offer my hand, knowing that his religious practice forbids him from touching any woman other than his wife.

I compliment him on the beauty of the sanctuary, and he gives me some details about its size and how many families it could hold. Then he invites us back into the lobby to sit.

"Well, what can I tell you?" he asks. From his accent, I know that he is from Israel. "I myself have only come here in 1999. But I will tell you what I know."

He tells us that most of the Jews of Ulm wound up in the concentration camp Theresienstadt. "The old *shul* was destroyed on Kristallnacht, the 9th of November 1938. After the war, from 1946 to 1949, the Jews who returned had nowhere to pray. They would pray in small rooms, you know, *Zimmers*," he says, using the German word. (In Yiddish, we would say *shtiblekh*.) "There were not many Jews from Ulm who survived the *Shoah*." (*Shoah* is the Hebrew word for the Holocaust, meaning "The Catastrophe.") "Of those who did, it was not long before they all left. No one wanted to stay here. Maybe five or six people stayed, but that's all. And now? Maybe two are still left. In 1990, the Russian Jews arrived here, and that is our membership now. All Russian. We began with eighty people, and now we have over five hundred. These men you saw tonight come to me five times a week for Torah study. We have a *mikvah* (a ritual bath) and a large ballroom space upstairs for events—bar mitzvahs, weddings. This new *shul* was built in 2012. Except for this, there is nothing I can tell you."

I congratulate him on his extraordinary work and successes. On one hand, it is miraculous that the synagogue seems so vital but on the other hand, tragic that hardly any German Jews still exist here.

He goes on. "The real information you seek is in Stuttgart. There is a woman there, a Mrs. Warscher. She is in the Jewish Community Center, and she knows everything. I will give you her number and email address."

He looks at his phone. I take out mine.

"How do you spell that?" I ask.

"W.A.R.S.C.H.E.R.," he says.

Wait. What? A light bulb bursts in my head, and I'm freaking out. I looked at Yeva to see if she heard what I heard. She didn't seem to catch it and doesn't know what I'm thinking.

The Rabbi gives me Mrs. Warscher's number, and we stand up to leave. Before we go, I tell him that I am a Yiddish singer and perhaps he would like me to do a concert here sometime. I'd be happy to do a benefit for the *shul*, I tell him. He says that he is not opposed to such an idea, even though we both know it is forbidden by his religious sect for men to listen to a woman singing. (A woman's voice is considered sexy and too much of a temptation for men. Don't get me started....) But these days, especially with Russian Jews, he says, one has to be more "flexible" in order to not to alienate anyone and keep the congregation growing, sometimes quietly doing things that are not quite so kosher.

The Rabbi and I look at each other and have some kind of connection. He is a good man with an open face and eyes that are alive. I ask him if he will be around tomorrow because I would like to give him a CD of my songs (even though I am sure he will not listen to it). He says to come by at ten.

We say our goodbyes and walk through the double security doors into the night. I turn to Yeva. "Did you catch the name of the woman he mentioned from the Jewish Community Center in Stuttgart?"

"Warscher?" she asks.

"Yes." I grab her eyeballs and I don't let them go. "Sound familiar?" We stop walking. "No, what?"

I take out the FedEx envelope with the photos. "Look at the signature on the back of these two photos—of my father with a man at a train station, and the one with the man driving the convertible."

I show her the German inscription on the back.

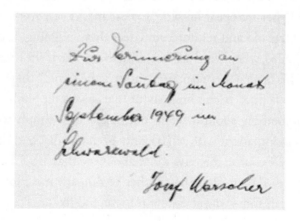

She translates the writing: "'To remember our time in Schwartz-wald, Stuttgart. September 1949, Josef Warscher.'" She stops. "Wait. Is that name from your father's letters? That friend of his, whose name I must have misread as 'Wachler'? Oh my God, he's the guy from the letters! Warscher! Of course!"

That name is in so many of my father's letters, but none of the translators could make out the correct spelling. In Warscher's own hand, on these photos, his name is clear.

Mrs. Warscher? Could they possibly be related? Do we dare to imagine that there is some connection? Yeva will email her tonight when we get back to the hotel and see if we can meet her when we are in Stuttgart. (I have not yet made the connection that she is the same woman that Hardy has already scheduled for me to meet on Wednesday.)

And this is only the first day?

I decide that tonight is "date night" and plan to take Yeva out for a nice dinner. We both deserve something special. We go back to our room to rest and do whatever email business we each need to do for the real world.

Even though we have only been together for this one day, there is something about Yeva that is making me uncomfortable. She speaks to me in very hushed tones, in a precious voice, as though everything is secret, as though it's all bad news that she is afraid to share. I have to keep asking her to repeat herself. "Excuse me?" I say, over and over. It makes me feel old and reinforces my fear that I'm going deaf. (Is that *her* fault?) Also, whenever I ask her something, like if she's ready to eat or wants this or that, her response is always the same. "That's fine." Or, "Either one is fine." Something about that makes me—what? Crazy? Angry? Something about it seems not honest or is simply too passive for me. I am impatient with it. (It's only been one day, and I'm *already* impatient? Of course, this says more about me than her.) I'm worried that I have made a mistake having her accompany me. Hopefully, we can connect in some way at dinner tonight and fix it.

We walk around looking for a place to eat. There's a restaurant near the hotel with nice lighting and people inside, but the menu has pictures of food, which seems touristy to me and not a good sign. Still, we go in. I am a sucker for candlelight.

We should have left as soon as the hostess was curt with us and moved us to the back of the restaurant near the kitchen. But we did not. We were tired and hungry.

It was a steak place. We both felt that we deserved red meat for whatever revitalizing properties we thought it might provide, even though that's probably contraindicated.

She would have red wine; I would have water. The waitress said there was a fifty cent (Euro) charge for water. Again, we should have left, and again, we did not. We both ordered the small steak.

It took way too long for the food to come. Yeva and I had little to say to each other. We just sat there making fake jagged conversation, interrupted by long bits of silence. In hindsight, we were both simply exhausted. And even though we were engaged in this very personal, intimate journey, we did not really know one another at all.

Finally, the food arrived. Both steaks were completely cooked through—brown on the outside and brown on the inside. They tasted like meat—not like steak—but like a slab of dead animal (which of course it was). It would have been enough to turn me into a vegetarian except that the vegetables were no better. The lousy meal was not helped by our lousy interaction. We were as dull and bland as the food. The conversation consisted of "What," "Fine," and "Whatever you want." It was exhaustingly boring, and I am certain that it was no better for her. Finally, thank the Lord, the meal was over and I paid the check. We left, each of us saying we were going to walk around on our own for a while.

I breathed a sigh of relief at her departure and wondered how I would get through the next three days. Maybe I needed to cut her loose and be on my own. I called John to complain and ask for advice. In general, his advice was usually helpful. What he might lack in heart, he made up for in brain.

"Try speaking to her authentically," he said. He reminded me that this was only our first day together and that it would get easier. I thanked him. He sounded distant and detached—not particularly warm. That was sometimes the case with him. It was hard to know how he was feeling, especially about me. I rarely knew where I stood. But I was thankful for his help. We said our "good nights," his "sweet dreams," and both of our "love yous," and I went back to the hotel.

Yeva was not back yet. I lay in bed and continued reading *The Saving Remnant*. It was not exactly light fare, but it was captivating and spot-on for this trip. After the war, according to the book, the Jews, so fed up with the brutality and inhumanity and indifference of the world, became emboldened by the cruelty against them. They were organizing; smuggling Jews to Palestine; raising money to feed and clothe the refugees; persevering despite international apathy, continued anti-Semitism, and exhaustion from post-war horrors. For me, lots of learning, lots of underlining.

Yeva returned. She washed up, put on her pajamas, and got into her bed. We talked about the letters. There were still letters that had not yet been translated. The project was plenty disorganized and whatever story narrative I was looking for, hoping for, was scattered and incomplete. Part of that was certainly my fault as I was—and am—nearly every synonym for disorganized: muddled, unsystematic, chaotic, distracted, and of course, messy and sloppy. Because of all this, plus my impatience and haste, I even had some letters translated twice. By two different translators. An interesting experiment—if only it had been intentional. I was frustrated, to say the least. Yeva and I talked about trying to rectify that and find a way for me to become better organized. She recommended a new organizing app. Yeah, good luck with that.

I told Yeva I wanted to talk to her about something else. I don't know how I found my way to it, but I did.

"I want you to know something, Yeva. I want you to know that I wouldn't be here if it weren't for you."

Yes, that was the right way to begin. And it was the truth. I would not be on this journey if it weren't for her.

"That you recognized the address on my father's stationery and offered to accompany me here absolutely persuaded me to take the leap into this world. I cannot ever thank you enough for that."

I could see her face soften. This was a lesson for me. *Say the positive truth first, Eleanor.* I am grateful to be reminded of that even now, a lesson I could benefit from daily.

"And something else." I went on. "I'm going to say this because I'm older than you and feel like I know a thing or two after all this time. I would like to tell you what I observe." I took a breath. "Often, when I ask you how you feel about something—about anything and about everything—your response is always 'Fine.' To me, the word 'fine' means 'not so good.' To me, it is a way to avoid saying what you actually think and feel."

"Really?"

"Yes. To me 'fine' is a placeholder. In my mind, it's rarely a truthful response; it means there is something you are not saying or are afraid to say. Or that you don't care. That makes me wonder what's really true. I am not sure how you feel about anything because to everything you respond, 'fine.' Yeva, I really want to know what you think and how you feel because you're a smart woman whose thoughts and feelings are important to me. I want your input. When you say 'fine,' I find myself shutting down. To me, it's like when I say 'I don't care.' Whenever I hear myself say 'I don't care,' I stop myself because I know that not caring is a defense against something that I probably care very much about."

I stop. "Forgive me if I've gone too far. It's just that I feel that you are hidden from me. I want for us to know each other, but I can't quite see you—and I would like to. I hope you're not angry."

She looks at me with tears in her eyes. "You know, when I am with my boyfriend, I sometimes leave everything to him and don't express my feelings. I understand what you are saying, and it is partially true. But also, to me, 'fine' is not a bad word. Maybe the problem is in translation. After all, I am translating my English through the Russian."

I look at her and take that in. "Ha, yes, of course, it's in the translation," I laugh. (That's ironic coming from the translator, no? She is a very smart woman.)

"Actually, Yeva," I go on, "when I think of the word 'fine,' I am now remembering what it used to mean: 'fine' used to mean excellent. Exceptional. Worldly. Like 'fine dining' or 'fine jewelry.' It hasn't meant that for a long time—at least to me. These days, it means something that's barely average, the lowest common denominator, basically less than good."

"Oh no, I don't mean it that way, as something 'less than,'" she says. "But you are right also, there is a part of me that acquiesces, that tolerates."

I told her I wanted her to be herself, her true self, so that I could be my true self. I wanted to share this journey with her and not some obedient beige woman. She wanted that too, she said. We smiled deeply and warmly at each other across the little lane separating our narrow but comfortable beds.

That night, we restarted our journey. We were now on the same page, speaking the same language. It took one whole day for us to get on track.

We continued talking deep into the night; about the letters, for one thing. How and when could they be completed? I still owed her money for them. And to make matters worse, I owed her additional money for her time accompanying me on this trip. The money didn't seem to matter to her, but we had a deal, and I needed to be responsible. Foolishly yet innocently, I had traveled to Germany with only enough cash to pay Yeva. Nothing extra. It wasn't that I didn't have the money. I just thought I could pay for everything with plastic and give her all the cash. Well, I was totally wrong. In New York City, I am completely reliant on credit cards. But in Germany, I had no idea that so many places would not take plastic. All the daily items—coffee, snacks, meals, transportation—had to be paid in cash, and my bankcard was unfortunately forgotten, sitting in a drawer in my kitchen. It is absurd, but by the end of the first day, I was broke. Not only was I not able to pay Yeva what I owed her, but I actually had to borrow cash from her! She was understanding, but I felt ridiculous and ashamed.

It was hard to sleep that night. Our conversation, as well as the images and experiences from our first day, were bringing up feelings of excitement as well as renewed grief and sorrow. My family. Dead for so long and yet so present to me, in me, with me. I am searching for them even though I know where they are: in the ground, long gone. Nothing would bring them back. And yet, I could feel them here. I swear, I could hear them speaking to me.

CHAPTER TWELVE

Day Two: Ulm to Stuttgart
(Tuesday, 16 January 2018)

We awoke to another rainy, gray German day. Does the sun ever shine here?

We both had a fitful night's sleep. Three or four hours, at the most, which would become the norm for the remainder of my trip.

Our plan was to go back to the archive to pick up the photos that I had left with them yesterday, and then walk along the river to find the exact spot where my parents had taken their photos—which seemed doable and was one of the few original ideas I had from the beginning. Then we would leisurely catch an afternoon train to Stuttgart.

I was hungry and really wanted some protein like eggs, but to dawdle in a restaurant felt like a waste of time. We picked up a coffee and croissant from an unwelcoming, overpriced delicatessen. So far, no one—no clerk or waiter—has been friendly, except for the receptionist at the hotel, who was herself a foreigner. Yeva said it was because we look like Jews. Really? Still?

We headed over to the archive. Josef welcomed us with a strong handshake and warm smile. He seemed happy to see us, more relaxed than yesterday. "I have found some things for you," he said. "Come, let's go upstairs to the office. But first of all, here are your photos back."

He gave me the photographs I had given him yesterday, but now they were inside an onionskin folder, as though they were actually valuable—which of course, they were. He did not treat them like a casual birthright, disrespectfully, as I had.

"These photographs," he said, "we don't have anything like them. They will be extremely helpful to us in continuing to tell the story of how these people lived here during that horrible time."

My family's lives would be remembered in this place, contributing something to history in a broader way than just affecting my life. This pleases me enormously. Their lives will be repurposed and useful, even in death.

Excitedly, Josef told us he had contacted the main archive in Ludwigsburg, just outside of Stuttgart, and found links to files about my family. We should go to the archive, he said, and give them these links, and they will be able to give us the files. Having these links will make it much easier for us than to begin a search on our own, and he gave us their hours of operation. They were open today from 9 a.m. to 6 p.m., but the last request for files ended at 4 p.m.

I thanked him but didn't really understand the importance of what he was saying. However, Yeva did. She looked at me sternly and said that we must leave right away. We put on our coats, shook hands, said goodbye to Josef, and thanked him. And he us.

As soon as we walked out the door, Yeva said, "Look, I know you want to go to the river to find the place where those photos of your parents were taken, but—I think we need to get to Ludwigsburg as quickly as possible. There is too little time and too much to do. Is that okay?"

She caught me off-guard. Finding that spot by the river was practically the only idea I wanted to accomplish on this trip. That, and going to the address on my father's letterhead.

I looked at her and thought for a second. Of course, Yeva was right. We didn't know what we would find at the archive, and so that was where we needed to be. We had very limited time and needed to make the most of it. Taking photos at the river was more like a Disney moment.

97

We went back to the hotel, quickly packed our bags, checked the train schedule, and dragged the accursed luggage to the station through the pissing rain. The lack of sleep from the night before had me bleary-eyed, and my body hurt plenty. But we had a train to catch. Yeva was moving quickly while I was feeling my age. I am nearly thirty years older than she is, damn it to hell, although I feel like her contemporary.

The train ride would take ninety minutes. Our hope was that we could leave our luggage at the train station in Stuttgart, take a commuter train to Ludwigsburg so that we would not waste any time, and get to the archive with some hours to spare before it closed for the day.

On the train, Yeva checked her email to see if Mrs. Warscher had written back. She had not.

That train ride from Ulm to Stuttgart put me square inside my father's head. I looked out the window at the fields and barren winter landscape, and pictured my father at the same window. In his letters, he writes about his train trips from Stuttgart to Ulm. He would go there practically every week to see my mother.

I wondered about his own reflections on these train trips: his life, his love, his past, his future, and the huge elephant in the room: the Holocaust. All that he had lost—so much. Everything. *My poor father.* My whole life, I thought that. (And I didn't even know the half of it.)

We arrived at Stuttgart Hauptbahnhof, a bustling train station hub. Thankfully, we found lockers for our luggage. We would leave our bags there until later, go to the archive in Ludwigsburg, and then Yeva would go on to her brother's, and I could walk to my hotel. Perfect.

Since we hadn't heard back from Mrs. Warscher, I decide to phone her. We have a drop of time until the train leaves for Ludwigsburg. From a quiet corner in the vast lobby of the station, I call the number that the rabbi had given us last night. The phone rings. Before I know it, a woman picks up.

"Uh, Mrs. Warscher?" I stammer.

"Yes?"

Wait. What? I was definitely not prepared for her to answer. *Come on, Eleanor, talk....*

"Hello. My name is Eleanor Reissa Schlusselberg."

"Yes?"

"My friend sent you an email yesterday. I'm not sure if you received it."

She says nothing. I go on.

"The rabbi from Ulm suggested that I contact you; he said that you knew a lot about the Jews of Stuttgart after the war."

"Yes."

"My father lived in Stuttgart."

"What was his name?"

"Chaskel Schlusselberg. Do you recognize that name?"

"I'm not sure."

"My father was friends with a man named Josef Warscher. By any chance, do you know who that is?"

Pause.

"He was my father."

I stop breathing, my eyes blinking tears away, like windshield wipers in the rain. Yeva is standing beside me, looking at me, awaiting the outcome. I lock onto her eyes with all of my telepathic skills. *"You will not believe this,"* I try to say.

And then into the phone, as calmly as possible, I say, "Oh, he was your *father....*"

Yeva's jaw drops, her eyes go wide, and she starts to cry, too.

"What are you doing here in Germany?" Warscher asks.

"I found letters from my father, from when he lived in Stuttgart in 1949, and so I came to see and try to retrace his steps. Your father is mentioned in many of the letters: the times they spent together on Sabbaths and weekends, where they went, what they ate, things they did and said."

"Is he still alive, your father?" she asks.

"No. He died in 1976."

"Your father died too young."

"Yes, he did." Wait. "Is *your* father alive?" I ask. (Oh my God, is that even a possibility?)

"No, he died in 1998."

"Oh, I'm sorry."

"But my mother is alive."

"What?"

"Yes, she is eighty-eight."

"Your mother is alive?" I repeat this so that Yeva can hear. She whispers, "Wow."

"Yes," Warscher says, "but she is not so clear in her head."

"I understand." (Do I?)

I don't know where to go from here.

"What is your first name?" I ask. I don't want to keep calling her Mrs. Warscher.

"Eve," she says.

"Eve. Eve, can I come see you tomorrow? I have only two days in Stuttgart; I would very much like to meet you. I also have a few photos of your father, plus there are so many references to him in my father's letters. Can I come by tomorrow?"

Silence.

"I won't stay long," I say quickly.

"Yes. All right. Can you come around nine in the morning?"

"Yes, yes. Great."

She gives me the address, and Yeva writes it down.

"Thank you, Eve. I will see you tomorrow then."

"By the way," she asks, "how old are you?"

"I'm sixty-four."

"Me too," she says. "And are you married?"

"No."

"Me too." (I guess the rabbi in Ulm just assumed she was a "Mrs.")

We pause.

"Well, thank you so much, Eve. I look forward to meeting you tomorrow."

"Yes, me too," she says.
Oh my goodness gracious.
And then we catch the train to Ludwigsburg.

CHAPTER THIRTEEN

Day Two Continued: Ludwigsburg
(Tuesday, 16 January 2018)

Nobody can say Germany is inconsistent: it is bone cold, gray as slate, and drizzling ad nauseam. We are on the train from Stuttgart to Ludwigsburg.

There are more than twenty references in my father's letters to Ludwigsburg. He writes of going there to try to sell his car, to get his passport, his visa for England to retrieve his son—which was weighed down by delay upon delay—and to buy jewelry for my mother, to sell furniture, to mail packages and letters, and to see friends. When I initially mentioned Ludwigsburg to Lutz in Berlin back in November, I thought nothing of the place. I thought it was some small burg or suburb and was surprised that Lutz had even heard of it. Turns out that it's Germany's version of a county seat with a population of nearly 100,000. Not such a small burb after all.

It takes about forty minutes for us to get to the Ludwigsburg station. I feel like I am furiously rowing backwards, upstream.

Everything I look at, everything I see, makes me wonder what he saw. From on board the train, looking out on that shed or this garage or that row of trees. The platform, the stairs, the street. Did it look like this, Dad? What was he thinking, feeling? My heart calls out to him. Oh, Dad! I want to see him, I want to watch him, walk quickly with him through the streets in his black overcoat and fedora. I want to be the kind face in the sea of hardship and inhumanity and misfortune that was his life. That is why I am here. To walk with my father. My eyes well up again. Mourning. Longing. Re-mourning, re-longing. All of these days here, I weep with the rain.

And then I remember: how many days, Eleanor? Two? Two days? And the second day has only just begun? That does not seem possible. I have been traveling toward this place all of my life.

Yeva and I leave the train station. We head up the stairs and stop at the corner. We look around and try to get our bearings. This is much more of a city than Ulm, larger and more modern. It bustles and moves faster. More cars, more people. That church in Ulm and the beautiful Danube gave Ulm a folksy, timeless character. This place lacks that particular charm, although it is known for its Baroque architecture and palaces, none of which I will get to see.

We ask for directions. It's half a mile to the Staatsarchiv. We walk.

After some trial and error, we find our way to the two officious white stone buildings that make up the archives. They used to be,

I learn later, the Arsenal Barracks and the Armory. Both buildings have been "repurposed" to hold the massive amounts of archives. My father's documents are in the Arsenal Barracks. The guard there tells us we must check our bags and coats in a locker before we go in, and so we do.

We enter what looks like a reading room in any library. A smattering of people seated at long tables: intently looking, reading, writing. We go up to the front desk manned by two officious women. Yeva speaks to them in German and gives them the file numbers that Josef gave us in Ulm, only a few hours ago. I stand there intuiting what I can. Yiddish is similar in some ways to German, so I can catch a few words here and there. The women are saying that we can have these documents tomorrow. Yeva firmly tells them that I am a visitor from the United States, only here for a few days, and could they please give us these documents *now*; documents about my family that was in the Holocaust, including my father, who was in Auschwitz.

Aha! Auschwitz. The key to the kingdom. "Just say the secret word," as Groucho used to say.

They ask us to fill out some papers while they look for the files. It's just after 2 p.m., and the place closes at six.

We choose a table near the window for the additional daylight, and we wait. Within fifteen minutes, one of the women walks toward us with a stack of files about a foot high and gently places them in front of Yeva. She whispers something to Yeva and then walks away. We look at each other with our now familiar "wow" expression. "She says that there are more files and she will bring them out to us as soon as they collect them," Yeva tells me.

More files? Are you kidding? How will we even get through all of these?

Each of the files have different names on them. The largest one says, "Chaskel Schlüsselberg." There are two other folders with his name on them, as well. The next largest says, "Isak Hoff"—my grandfather, my mother's father, whom I loved so, and grew up with as a child. Then, "Chana Schlüsselberg née Rubin," my father's first wife.

And then thinnest file of all: "Frida Schlüsselberg," my father's other daughter, Harry's young sister. She gets a file too?

No, we never, *ever* expected this; never imagined, hoped, dreamed this; that we would find such files. We didn't know what the files contained, but it was clear that we had found the mother lode. Of something.

Now that we found them, now that they were resting on our table, out of the vault or wherever they had been stored for these many years, well, now what? Hundreds and hundreds of pages. We were stupefied. And more than a little panicked. We have three hours left to us today, and tomorrow is Yeva's last day with me. There is absolutely no way we will get through all of these papers. They are all in German, which means we cannot tackle them independently. We will have to go through each page, each line, each word—together. I am completely dependent on Yeva.

Just as we are about to open the largest file, the one that says "Chaskel Schl*ü*sselberg," the librarian returns. With more files. Another one with my father's name; one with my father's brothers' names; and one that says "Leah Hoff," my mother's mother. Her too?

Yeva thanks the librarian. We look at each other and at the stacks of files, and have our second real laugh of this trip. And then some more crying.

Ever since that late night conversation in our hotel room in Ulm, Yeva and I are more of a team: open, honest, comfortable. I count on her, bounce my ideas off her, trust her. She knows the players, under-stands the mission, and is moved by the depth and tragedy of it all.

Wait a minute. Was that conversation in Ulm only last night? Last night! Haven't we been friends for years and on this journey for months?

Our task is impossible and overwhelming. How will we get through these papers now that we have exposed them to the light of day? For whom were they waiting? What if I hadn't come here?

We open the largest of my father's files. The papers, brown and crispy with age, look like standard government documents: printed questions with blank spaces for answers. Yeva looks at the first page.

"What does it say?" I ask.

As she reads, she mouths the words to herself and then translates to me: "The questions ask for the dates of your father's time in the camps. He answers that he was in Auschwitz from February 1943 until January 1945. Then he went to the other camps—Buchenwald, Schönebeck, and Oranienburg."

Did I know the dates of his internment in Auschwitz? No.

Did I know he was also in other camps? No.

I did not know anything.

I am sixty-four years old and my ignorance is rigorous and comprehensive. "Man is responsible for his ignorance," Milan Kundera writes. "Living is easy with eyes closed," says John Lennon. "Facts do not cease to exist because they are ignored," chimes in Aldous Huxley. Take your pick.

The archive ladies, when we initially checked in, told Yeva that they could make copies of whatever documents we wanted for a per-page fee and then either mail the hard copies or send us email links of the pages. I told Yeva I wanted hard copies. She stared at me like I was nuts. "No, it's too much paper, and besides, then only you will have the document. No. Let them send the email links; then we can both look at them. I or someone else can continue to translate them." I argued that I like reading from actual paper. She shook her head and shrugged, as if to say, "I strongly disagree, but do whatever you want, it's your rodeo," even though she probably didn't know that expression. Thankfully, when I thought about it for another minute, I realized that Yeva was right again. We would ask for the email links, and mark each of the papers we want copies of.

And so, we mark that first page. It takes us ten minutes just to get through that one paper, and there are hundreds more. This is a very bad joke.

Yeva looks at the next page.

Antrag auf Widergutmachung. "Application for Restitution," she says. "Do you know what that is?"

106

Ah, yes. Now I believe I understand this, all of these papers, and why they exist. When he was alive, my father received monthly checks from Germany. *Wiedergutmachung.* It was a long time ago, but I remember that it was something like $362 or $348 per month. Decades ago, in the early '70s, when I put him in the nursing home after his strokes, I had to manage all of his finances. At that time, none of his bank accounts were in my name or in joint accounts. Everything was in his name only. It took some creative finessing to get myself onto his accounts, but I did.

At that time, the cost of getting into a nursing home was prohibitive, something like $3,000 a month, which was an enormous amount of money for us. In order to be admitted, a person had to pay that money, $36,000 a year, until they ran out of their savings—except for $2,000, which the government allowed you to keep so that you could bury yourself. Only then could a person qualify for Medicaid, which would subsequently pick up the tab to the nursing home for remainder of their days. (So, a person who worked their whole stinking life and saved every damn penny for their retirement or for their children, would have to give all their money to the nursing home before the government would chip in for the privilege of living their sunset years penniless in a shithole institution.)

As his next of kin, I had to fill out all the documents and applications in order to get my father into the nicest nursing home I could find at the time: Shoreview Nursing Home in the Sheepshead Bay neighborhood of Brooklyn. The name, Shoreview, is an unfunny joke as the only view from the windows was of the parking lot. It should have been called Parkinglotview Nursing Home.

It was a challenging task for me. I was barely nineteen. I got lots of advice on how to do it, how to handle my father's finances with regards to his nursing home application. People said that only fools told the financial truth to the authorities. They said, what smart people do is hide the money from the nursing home or spend the money or put the money in other people's names, and then apply for Medicaid. Everyone said I should do that. And so, I did that. All of that. I acted in a rushed, haphazard, chaotic, disorganized, willy-nilly way. Best intentioned but not unlike my chicken bones in nature, and in outcome. As my karma would have it, there was a gigantic exposé of nursing home financial fraud that very year. Yup. My timing could not have been worse. The New York State Attorney General at the time, Eliot Spitzer (of the later infamous prostitution scandal) said:

"New Yorkers were shocked by revelations of widespread financial fraud, patient abuse, and official corruption plaguing the State's nursing home industry. In response, New York became the first state in the nation to establish an office—the Medicaid Fraud Control Unit—to thoroughly investigate those engaged in health care fraud and abuse in order to protect both patients and taxpayers."

That was me! And they caught me. Of all the people who ever committed fraud in modern times, the year I try to commit just a tiny little bit of fraud is the year they crack down.

I was petrified. I was called into a government office and questioned by some unsympathetic official. In order to avoid going to jail, I gave all of the money my father had saved and slaved for in Germany and in that fucking paintbrush sweatshop—all of it—to the government and the nursing home.

These files existed because of the *Wiedergutmachung*. Literally, that means "to make it good again." In English, it's called "restitution" or "reparations." Germany was going to try to "make it good again." (Well, they couldn't exactly make it good again considering how bad they had made it, but having a few extra dollars certainly could make it—life—somewhat better, although I have known people who said they would never touch this blood money. But each to their own.)

The stacks of files in front of us were filled with applications and explanations from my family, trying to prove that they deserved German money to make their lives good again. (Talk about entitlement.) But the German government put the onus on them, the victims, to document and prove that their time, their property, and their lives were stolen, and that unimaginable harm was done to them. Yes, you just go ahead and try to prove that.

Because of the letters that he wrote to my mother, I could place my father during that time. While he was writing to her in the New World from Stuttgart, he was also writing to the newly formed German government, trying to get reimbursed for his world that they had destroyed.

If I ever wondered—which I always did—what my father was doing from the time he got out of Auschwitz to the time he came to America, I was certainly on the road to finding that out now.

Yeva turns the page. "In this paper, it says he arrived in Stuttgart from Poland in 1918."

One hundred years ago. Just after World War I. My father would have been seventeen years old.

She continues. "The paper says where and when he was born." I knew the name of his town, Strzyżów, and the date, 27 October 1901.

"It also says that he was a *Jude*—a Jew." Yes, I knew that, too.

"It says he was in the camps for two years and three months."

Two years and three months. No, I didn't know that. I do the math. 820 days. And nights. How many hours? How many frigid winter nights and scorching summer days? There is no time now at the archive for me to really think about this, to think about my father's days and nights in Hell. There are too many papers. It is overwhelming and my head is already spinning. But we cannot stop the clock and must plow ahead.

We mark that page. We want it. We move on to the next page.

Yeva says this next document asks about my father's bodily injuries. What?

She translates. "Your father says that he had a 'sick heart.' It also lists the doctors that he saw, including a doctor in Stuttgart as well as a dentist." (I don't understand the importance of that, but I will later.)

Another paper says that he was a partner in a business called Brothers Schlüsselberg, but it was sold in October 1939. Yeva asks, "Did you know about that?" No. I know absolutely nothing.

Yeva reads on and then laughs in a creepy, sardonic way. "These Germans. Can you imagine? It says his business was sold in 1939. I mean," she says bitterly, "it was not sold. In 1939, Jewish businesses were not sold, they were stolen! Jews were forbidden by law to own businesses."

Besides translating, Yeva was also educating me, helping me understand some of the context, the history. She was also looking for corroboration of her own feelings about the heartlessness and rigidity of the German government. She believed that although they appeared to want to make amends, they just kept putting stumbling blocks in the way of the survivors, asking for documentation of their injuries and losses at a time when there was no possibility of documentation.

We would keep that page.

Next.

The following paper says, "Certificate." She scans it with her eyes as she simultaneously translates it to me. "Your father was called in by the Gestapo on 23 February 1943, and one day later, he was deported to Auschwitz in a transport with twenty-three other people from Stuttgart. From this transport," she reads, "only Herr Schlüsselberg came back alive."

Yeva looks at me in her deep, empathetic way. We pause and give weight to that sentence: my father was the only one from his transport to come back alive. My father? Who was my father that he was the only one to come back alive? How are we supposed to go on? How can we not stop and give this information the respect and dignity it deserves? But we cannot. There is no time.

She continues.

"The number tattooed on his left underarm was 105151."

Full stop.

Over the years, since my father's death, I have tried to recall the number on his left arm that I had seen for the twenty-three years that I knew him. I saw it so many times. You would think a daughter would remember such a thing. But I didn't. I recalled a seven.... Ha, I guess not. Although, to my minimal credit, the European way that the number one is printed looks a lot like an American seven. (Printed. On his flesh.) And there were three of those funny looking ones/sevens: 105151. No, I will not forget that number again. (But of course, I probably will.)

We were moving through these documents slower than a snail's pace. At this rate, we would never get through my father's files, not to mention the other files. We start to move quicker. Yeva would look at a page, try to quickly sum it up for me, and like our own version of Nazi selection, we choose which papers will live and which will die.

"Keep it."

"Leave it."

"Keep it."

"Leave it."

"Do you want this one?"

"No."

"This one?"

"Yes."

Document after document. We were not even close to halfway through my father's first file. So much. So many pages. And in German, damn it. Their attention to detail was overwhelming and absurd. The information, the documentation, the authorizations. Page after page. Stamped by this bureaucrat, signed by that official. Typed questions, handwritten answers. On and on. Signatures. Red ink. Blue ink. Relentless and endless.

We decide to take a break from my father's papers. Perhaps we should try to glean something from a different file. We look inside the "Chana Schlüsselberg" file, even though I am not related to her. My father's first wife and Harry's mother. We picked her file because it was smaller, and we thought we could digest information about her situation in a shorter amount of time—which proved to be true. The reason her file was so small was because her life was so short.

According to all of the papers in her file, she and her daughter, six-year-old Frida (sister of Harry/Heiner, daughter of my father) had been deported by train from Stuttgart on 5 April 1942 and brought to a place called Izbica, a town in Poland that served as one of the largest transfer points to various concentration camps. The documents in her folder said that she and her daughter had "died" sometime between 5 April, the day they were transported, and 2 November 1942, seven months later. They didn't know the exact date or the exact location of their murder. (No, they did not use the word "murder.") During that period of time, 15,000 Jews had been transported to Izbica from across Europe. Beginning November 2, 1942, the entire Izbica ghetto was "liquidated"—also known as erased, eradicated, eliminated, executed, slaughtered, butchered, and of course, exterminated. It is estimated that 4,500 Jewish men, women, and children were massacred assembly-line style and dumped into hastily dug mass graves. All of this was done at the direction of the sole commander of that ghetto: a career Nazi known for his exceptional cruelty, Hauptsturmführer Kurt Engels (SS), nicknamed the "Devil of Izbica." (Yes, he had a nickname, not to mention his own Wikipedia page.) It is said that he could not have breakfast without first shooting a Jew.

Chana and Frida Schlüsselberg were murdered between the time they were transported to Izbica in April and the time the ghetto was liquidated in November. Perhaps they were dumped into that hastily dug mass grave. Perhaps not. There were so many other options.

No one from their transport returned to Stuttgart alive.

No one. Not one person.

I'd never heard of Izbica before. You?

Fortunately, Wikipedia had. When I looked it up, I saw that the name of the town, Izbica also had another spelling—in Yiddish, "*Ishbitza*." That sounded familiar. Wait, yes, I *had* heard of *Ishbitza*.

In 1986, after my mother died, the hole in my heart was massive. I started going to different synagogues, hoping to find my family's soul resting in some House of God somewhere. I was not successful until 1990, when someone brought me to the little *shul* of Reb Shlomo Carlebach, a Chassid who spoke like a hippie from the '70s and whose message was inclusive, especially to women. He found holiness in everyone. His House of Love and Prayer was filled with warm, rose-colored light that seemed to have access to Heaven. It was close enough to what I was looking for, and I found some comfort there until he died in 1994.

Reb Shlomo spoke often of the teachings of different wise men from Jewish history, but especially of the *Ishbitzer Rebbe*. Reb Mordechai Leiner was famous: an important leader of a Chassidic dynasty in the late 1800s, whose teachings and commentaries on Jewish law and Torah are still studied and revered. Among many other things, he taught that mankind's surrender to despair and darkness are the ultimate blasphemy. (I knew I was a blasphemer, but I didn't know that was one of the reasons why.)

Rabbi Leiner is, in fact, buried in Ishbitza/Izbica. His disciples in Israel and all around the world still visit his holy grave to this day. And now we know that besides Rabbi Leiner, there are thousands of *other* holy Jews buried there—in *unmarked* graves—including possibly Chana and Frida Schlüsselberg.

Yeva and I look at the dates of their deportation on page after page. When we close the file, I look to Yeva, wondering if she is thinking what I am thinking.

"Do you see something weird about these dates?"

"What do you mean?"

"Yeva, my father was transported from Stuttgart to Auschwitz in February 1943. His wife and daughter were transported to Izbica in April 1942."

We look at each other like dopes. Why were they deported in 1942 and he in 1943? Why were they sent to Izbica and he to Auschwitz? How did he live through Auschwitz while they died in Izbica? These pages were eliciting more questions than answers.

We decide to open little Frida's file, the smallest one of all. It's late, and we are running out of time.

Frida's file is full of papers repeating the info about the transport to Izbica with her mother. But then we come upon something else. Yeva is reading to herself. She picks up her head and looks me square in the eye.

"This is so fucked up," she says. "You know what these papers are? You won't believe it."

"What?"

"It seems that you could get extra reparation money if you could prove that you wore the yellow star. These papers, submitted by your father, were trying to get this extra money for Frida. But," Yeva spits, "you have to fucking prove it. You have to prove that your dead five-year-old daughter really and truly wore a yellow star. Got any photos?"

We were weeping with rage.

It went on to say that extra money would be granted for children who were not less than five or six-years-old and wore the Star of David for over three months or some such absurd detail.

And now it was 5:45. We had to stop.

Yeva argued that we still had fifteen minutes. We were not moving through these papers quickly enough. "No," I said, "it's time to stop. We have to organize our thoughts and ourselves before we leave here. We have to figure out a plan."

We'd been going without a break since we got here, trying to tear through it all because of our limited time, but we simply could not. We looked at the stacks and stacks of still unopened files as well as the piles of papers still unseen from my father's huge file. Hundreds of documents. In German. The task was beyond mind boggling. How in the world should we proceed?

We took a breath. We looked. We thought.

We would come back to the archive first thing in the morning—at least Yeva would. I could not because I was seeing Eve Warscher, the daughter of my father's friend, at the Jewish Community Center in Stuttgart. I wanted to be with Yeva, but it was impossible. I was reassured that she understood, more or less, the kinds of information/ documents I was looking for. I would have to trust her with those decisions.

After my visit with Warscher, which I imagined would take an hour or so, I would join Yeva back at the archive and we would continue together, at least until I was scheduled to begin Hardy's agenda for me tomorrow afternoon.

Before we left, she told the librarians that we would be back first thing in the morning and to please keep our files available for us. They agreed.

We put on our coats and hats and gloves and walked out into the night. The freezing air slapped us awake. And alive. It was 2018, not 1943. We returned to the World of Today, to the World of Alive, to the World of Now. We had spent the last four hours in the World of Yesterday, the World of Dread and Horror; sitting hunched over, analyzing and scouring page after page, sentence after sentence, trying to make sense of the senselessness. During those hours, we had left our chairs only once to use the bathroom. Except for that break, our heads and hearts and eyeballs were being squeezed like slaves through the rubble of history, categorizing the uncategorizable; which information was important and which not important enough. (How dare we! Truly.) At first, we didn't know how to distinguish one delicate onionskin from another. There were so many details on every page.

Somehow, we figured out a method to this madness: Any direct information about my father was a keeper. Things that happened to him or things that he said or wrote in his own hand—which was a lot—we would try to save. Also, documents that described the abnormal normalcy of the Third Reich and its aftermath, such as the Germans offering restitution on the one hand, while putting up massive road-blocks on the other, making it brutally difficult to receive reparations. Papers that required documentation of the horrors—which were impossible to provide—we'd keep those too. (Documentation? Talk about a catch-22, over and over again.)

But now we were outside, and we were gratefully in the present. Cold, hungry, deserving. Yes, definitely deserving.

What now? We had no plan for tonight. Although Yeva was sleeping at her brother's place, she was not expected for dinner. I thought we should go back to Stuttgart to eat, but Yeva suggested we eat in Ludwigsburg. Another good idea, Yeva. She checked her phone for places to eat. Nothing sounded good, so we just walked around in the dark bracing night.

We found ourselves walking through a kind of park. At the end of the park, we came upon a square—literally, a square—outlined in paint on the cement pavement. Within this square, we saw old-fashioned life-sized suitcases, seemingly abandoned helter-skelter on the ground. The suitcases looked like old brown leather valises, but upon closer inspection, we saw that they were made of metal. Each one had writing on them, as though written in white chalk, with different names and dates. It took us a minute to understand what this was.

Yeva and I, it turns out, had stumbled upon the Ludwigsburg Holocaust Memorial, which was on the site of the former synagogue that had been burnt down on national bonfire day, Kristallnacht, 9 November 1938. We laughed at our macabre good fortune instead of weeping, and continued our search for someplace to eat. We had not eaten since we left Ulm this morning. (Ulm? This morning? Was it only this morning that we were in Ulm?)

We passed by what looked like an actual Italian restaurant. We went inside. It was warm and smelled good.

We ordered wine and food. Even I would have wine tonight. Yeva went off to phone her boyfriend for a few minutes. I sat and rested and waited. When she returned, we toasted ourselves and raised our glasses to my dead family. We wept, and then we ate. (It's like that old Passover joke: "The Egyptians tried to kill us, we escaped, let's eat.")

Afterwards, we took the commuter train back to the main station in Stuttgart. It was raining, of course. We got our luggage, and Yeva insisted on walking me to find my hotel, which was, as promised, right across the street from the station. She would take a different train to her brother's apartment, about half an hour away. We kissed and hugged and wept some more, wringing the last bits of salt water out of our souls, and then went our separate ways, until we would meet tomorrow.

I rolled my overstuffed luggage across the street to the hotel. Thank the Lord, it was a proper hotel. Elegant and grown-up. I felt a warm glow from the kindness and thoughtfulness I had provided for myself. "Good for you, Eleanor," I said out loud. "Good for you, my girl."

The clerk at the front desk was kind and lovely. I had asked for a quiet room with a tub, and that's what I got. My room was large and appointed in an old luxurious European manner, with a view—and a tub.

I was completely drained, beyond tired. I arrived in Germany on Sunday, and today was Tuesday. The third night. Really? Unbelievable.

I called John. It felt like we hadn't spoken in weeks, and yet it was only one night after yesterday's conversation from Ulm. I was feeling so alone with all of this sadness and death. I tried to explain to him a bit of what we had been through today and what we had found and how I was feeling, but it was very hard to put the day into words. It was too much. Fortunately, he didn't press me for details. Instead, I asked him about himself and his kids and let him do most of the talking. I can't remember now what he said except for "sweet dreams," which, when I think about it, was a grisly joke.

I was too tired to take a bath, but because of all of the fuss I had made about getting a tub, I felt obligated. I threw myself in, and then very quickly, I threw myself out. Like the hokey-pokey. I did not have the energy to sit still and give myself to the water.

Then I went to bed, but not to sleep. "*Sweet dreams?*" No, sleep would not be my friend on this journey.

CHAPTER FOURTEEN

Day Three Morning: Eve Warscher—Jewish Community Center (Stuttgart)
(Wednesday, 17 January 2018)

It was a lousy night. Tossing and turning. Awake till dawn's early light. When it became clear that I could not sleep, I tried to be productive and took out my father's letters. I went through all of them and highlighted wherever the name "Warscher" appeared—which was a lot. Eve Warscher would be interested in that, I thought.

It was time to get out of bed, but I was dragging my ass, moving very slowly. Even though I was awake all damn night, I somehow wound up leaving the hotel late. I wanted to be at the Jewish Community Center by nine, but now, I would arrive at least a half hour later. That meant I would also be late to meet Yeva at the archive. I was very tired and very angry with myself.

It was also my first day without Yeva; completely on my own and responsible for my own travel. I had no ticket for the train and had to buy one. Plus I had no cash. That made everything more difficult, and it took extra time for me to find a ticket machine that accepted credit cards. Grrr. They all took debit cards but not credit cards, and my debit card was still in Manhattan.

After looking at Google Maps on my iPhone again (and again), I took what I hoped was the right train. Once on the train, I asked and learned that the stop I thought I was looking for was called by a different name. And oops, hello, it was this upcoming stop. Glad I asked.

Up on the street, again glued to my Google map, I begin walking. I go one block and decide to ask an actual person. Of course, I am walking in the opposite direction. I should probably just count on that in the future—that my instincts are wrong and I should always walk in the opposite direction of my initial inclination.

I get to the street of the Community Center, *Hospitalstraße*, and find the address, "number 36." The building is completely boarded up with signs in German that I understand to mean, "Due to construction, the main entrance is around the corner." I will now arrive for this meeting even later. Not a good way to start the day.

You would think that of all places, there would be tight security to get into the Jewish Community Center of Stuttgart. There certainly was in every other Jewish building all over Europe. Well, not here. Construction had the whole place in disarray. I entered the building on the heels of some worker and was allowed in without any examination or question. The lobby was filled with baby carriages lined up against the wall. I asked a woman where I could find Miss Warscher. She asked, in English, if I was expected. I said yes, and she walked me up five flights of stairs, apologizing all the way that the elevator was not working due to the construction.

The staircase leads directly to a large room where three women sit quietly at their desks. Off to the right is a private office. My escort looks inside, "Someone here to see you," she says.

From behind the desk, a woman comes toward me, her face round, like a dumpling. Her hair is the blackest black, a frizzy mop of fine curls, beginning high up on her forehead. She looks me over, we exchange hellos, and shake hands.

"Come, let us go somewhere we can talk." Her English is nearly without accent. We walk down a hallway and find chairs in a barren conference room.

I explain about the letters: how I had come upon them and what I was learning from them; how it was not until I got to Ulm two days ago that I connected the name in the letters to the name on the back of the photographs, and then miraculously connected it to her.

We spoke first about ourselves. It turned out there was a great deal we had in common: We were both turning sixty-five in May—she was five days older. Her mother was a lot younger than her father—twenty years—just like mine. And her mother was related to her father—a cousin—as was mine. Different, yet nearly parallel lives.

She had stayed in Stuttgart all these years because her mother needed help. I was incredulous that she still had a mother. She made a point of telling me that her brother was of no help, so she had washed her hands of him, and they no longer spoke.

I took out the two photos I had of my father with her father, Josef Warscher. I don't know what I expected exactly, but she did not betray any emotion at all upon seeing them: no excitement or surprise or delight at what I imagined were new discoveries about her father. I assumed she had never seen these photos—and she hadn't. She looked at them impassively, betraying nothing.

I took out the letters and rifled through them until I found the ones with her father's name that I had highlighted the night before. She took a page and began reading the German easily. "Your father had a beautiful handwriting," she said. Really? To me, the letters were unintelligible. How beautiful could the writing of an uneducated factory worker be? Yeva had been struggling with the translations. It was such slow going for her, I just assumed that the letters were hard to read. Well, not for Eve Warscher.

As she was reading, she remarked casually, "Oh look, he refers to Helfer." "Helfer" was another name often mentioned in the letters, another person I had no idea about. In my wildest dreams, I never expected to learn who those names were, those names from my father's life, seventy years ago.

"You know who Helfer is?" I ask.

"Yes, of course. He was my great uncle."

"What?"

"Yes, he was my mother's uncle. My mother, her maiden name is Helfer."

I am completely blown away. The dead are screaming in my ears. Eve Warscher is my father's best friend's daughter! She knew the people in those letters.

"Was your mother with them then after the war?" I ask.

"No, no. She was in England during the war, sent on a *kindertransport*."

"Wait," I interrupt, "my father's son too, my half-brother...."

But she doesn't wait. She keeps talking.

"My mother did not want to return to Germany after the war. She was happy in England. They forced her to come back."

"Wow, my brother too," I say. "He didn't want to come back either, but my father allowed him remain in England."

"That was very kind of your father. My mother resented—always— that she had to come back to Germany. She hated Germany. As do I."

Breathe. I am trying to take this all in.

"This 'Helfer,' who my father talks about, your great uncle, is *he* still alive?" All of a sudden, every unimaginable possibility is possible.

"No, no. But that doesn't matter; my mother stopped speaking to him when she returned to Germany. She believed that Helfer had betrayed her father—his own brother—to the Nazis, which cost him his life."

I sit there with Eve Warscher as though this is normal, as though we are having some kind of getting-to-know-you chat over tea and cucumber sandwiches. My brain is in a backward spin. The skeletons refuse to rest quietly in their wooden boxes. Oh, no. They have been waiting patiently for this opening, for this small crack in the darkness.

Eve goes on. I learn from her that the three of them—my father, her father, and her mother's uncle, Helfer (which in Yiddish, ironically, means "helper") were the best of friends at that time, in '48 and '49, as well as with another man, a name she recognizes in the letters— Orfner. Another name identified. Impossible.

Eva knew these people because they were all still living in Germany in the 1950s, '60s, and '70s. She would have known my father, too, if he had stayed. If...

I ask if they were friends from before the war. She does not believe so. After surviving the Nazi horror, they all miraculously returned to Stuttgart. They had lost everything and everyone, and they were now single men—"bachelors," she calls them—who found some paltry yet necessary comfort in one another, determined to live as best they could in a country that tried—and succeeded—in completely mangling their lives. At least they would have each other. Until they wouldn't.

The letters take on new meaning. Names are attached to real human beings. Friends. My father had friends! I try to imagine what it meant for him to leave these people behind—these comrades, brothers—who lived lives aligned with his, with whom he might have shared a future.

In his penultimate letter, dated 19 December 1949, just before he leaves Stuttgart for Bremerhaven where he will take the boat to America, my father writes:

> *In my last letter, I already mentioned that the farewell from here weighs heavily, not only from my side but also from my friends and acquaintances. I've been already twice to Helfer's to say goodbye. He bemoans my leaving, and he begs me to visit one more time.... All the others also insist on seeing me once again before I leave for good. I must do it. I am not happy with the weight of it.... Tonight I will be at Felsen's with Warscher, Stuetz, Zimmermann, and the others. Tomorrow night I am invited to go to Gehring's.*
>
> *I have banned everyone from coming to the train station in Ludwigsburg to see me off. I hope they will heed my request.*

How many times can you say goodbye to loved ones? My poor father: goodbye, goodbye; gambling that this new unknown life with strangers will be better than his known life with friends. Risk/reward. The Devil you know. How do you calculate that? Especially in 1949. Of course, he couldn't see into the future, but I am here to tell you that nothing was improved in this trade-off for him. Nothing. Except if you count me. I was all he got out of this deal.

I give Eve a few other letters, asking if she knows of this person or that place that my father referred to. Yes, she knows some of the other people mentioned and places that they went to. She reads the letters handily but with little surprise or wonder. Unfazed. If it were me, if I had just met someone who brought me documents and photos from the past about my parents, I would have been in awe and amazed.

It took a little more than an hour to show her the references to her family and for her to answer whatever questions I could think of on the fly. I was not at all prepared for this miraculous meeting. I had not connected enough dots for a more meaningful visit. However, in my defense, who could have expected that I would meet the daughter of Josef Warscher?

I am already more than half an hour late to meet Yeva back in Ludwigsburg at the Staatsarchiv—for which I was also unprepared. Because of the lateness of the hour, I have to finish up with Eve Warscher, the daughter of my father's best friend.

I put the letters away. We continue talking.

Had she ever married? No. As the sole caretaker of her mother, who is suffering from dementia, Eve had no time for herself. Plus, "there was no one to marry here in Stuttgart." She was tired of her job, which included the responsibility of providing burial services for Jews who could not afford funeral expenses. "There are no German Jews left anymore," she says. "What we have here now are the Russian Jews, and they are different from what I am used to. And I have no friends here anymore. I am just waiting until I am sixty-five, and then I will retire. This is my last year here. I have had enough."

She seemed so sad.

125

"I'm sorry," I say and she looks at me deeply.

"Yes, this is what I miss: someone like you," she says. "*Yiddishkayt*—the Jewish soul." Then, at last, she weeps. I join her, and we sit like that for a few minutes.

It is time to go.

She takes off her glasses, dries her tears. We stand and hug. I had brought along one of my CDs and suggested that perhaps her mother, who she said used to speak Yiddish, might enjoy it. She thanks me and asks if I would forgive her for not seeing me out, down the five flights of stairs. Her knees are a problem. Yes, mine too. I assure her that I can exit on my own. We hug again, and I leave, heading toward the train for Ludwigsburg.

My father's friend, Warscher.... An unknown name in so many of the letters, one that meant nothing to me. Now he is a man. Now he is alive. Now he has a wife, and a son, and a daughter—who is my counterpart, like a sister. Never did I dream that she would exist and that I could or would ever find her.

How could I find her? I wasn't even looking.

CHAPTER FIFTEEN

Day Three Continued: Staatsarchiv (Ludwigsburg)
(Wednesday, 17 January 2018)

My second time today alone on the train. I'm feeling more comfortable now. I get to Ludwigsburg and easily find my way back to the archive. I congratulate myself as though I were a child. Or a dog. Good girl!

When I arrive, Yeva already has the stacks of files on the desk. It is eleven-thirty, and I am being picked up at one-thirty by Hardy to begin the official itinerary he had so thoughtfully prepared for me a month ago.

Yeva and I have two hours left together to go through as many of these papers as possible, to figure out which ones to keep. Our task is impossible. The material is infinite; the time is not.

We are examining my father's file once again. We come across his tax returns for the year 1965. Everything plus the kitchen sink seems to be in these folders. This is an example of where my presence is valuable. Yeva would have understandably ignored these tax returns, whereas for me, they are important and provide me with details about the past and about my father.

My father's federal tax returns from fifty years ago. Who would have thought that tax returns of any kind would be of the slightest interest to me? But they were. What did he and the world look like in Brooklyn in 1965? I was twelve. My parents were no longer together. What did he earn? What did he spend? This was another way for me to know him.

Looking at those papers makes me realize that I also needed to learn about Germany. What was the mark worth in 1949? (For one dollar, you got 3.33 mark.) What did that government look like during those first years of its re-creation? Before today, I didn't know or care that Germany became a nation again in 1949. Now, everything is a piece of the puzzle that I am trying to solve.

My father's tax returns were rich with details about his life in Brooklyn, a life that I lived through but was too young to understand or remember. I look at the stocks he had: Pan American, J.W. Mays, S. Klein Department Store. Blue chips that were supposed to last forever, all thriving at one time, and now all gone. Like him. Like everything. Dust to dust.

(When I was a girl, he used to buy me gifts—blouses and sweaters—from S. Klein. I didn't know that he owned the company. At least a hundred shares, anyway.)

The long-term gains from his stocks in 1965 was $343.97. To me, that was worth knowing. Why? Then versus Now? My father made $343 for the entire year from his stock profits. That's what my monthly phone bill costs me today.

On another page was his wage statement, his W-2 from the paintbrush factory, where he sweated and slogged for all his days in the United States of America. In 1965, my father earned $5,436.17, paying $379.10 in federal taxes. To put this into perspective, my rent in Manhattan is currently $3,400 a month. Does anyone care? I do. My father was a real person, like us, who paid real taxes and had a real life. He has been dead for so long that sometimes it seems possible that he never really existed. But he did. Not just in my memory. The guy paid taxes! That proves he was real. He fulfilled both of life's two guarantees.

This also gives some credibility to my memory, which I fear is often suspect. Tax returns are practically the definition of "just the facts." There is nothing subjective about a tax statement. It says right here, he worked in a paintbrush factory. His employer was Adams' Brush Manufacturer. Yes! I had forgotten their name. And his profession:

"dyer."Thank you, that is what I remembered and what I believed, but it was all so long ago, I couldn't be sure anymore if it was true. Sadly, my father had become more of a memory to me than a flesh and blood human being. Time can do that.

My father claimed four dependents. Really? My parents were already divorced by then, and my brother Seymour was twenty-four and married. So, how did he come to four dependents? I guess that's even more proof of him being human—that he cheated on his tax returns.

Alimony was listed at $1,300 for the year. For the year? A hundred dollars a month? No wonder I went to public school.

Charities? Three hundred dollars total. To the following charities: Synagogue, UJA, Red Cross, Leukemia Society, Xmas Seals (Yup, that's what it says), March of Dimes, and the Muscular Dystrophy Fund. Ha, that was definitely pledged during the Jerry Lewis Telethon, which was on TV every Labor Day. We were big fans of Jerry Lewis, my father and I. On some Sundays when I was a girl, after he made lunch, he'd take me to the latest Jerry Lewis movie, which he managed to sleep through. I never understood how legitimately tired my father must have been. Never until now.

We flip through the other pages. Expenses and earnings, and then the ever important, "Line 18—Balance Due." In the year 1965, my father got back a refund of $37.48 in federal taxes. A windfall.

We were trying to plow through the massive amounts of documents, and yet, I was interested in tax minutiae. We were playing "Beat the Clock" and losing; going as quickly as we could, picking and choosing, but not really making a dent in the many pages that were still left to look at.

We are overwhelmed and becoming distracted and numb. Let's look at a different folder. We open my grandfather Isak Hoff's folder. The war years found him and my mother's family in Uzbekistan. Date of birth, place of birth, a little bit more than that, but nothing we found at that time seemed particularly illuminating. Only later would I learn what secrets were resting deeper in that file.

It was almost 1:30. Hardy would be here in a minute.

Yeva and I agree that she would carry on, selecting documents on my behalf. My instruction to her was: when in doubt—save it. (We didn't yet know how much each copy would cost.)

We said our goodbyes. I felt wretched, trying to absorb the unabsorbable. I wanted to stay with Yeva and the papers. That was where my family was.

Yeva went back to work as I trudged into the lobby, opened the locker, and put on my coat. As I was getting ready leave, a man who appeared to be somewhere in his sixties was approaching the entrance. "Eleanor?" he asked. "Hello, Hardy!" I answered. We looked into each other's faces, searching for some commonality, for Kipling's words: "We are of one blood, ye and I." Were we?

He looks kind. Slight but not unattractive. Well put-together in slacks, sports jacket, and turtleneck. Very European.

We shake hands, and I follow him to his car, a recent middle-of-the-road black sedan—nothing fancy.

He gives me the plan for the day.

First, we will go to the *Zentrale Stelle zur Verfolgung von NS Verbreche*, also known as the "Central Bureau of the State Justice Administration for the Investigation of National Socialist Crimes." Or as I was calling it, "The Nazi Department of Justice." (An oxymoron.) There, we will meet with the head archivist, Dr. Peter Gohle. Hardy tells me that they have found "a document about your father."

The reporter that I had agreed to a month ago will join us there, he goes on to say. From that point on, she will accompany me to all of my meetings for the rest of my stay in Stuttgart.

"Great," I say with secret regret. My emotions feel way too raw and private now to have some journalist following me around. Too late, I should have thought of that earlier.

She would also like to interview me for her upcoming article. Sure.

Tonight, there will be a dinner at the Theatre Haus restaurant with the renowned costume designer, whose name I didn't catch, and her husband, also of unknown renown, who is the director of the theatre. She, the costume designer, will look at my family photos then. "Terrific," I say. But in fact, I am so tired and so sorry not to be at the archive desk with Yeva.

I ask him about himself and why his English is so good. He was a copywriter in the States for many years, he says. How does he know Lutz Engelhardt, whom I'd met in Berlin and had connected us? Well, it turns out that he doesn't know Lutz at all, that they'd never met. Both were involved in Stuttgart's music scene, and Lutz had simply contacted him out of the blue.

Great.

And it is great. Such an amazing circumstance/opportunity, and I am able to recognize it at this very moment that it's happening. Here is this guy who I don't know from Adam, connected to me by another guy I know a drop more than Adam; taking me, guiding me, shining a light for me down into the black hole of my past. The mere offering is a gift and a wonder.

We arrive at our destination, still in Ludwigsburg. I'm not really clear where we are or who we are meeting. Hardy keeps calling it the Ministry of Persecution. Well, that's bound to be a pretty big fucking ministry.

He parks his car, and we walk to a stone-walled entryway with a steel door blocking the way. Hardy takes a paper out of his attaché case, looks something up, and chooses one of the bells to ring. We wait. It's cold and grey and still/again/always raining. A woman's voice on the intercom asks something, and he says something that includes his name and mine, and then we are buzzed into an inner courtyard. In front of us is a four-story building, neither old nor modern. Again, he rings, says something, and again, we wait.

Soon, the heavy door is opened by a large, full-faced man of indeterminate age, sporting actual muttonchops. (Yes, muttonchops!) He addresses Hardy. I am unclear who he is, but I suspect he is the security doorman. We follow him up a flight of stairs and walk into an office, where the doorman takes a seat behind the desk. Oh. I guess he's the archivist—Dr. Peter Gohle.

He and Hardy say some more things in German that I can kind of infer thanks to my Yiddish. The archivist asks about the reporter, and Hardy says she should be here any minute. As if on cue, the bell rings and someone shows the reporter up to join us. She is a thin blonde with glasses, late 40s or early 50s. Her presence immediately brings a different energy into the room: frenzied, lively, impatient. Rather than sizing up the room, she shifts the focus of the room to herself. She apologizes for being late and begins. Her name is Hilke Lorenz, and she writes for the *Stuttgart Zeitung*. She takes out a pad and her camera, and she leaps in. "You won't mind if I take photographs." She doesn't intend this as a question. The archivist asks her to please not photograph him. Perhaps I should have thought this through more carefully; having a reporter follow me around on this trip. I am already sorry.

Dr. Gohle begins. He explains what the organization is and what they do. "It was learned, after the war ended, that there were many Nazis who returned to Ludwigsburg after the German surrender. They went on with their lives as though nothing had happened. But since 1947, the job of this department has been to conduct investigations into National Socialist crimes. Of course, we knew who the leaders were, but we were interested in the underlings, the less well-known Nazis. Our job is to find those who committed crimes against humanity and to continue to prosecute the guilty, to this day. Even though people are dying off, we continue with our investigations. Despite this long period of time, we are still able to prosecute crimes from the Nazi regime today." He points to a chart on the wall that looks like a genealogical map, listing the hierarchy of the Nazi Party, beginning at the top with Himself—the Fuhrer, of course—and then moving down and across to the masses of the lesser-known murderous barbarians. The family tree of the Nazi Party.

The reporter, Hilke, asks if she can take a photo, not waiting for an answer. I am now seriously regretting my decision to allow a reporter to follow me. What in the world was I thinking? (Or not thinking?) I imagined that she would just be a fly on the wall. There's no such thing as "bad" press, I used to think. Wrong.

Finally, the archivist gets down to business. He tells me that they have a document of my father's in their possession: sworn testimony that he gave to this very office in 1947. 1947? That was earlier than any of his letters to my mother, earlier than any of the documents Yeva and I had found at the Staatsarchiv. That was less than two years after Auschwitz.

The archivist continues. "At that time, this office was trying to identify the average German citizens who had collaborated with the Nazis. Since your father was one of the few Jews deported from Stuttgart that returned to the city after the war, this office interviewed him in 1947. And these are his words, your father's words."

My eyes are blinking like crazy. I want to put my hand over them to calm them. But I don't. I just blink. His voice bounces back and forth in my head. *"Your father's words."*

Then he opens a manila envelope and hands me a document. Three pages. Written in German.

Of course, Hilke is the first one to speak. "What's in it?" she asks. The archivist replies that he has not read it. (Really? Can that possibly be true?)

We stay and chat for a bit longer, although all I want to do is find out what's in that document. The archivist asks me what exactly I am doing here in Germany, why I have come. (Yes, good question.) I explain about the letters. Hilke is taking notes. Dr. Gohle seems to be interested.

After about an hour or so, he tells us there is a photography exhibit next door about the Nazis that he would like to show us. Hilke begs off. She has a deadline on a story that she needs to submit today, she says. I wish I had a deadline too. I think, *Oh God, must I? Can't I tell him that I gave at the office?* No, I cannot.

We go: Hardy, Dr. Gohle, and I. I look at the photos and the displays politely. I "ooh" and "ahh" at yet more photos of the nightmare. I am hungry and tired and if I didn't see another picture of a

Holocaust victim or a Nazi for the rest of my life, that would be okay with me.

Finally, we give our thanks and say our goodbyes to the archivist. The envelope with the three pages of my father's testimony is burning a hole in my little hands.

Hardy and I walk a few blocks to a bakery where Hilke is sitting with her computer, feverishly typing. It's an unadorned, nondescript little shop with two or three small café tables and chairs, a brightly lit counter with breads and pretzels, and an old white-haired woman with an apron. (What was *she* doing during the war?)

Hardy asks if I've had any pretzels since I've been in Germany. No, I tell him. "Oh," he says proudly, "these pretzels are what this county is famous for." I would beg to differ, but I don't want to be rude.

"Every neighborhood boasts of their pretzels and claims that their pretzels are the very best," he says. "But here, at this little shop, they truly are the best ones." He buys me a buttered pretzel and a coffee. By gosh, he is right. It is terrifically delicious: soft, chewy, warm. The sweet butter alone is worth the price of admission. I was hungry as all hell, so what could be bad? (I realize that I hadn't eaten since this morning, before my meeting with Eve Warscher. Wait, was that today?)

He and I sit at one of the little tables having forced, idle conversation while Hilke is sitting at another table, hammering away on her keyboard. After about twenty minutes, she is finished. I realize Hardy has just been babysitting me until Hilke was done because he now respectfully excuses himself. He confirms that we will both be at dinner tonight at the Theatre Haus. Hilke agrees to see that I get back to my hotel in Stuttgart before then, and in a flash, he's gone.

Hilke joins me at my little table. She asks some questions about my parents and the letters. Then her eyes light up and she says, "You know, I would love to see what is written in that testimony you got today. Would you let me see it?"

I was so tired that I had practically forgotten about the testimony. I, too, would love to know what was written in it. I think for a quick second. I look at her and say if she would allow me to use her computer while she translates the testimony into English as she reads it, sentence by sentence, I would be happy to let her look at it.

She agrees.

The computer was not a Mac. It also had a German-based keyboard, so there was a small learning curve for me. But I made do. As Hilke read to herself, she simultaneously translated aloud for me. I entered the information as quickly as I could:

Württemberg. The Testimony of Chaskel Schlüsselberg, Importer of Eggs and Chickens.

In former days, I owned a business of collecting things in Stuttgart-Bad Cannstatt. Because of the laws against Jews in the former German state, I had to give up this business in July 1938, which meant I was forced to sell it. For a certain time after that, I lived on my money until the Gestapo stopped my access to this money. I began working at the heel factory on Taubenstraße 4. There, I worked until February 1943. On the 21 or 22 February 1943, I got a letter that said that in two days, the ghetto would be evacuated and to go to Hospitalstraße 36. (I did not connect the dot at that moment, but Hospitalstraße 36 was where I met with Eve Warscher—that very morning.)

The transport was created there. It was seventy-nine people, including the superintendent of the Jewish Community: Lowenstein, his wife, and child. Also, the jeweler Oppenheimer was there with his family. In a closed train, we traveled to Trier, where a larger transport of a thousand people was amassed. This transport of about 1,000 people was driven via Berlin to Auschwitz.

The organizer of the transport in Stuttgart was the Police Inspector Koch. Together with him worked the Gestapo-men Ott and Amther. Those two men gave us declarations to sign, which said that we permitted them to take our money because of our Communist activities. For that reason, the state could take our money, they told us. Not one of us Jews objected to signing these declarations. At this point, it no longer mattered whether or not they had our signatures or permission in order for them to take our money.

135

I asked Ott where we are going to, and he told me that the place where you are going will be much better for you than it is here. I told him I wouldn't mind if they kept me here.

When I smoked a cigarette later, I heard Ott talking to Amther. "Look at this disobedient Jew. He's smoking." The Jews didn't have smoking cards. Amther answered, "Let them do it. At the place where they are going to, they will smoke the shit from horses."

Who took our baggage, I don't know. I remember that the women participants were frisked physically, but I don't know who did this. Ott and Amther brought us, along with other policemen whom I did not know, to Trier and put us into the hands of the Gestapo there.

From Trier began a very severe time of suffering for us. The victims of the transport were not discriminated there by age or gender, male or female. They were all just put into cattle cars, about 150 people. They were using violence to put us into the cars. In the cattle wagon, there was no toilet, and neither could we lay down or sit. Two days and two nights long, we didn't get anything to eat or to drink. Some of the children were so thirsty that their mothers spit into their mouths to quench their thirst.

After two days, the transport arrived at the station to Auschwitz Birkenau. The train stopped there and waited until it was dark because all the actions of the SS only took place in darkness. Then that night, the SS men tore open the doors and we were hit with rubber batons and with shouting sentences like: "Get out, you pig Jews!" and thrown out from the train car. Because of this treatment, we lost our baggage. No one was allowed to take it with them. The whole action was organized so that we had to leave our luggage. Later on, we saw how German prisoners collected the baggage and with trucks took them away. Not one of the transported people ever saw his baggage again.

Then, in the light of very bright lamps, they made their selection from the people in the transport. The men were put together. The women and also the children were selected apart from each other. It was a crying like in a cattle market. Screaming. Shouting. I was separated from my wife and my six-year-old little daughter. I never saw them again.

When Hilke translated that sentence, I stopped. Up until that moment, I was just typing away, detached, like a court stenographer, transcribing every word that she had said. When she spoke the words about my father's wife and daughter, I froze. Hilke stopped too. She looked at me. She must have thought that I was finally moved by the horror of my father's story. She asked if I was all right. She herself seemed quite moved by it all and was giving me as sympathetic an eye as a reporter could—sympathetic yet excited because she smelled the blood of a story here.

I did not tell her why I had stopped. I would not tell her that at the archive earlier today and yesterday, all of the documents Yeva and I found about my father's wife and daughter said that they had been transported in 1942 and had died that year, sometime between April and November. All of the many documents said that same thing. But here, my father's testimony seemed to be saying something different: that the last time he had seen his wife and daughter was after he got out of that train in Auschwitz in February 1943. I didn't understand. I concluded that somebody was not telling the truth, and I had the scary feeling that it was my father. The possible repercussions frightened me. Being caught in a lie or in a crime is something that, rationally or not, I have been afraid of my entire adult life. I imagined the headline of Hilke's upcoming article in the *Stuttgart Zeitung*: "Holocaust Survivor Exposed as Liar! Further Investigations to Follow." Paranoid? Guilty? Me?

I looked at Hilke. I told her I was all right. She asked if we could go on. Yes, of course we could.

Men were selected by how strong they were, by their physical power. Men with injuries from the first war, they were forced to throw away their walking canes. Those men lay crying in the snow. Me being strong went to the so-called "100 percent commando." There were other commandos: for example, 10 percent commandos for less strong people or 40 percent, etcetera.

By end of February 1943, I was working as a bricklayer for Buna Werke factory in the concentration camp, Monowitz, part of Auschwitz.

[Monowitz was the slave labor camp financed by IG Farben—the leading manufacturer of German explosives as well as Zyklon B, the gas that murdered millions.]

We were able to live there, but food was not enough. Very not enough, so that even stronger persons couldn't stand it. Every two months, there was a reselection by the SS where the weak and undernourished were selected. It would happen in this way: at the reselection, they wrote down the names and then called them out. This was easy because just a few days after arriving in Auschwitz, we got a prisoner number tattooed on our left forearm. I, for example, had 105151. Those who were selected were later gassed. What this gassing means, we got knowledge of only three months after our arrival. The selected ones were brought naked to closed transportation wagons in Auschwitz, where they were gassed. The corpses were then burned. The prisoners were exposed to the will of the SS. I personally saw during the morning roll call, with thousands of others, prisoners who were hanged because they had stolen food.

On the 16th January 1945, they took us from Auschwitz to Buchenwald. This happened because of the Russian advance, and Auschwitz was no longer being protected by the Germans. Our transport occurred as a land march. We marched for nearly eight days. We came to Prague and then were transported in an open coal wagon to Buchenwald. On the way, a lot of people died of cold. Those people were just thrown out from the wagon. In Buchenwald, there was not much work because the breakdown was approaching. The camp was terribly overcrowded. And also there, we had terrible suffering.

Four weeks later, I came to Schönebeck near the River Elbe, where we were again forced to work and build barricades against tanks. Panzers. We were there for about fourteen days. Then we went by marching to Oranienburg. From there, we were supposed to go on further. We got bread for yet another march, but I felt so hopeless that I didn't want to go on anymore. I hid with my bread under a sack of straw. I ate the bread there in that position and said to myself that if I would be caught, at least I would die with a full stomach. My hiding wasn't discovered, and later on, I was liberated by Russians. I am the only survivor from the Stuttgart transport from February 1943.

That was that. My father, in his own words. In 1947.

"I am the only survivor from the Stuttgart transport from February 1943."

My father stares at me from behind my eyes. And now that he's gone, I feel that *I* am the only survivor of that transport.

But in this brightly lit bakery with this German stranger—a reporter, no less—I realize that I need to come back to earth and be careful. Everything I do and say is potential fodder for some newspaper article that I will have no control over. I have to watch myself and think before I speak, which is not such a bad idea in general. Isn't that something parents tell their children? "Don't say anything you wouldn't want printed on the front page of *The New York Times*." Or the *Stuttgart Zeitung*.

Hilke is looking at me, trying hard to read me. "What are you thinking?" she asks. "This must upset you."

(Do you think?) "Yes, well, it is a lot," I mutter.

"Did you know any of this before? Did your father speak much about the war?"

"No. Not really. Just a few things." I do not elaborate.

"You know," she says, "I would love to read the letters from your father. It would really help me in this article to have the flavor of his writing style. Would that be possible?"

I had his letters in my backpack from earlier in the day when I showed them to Eve Warscher. So, yes, I did have them with me. Every single one of them.

Then the oddest thing happened. After just telling myself to think and be careful, I spoke without doing either. "Sure," I said. "Here." And I dug into my backpack and handed over the complete file of the fifty-six letters to Hilke Lorenz, reporter.

"I will make a copy in the office tomorrow," she said, "and give them back to you. Do not worry. They will be safe. I will take good care of them."

I can only imagine that I was beyond exhausted and in some state of shock. I had not shown anyone—*not anyone*—all of these letters. Not even the translators. No one. I had been so careful parceling them out, not giving anyone the entire narrative, if indeed there was a narrative. The letters were mine, and I am not a sharing type of person. But here I am thoughtlessly—literally without thought—giving the letters—*all* of the letters—to a newspaper reporter. A *German* newspaper reporter.

The bakery was closing. It was time to go. In a few hours, it would be time for dinner in Stuttgart with the costume designer. Yeva was still at the archive, which was also about to close. Hilke was going to drive me to the train. I asked if we could pick up Yeva on the way. She said sure.

I phoned Yeva, who was just packing up at the archive, and told her we would come fetch her. I asked her about her day. She said she had made some startling discoveries.

"Me too," I said.

"Wait till I tell you," said Yeva.

"Yes, me too," I said.

Hilke could see that I was excited and asked about it, of course. I told her that Yeva said she had uncovered some important information.

We went out into the cold rainy night. (Not one day of sunshine during my entire week in Germany.) It felt good though, the bite of the air and freezing drops spraying my face: alive and invigorating. All of this had happened in one day? One day—which was not even over yet. Day three?

We found Yeva in front of the archive, and she got into the back of the car. I introduced her to Hilke, and Hilke immediately started speaking to her in German, which bothered me since we all spoke English. To her credit, she quickly apologized.

"We really got something today," I told Yeva. "Sworn testimony by my father to the Ministry of Justice."

Hilke immediately corrected me: "It's called the Central Bureau of the State Justice for Investigation of National Socialist Crimes."

Whatever. (I would never remember that.) "Three whole pages," I babbled on, "from 1947!"

Yeva countered with, "Wow, that's great." She didn't say, ask, or volunteer anything more.

"How about you, what did you find?" I asked, excited to hear about her discovery.

"Oh," she said softly, "nothing like that; nothing very much." A completely different tone from the one I'd heard on the phone just a few minutes earlier.

Hilke, as she was driving through the traffic, didn't buy that. She turned around to look at Yeva.

"Come on, tell us what you found."

"No," Yeva said, "really, it was not that much. Eleanor, we can talk about it later."

And that was that.

It took me a minute to understand. She did not want to speak in front of Hilke. Perhaps Hilke understood that too. It didn't matter if she did or not. Case closed. For now.

Yeva was willing, however, to talk about other things. She spoke about finding lots of official German requests for more and more documentation to prove the impossible, which kept postponing reparation payments. Yeva said that these reparation claims were a very good source of income for the German lawyers who were required to help the poor Jews prove that they had actually suffered during the war. It was quite a scam, she said, a big payday for the lawyers who were getting additional fees by creating all these delays and postponements. She went on: It was also benefitting the German government, who could claim to be investigating reparation inquiries without actually paying out money to the victims until the very last possible moment—if ever.

Hilke, driving though the rainy stop-and-go rush hour traffic, spoke up, vehemently disagreeing. The lawyers in those cases were not working for the money, she said, but for the general good. Lawyers were not getting rich on restitution cases. Yeva sharply challenged that, and they got into a bit of a spin about it. They were trying to be polite, but their disdain for each other was clear. The traffic trapped us in the car for nearly an hour. It was exhausting and unpleasant.

Finally, we came to the train station and said our goodbyes. I would see Hilke soon at the Theatre Haus for dinner with Hardy and the costume designer.

As soon as we were alone, I looked at Yeva and realized that I had made a terrible mistake. Yeva wanted to talk, but I needed to do something first—and fast. I dialed Hilke's cellphone. It went straight to voice mail. I left a message, trying my best to hide my panic. "Hey, Hilke. I just realized that I needed something in that folder of my father's letters that I gave you. Please, would you bring them all with you tonight? Thanks so much." And hung up.

"You gave her the letters?!" Yeva was incredulous.

"Yes. I must have lost my mind."

"I don't trust her," Yeva said.

"Yes, well, I'm not sure. But I am sure it was totally stupid to give her the letters. I bet she'll bring them tonight."

I said that to Yeva, but in fact, I had no idea if she would or wouldn't. I had only just met her that afternoon, and didn't know a damn thing about her or her ethics or anything else. I had a sickening feeling.

The train finally came.

I asked Yeva about what she had found.

"Thirty pages."

"What?"

"Thirty pages of your father's sworn testimony. Everything. His whole history. Before the war, during the war, and then afterwards in America."

"From when?"

"The 1960s. Everything, Eleanor. About his life in Brooklyn, your mother. You…."

"Me?"

"Yes. Do you want to know?

"Of course, I want to know."

"It's really a lot. I've been crying all day."

She looks at me so gently, with such sympathy.

"First of all, he told everything about the camps. And the death march. Everything. Then about your mother." She pauses. "Well, that she had an affair after they were married."

Yeva waits for a reaction.

It's like everybody is waiting for a reaction from me, like I'm a science experiment: How will Eleanor react to this surprising horror and to that new nightmare; like putting electrodes on a fucking frog, upping the electric shocks and seeing how much pain the frog can stand before she, what? Breaks? Goes mad? Twitches to death?

I am in no mood to show anyone anything. I am tired and frightened and enormously sad. I am just taking it all in, period.

"Go on. What else?"

"About you. He says you were everything to him."

No. Stop. I don't want to hear about that. About me and him. I do not want to have been his "everything." I switch topics.

"Anything about my brothers, about Seymour or Harry?"

"Yes. About Seymour, he said that he was an ungrateful boy. That he had paid for him to become an engineer, and Seymour didn't even invite him to his wedding. He was very hurt by that. And Harry, too, was a disappointment. That he didn't remember his German and that the two of them had to speak through a translator and that it was a painful loss for him."

I just listen, staring at the floor.

"And his job was horrible. He hated everything about his life in America. Except for you. You were the only thing worth anything in his life."

That was it. I put my head in my hands. I am down for the count. Yeva touches my shoulder. "I'm so sorry."

I could only think: *My father, my poor father, so much anguish.* I was "everything to him." And what was he to me? An obligation. A burden. That was not exactly fair or completely true, but that was how

I felt then. Awful. And he hated his life in America? Yes, of course he did. How could he not?

Nothing more was said.

We came to the station where we both needed to exit. She was traveling on to her brother's.

"You ordered a copy of that document, Yeva?"

"Yes, of course," she said. "And of others as well, but that was the main one."

"Yes. Good. Thank you."

We were standing on the platform now.

This was our last day together. Oh my God, I forgot.

It was all unbelievable. To both of us. How could such a journey have come to pass? From nothing! From a mere suggestion. From a germ of an idea a few months earlier in the lobby of some hipster hotel in Berlin. From Monday to Wednesday. Three days.

For three days, I held onto her for dear life, as a child would hold a mother and as a mother would hold a child. And also as a colleague. And partner. And friend. And family. We walked separately and together through the darkest darkness of my family's life and into the barbaric history of the world. And she did her best, her very best, to be there with me, for me. For my family.

We stood there and looked at each other. I thanked her profusely.

It was impossible to believe we were parting. We hugged and hugged and wept and wept. How in the world could we say goodbye?

We would speak. We would write. But we would never be on this road again.

How would I get along without her?

The Yeva chapter was over.

CHAPTER SIXTEEN

Day Three Evening: Theater Haus (Stuttgart)
(Wednesday Evening, 17 January 2018)

I walk to my hotel in a daze. I look at the clock. There's barely an hour before I have to leave again to meet the costume designer. I am spent like a dog.

In my hotel room, I eye that tub longingly, but know there is not enough time. Damn. Maybe tonight. I lay down on that big bed, letting the day wash over me.

I check and recheck directions to Theater Haus. Before I know it, it's time to dress and go.

The address is in a different neighborhood on a different train. Fortunately, I am feeling more comfortable in the Hauptbahnhof. I figure out the stop, buy my ticket, and get on the train. Twenty minutes later, I find myself walking the few blocks toward the theatre. Huge signage painted on a rectangular modern cement building like a depot or a warehouse: "THEATER HAUS."

I find the restaurant and then see the table where Hardy is standing. He greets me and introduces me to two women already seated. One woman, about seventy or so, was beautifully put together, with large bold glasses and a colorful scarf. That was Gudrun, the designer who would help me with my family photos. The other woman, full-figured and Teutonic, was, well, I missed who Hardy said she was. I said hello. They were engrossed in a conversation—in German, of course—stopping only for a mini-second to say hello to me and then continuing on with each other.

Standing next to Hardy was Hilke, whom I hadn't noticed when I first walked in. She had also changed clothes and freshened up since we were last trapped in her car a couple of hours ago. When I turned to greet her, she immediately handed me the folder with my father's letters.

"I'm so sorry," she said.

"No, no," I stuttered.

"Yes. I am sorry. It was wrong of me. I got too excited. I know it was the wrong thing."

With her eyes, she pleaded with me to take her in; to believe her and forgive her. I was completely disarmed and felt enormous relief. I thanked her. And at that moment, something seemed to change between us.

We sat down at the table and waited while the two women opposite us babbled in German. Then Hilke turned to me and asked what documents in the archive had made Yeva so excited this afternoon. She caught me off-guard, which wasn't hard to do. I hadn't intended to tell anyone, much less Hilke, about the thirty-page testimony Yeva had found.

Answering quickly and without thinking—again—I said that Yeva had found out that my father's wife and daughter had died sometime between April and November of 1942. That was what came into my head, so that was what I said. It seemed safe enough to share.

Hilke looked at me kind of funny. "I thought they died in Auschwitz in 1943. That was what your father said in his testimony."

What? Oh, right. Damn. Yeva's thirty-page discovery so overshadowed everything else, I'd forgotten all about my father's 1947 Ministry of Justice testimony from earlier today. Ugh, too much information, and I was too tired. But Hilke was not too tired nor too overwhelmed. She was a pro and sharp as a tack, and doing her job meant that she would remember everything.

"Oh," I stammered, "that's what I meant. Yes, 1943. I just got confused. Yeva found documents that recorded their deaths between April and November of 1943."

Would she believe that? I couldn't tell, and it put me into another fearful spin. I kicked myself again for agreeing to have a newspaper reporter follow me around.

I suddenly realize that I am shockingly hungry. Maybe that's why I am so stupid. The only thing I had eaten all day—a day that began with Eve Warscher—was that buttered pretzel Hardy bought me hours and hours ago.

Hardy explains that we are waiting for the artistic director of the theatre, Werner, the husband of Gudrun, the costume designer. I had never heard the name Gudrun before. I keep repeating it to myself so that I will remember it. When I got home, I looked it up online and found that the most famous Gudrun was the fifth and last wife of Attila the Hun. It is said that she murdered their twin sons and served their hearts to Attila on a platter. Charming. Who wouldn't want to name their daughter after her?

About twenty minutes later, a handsome, bohemian, bear of a man, somewhere in his sixties, bounds in. He walks straight toward me and gives me a hug. He touches my face and says, in a rich German-British scented English, "You must be Eleanor. Please forgive my English." There was nothing to forgive. It sounded more elegant than my own.

That was, of course, Werner. He spoke a few words in German to the others at the table. Then to me, he said, "Please excuse me, but I am opening a show this week, and I have a meeting with my designers," indicating toward the long table in the corner next to us. He gave a short bow and joined that table, where a few younger men were sitting. He was lovely. Our interaction was warm and open, however brief. I was grateful for it.

Finally, the waitress came for our orders. I had no idea what to get except that I felt both deserving *and* entitled. The woman sitting next to Gudrun ordered the venison. What's that saying, "When in

Germany do as the Germans do"? And so, I did. German Bambi for me too, please.

When the waitress left, Gudrun directed her attention to me for the first time. She asked about my father, my family, the war. The woman next to her also spoke and asked questions. Then Hardy said something that included the words "my wife."

"Your wife?" I asked. "Is your wife here?"

"I introduced her when you came in. That is Cordelia." He said, pointing to the deer woman.

"Why didn't you say so?" I said jokingly.

"You didn't hear?"

"No," I said, "I've been thinking all this time that she was Gudrun's assistant!" They laughed and the ice started to break. Just as the conversation finally turned to the photos, the food came. We would wait until after the meal.

The food was so good, I cleaned my plate—as did Cordelia, an unlikely casting choice for King Lear's most sympathetic daughter.

The table was cleared, and then Gudrun asked to see the photos.

There were a number of pictures I had brought with me but two in particular that I wanted to show her. They looked like studio photographs of my father from before the war. He was young, in his late teens or early twenties. There was no date on them, no way for me to know exactly when they had been taken. In both pictures, he looked serious and wore very stylish suits, clearly tailor-made. Was that common? Unusual? I didn't know anything about them—or him.

I took the photos out of the FedEx envelope and gave the first one to Gudrun. She took it, looked up at the light, and angled herself just so. Everyone squeezed closer—Hilke, who would not be denied; Cordelia, who wedged herself in tighter; and Hardy, who stood, hovering at the edge. We were about to embark on a grown-up show-and-tell of my family's life; a circus curio for everyone at that table, except for Gudrun, who understood the purpose of this visit and took her task seriously. The rest of the gang was just excited to see the merchandise. My own Holocaust family on full display. Step right up.

The first portrait of my father that I showed Gudrun was definitely taken before the war. He was wearing a three-piece suit with a pocket on the left side, just above his heart. The pocket was not horizontal like most hankie pockets, but slanted on a diagonal, with a bit of a silk or satin handkerchief peeking out.

Gudrun looked closely at the photograph. "Remarkable," she said. Based on the collar of his jacket, she said it was from the late 1920s. "I've never seen such a beautiful, unique suit." She took out her iPhone. "Do you mind if I take a photo?"

I said "No," but I thought *Yes*. However, this was not a time for me to be stingy, petty, or selfish. It also did not feel like a frivolous request. It felt like one day, we would see such a suit in a film or play, and that felt all right to me.

"What do you think about that pocket?" I asked her.

Using the photo she had just taken on her phone, she zoomed in closer and closer. "Is that a pocket?" she asked. "A pocket cut on the bias?"

"Yes," I said, "that's what I think it is." I have looked at this photo hundreds of times over the last forty years since my father died.

"It is beautiful. It shows style and wealth," she said.

"Style and wealth?" I had never before connected those two words with my father.

I showed her the other studio portrait of him. He was clearly younger still.

"This," she said, "is definitely early 1920s. Look at the wing-tipped collar and the silk tie. Another beautiful suit. Do you mind?" she asked again, as she focused her camera on this photo.

"Can we see? Can we see?" Cornelia squealed, like a child looking at some worm we found in the schoolyard. I hated how the photos were being passed around: Hilke getting the first dibs, and Hardy's wife getting the second.

"These are pictures of my father!" I wanted to shout. "My father, whose life was destroyed by you Germans!" Hopefully I was wearing my poker face (which I'm told I don't have).

Gudrun was captivated, and her eye was sharp. I showed her another photo. This one of my father and Uncle Hershel, contemporaries, both in long winter coats, circa 1947. Again, a photo I've looked at so many times over so many years. For details, for clues. For them.

Gudrun looked carefully and then turned to me and said, "Do you see how much better your father's coat fits than the other man's? In all of these pictures, your father's clothes fit so him well. Look at the shoulders, the sleeves, the hem." She was right. I'd never noticed that. His clothes did fit him very well. Perfectly, in fact. Uncle Hershel's coat, I saw now, was tattered and too big for him. "And look here," she went on. "Look at your father's hat, how it's a bit tilted to one side. He fancied himself a lady's man, I would say. Stylish. I'm not saying a playboy, but a man who cared about his looks. Clotheshorse? Is that the English word, yes?"

Clotheshorse? My father?

But yes, I could see it now in the photos, even in the ones immediately following the war. A sport jacket, a bowtie knotted just so. There was nothing of the greenhorn-rube-factory worker-misfit-refugee-loser in these photos. He was manly. Sexual. Dapper. My father was dapper.

I think of the last years of his life, the six years that he spent in that nursing home, completely dependent on me and a few others—certain thoughtful workers there. But dapper? In that institution? What's the opposite of dapper? Utilitarian comes to mind. Chinos, short sleeve madras shirts, gray woolen vests. All of them stained. All of them coarsely, thoughtlessly marked with a thick black Sharpie indicating his room number, so that his clothes would find their way back to him from the laundry. (Or not.)

At that time, I didn't know—and I didn't bother to think—who my father was and what small pleasures I might have provided him. His clothes, his toiletries, small perks from the outside. He had asked for so little. Cigarettes and fresh bread. So, the precious cigarettes I provided? Tasteless and unsatisfying. Fresh bread from a bakery? Sometimes. Rarely. Yes, I was young, but right now I would have to confess that I did not take good enough care of my father—certainly not the care he was entitled to and deserved.

And now, I am sitting here with these Germans, whose parents or neighbors were Nazis; who were, in part, responsible for the inexcusable cruelties to my father's disastrous life, and I recognize now that I too was responsible. I really didn't do right by him. And as usual, I am sorry. I have been sorry my whole life.

I was glad that I had left some of the photos in my hotel room, especially the one of my father from the nursing home. I had brought it with me to Germany as a contrast, to show what had become of him.

It was a black-and-white photo of him in his wheelchair, smiling up at me, directly into the camera; his crooked, vulnerable, stroke-shaped smile with food in his dentures, wearing his shabby, stained plaid shirt. He didn't know what he looked like, only that he was looking at me, his daughter, whom he so loved. I would have felt terrible to have them, these curious Germans, ogling and judging my father at his most diminished and vulnerable time.

This reminds me of my father's funeral, of the Orthodox rabbi who officiated on that day. I didn't known him personally; he was the rabbi of a relative. But he understood, this rabbi, that I was the daughter and principal mourner of this man, this refugee, this concentration camp survivor. Before the other mourners—there were not many—came into the room, the plain pine casket was opened for just a moment, so that I could identify the body, to make sure they were burying the right guy. That didn't frighten me at all. It gave me comfort actually to see my father again. To be there with him, look at him, touch him, apologize to him again and again. I'm sorry, I'm sorry, Dad. For everything. But the rabbi interrupted me. We had to close the casket right away, he said firmly. I was not to linger there. I asked for, please, just a drop more time.

"No," he said. "It is not permitted. It is not fair."

I didn't understand.

"It is unkind to stare at the dead," he explained. "They cannot stare back at you. They have no choice in the matter, do they? They have not given their permission, have they? Your father may not wish to be stared at, and we must be respect him."

Yes, I understood. He was right. As much as I wished to remain with my father, to see him one last time forever, I understood the indignity, and we closed the casket.

This moment felt like that. I was embarrassing my father in front of strangers—nosy Germans to boot. He had no say over these people poring over his photos, examining and viewing and casually commenting on his life.

But Gudrun had great eyes, with a true designer's insights. She wanted to see the rest of the photos that I had brought with me.

I showed her one of my mother with her two brothers in Ulm, outside of the DP camp where Yeva and I had taken photos of me just two days before.

She remarked on my uncles' boots: one pair worn and tattered, the other pair—actual riding boots, she said—in better shape. I had

never noticed that. I didn't know to look at that detail, to notice that difference.

But I also pointed out things that she missed. One photo of my mother holding the purse—the one I found after she died, the one that contained the letters. "Ah yes, beautiful," she said after she had enlarged it on her phone.

"Look at this detail," I said, showing her my mother's initials "RH" attached in silver.

"Oh my, that is something. Do you mind...?" She was taking a lot of photos. Who was helping whom? But it didn't matter. I was grateful. She was giving me precisely what I had hoped for. She took me deeper, and I learned more about who my family was before I knew them.

We went on like that for easily an hour. Everyone was hungry to see the photos. More, more. My family was a fascination to them, like rare animals in a zoo. Real people from the war. Real Jews. Gudrun clearly had other motives, but the rest of them, well, I found it morbid and distasteful, although I know they meant no harm.

Everyone expressed disappointment when we finally came to the last photo. But I was relieved. It was enough. I put my family back into their FedEx envelope.

Then Gudrun asked me if I wanted to see their theatres. I jumped at the offer. Their theatre complex had four different impressive spaces, plus a costume and set design shop. I was in awe of her creative situation. Also, it was so refreshing to speak about art and theatre rather than the bloody Holocaust. You can imagine.

The evening was over. Werner and Gudrun drove me back to my hotel as it was on their way home. It had begun to snow, big fat hard wet flakes. We continued to speak about plays and work, and I thoroughly enjoyed their company. I would be thrilled to work with them someday if they ever asked.

Back at the hotel, I reviewed my agenda for my next—and last—day in Germany. Thursday. In the itinerary that Hardy had prepared for me, we would go to the Ludwigsburg Staatsarchiv (again) and meet with the head archivist - all of us: Hardy, Mrs. Hardy, and Hilke. After everything that Yeva and I had found there, what more could she possibly have to show me? But that was the prearranged plan. Then we would meet with the fellow from Ludwigsburg responsible for *Stolperstein* or "stumbling stones," one of the many memorials to the Holocaust. These were cobblestones engraved with the names of people who "did not return" from deportation a.k.a. killed. The stones were embedded in the streets near their former homes. They were meant to make you take notice; otherwise, you were bound to trip. Literally, "attention must be paid."

The final "official" event of the day would end with yet another memorial—this one at the railroad station where all of the Jews from Stuttgart had been transported to their deaths. Well, nearly all. Chaskel Schlüsselberg was one of the few who had returned.

Lastly, Hardy invited Hilke and me to a restaurant with him and his wife for an authentic Swabish dinner. That cuisine is world renowned for being hearty, hefty fare, which I don't mind: dumplings, hunted beasts, and no greens. Poor Hilke was a vegetarian.

Then early the next morning, Friday, I would take the train to the Frankfurt airport and fly to Israel, for my two-week writing retreat. That was the plan.

Okay. Breathe. (I am in never-ending conversation with myself: instructing, consoling, comforting—hoping to avoid berating.)

I had not slept all week. These days had been more ferocious than any I could imagine or bargain for. I was exhausted and bereft. The bags under my eyes were dark and deep, and I felt and looked like my actual sixty-four years—if not older. Still no proper bath. Just tossing and turning till 3 a.m., and then, finally, some sleep.

CHAPTER SEVENTEEN

The Fourth and Last Day: Germany
(Thursday, 18 January 2018)

Masochistically, I wake up before the alarm. Certainly not because I'd slept enough.

Hardy, Hilke, and I are scheduled to meet at the memorial of the former synagogue in Ludwigsburg, the one with the fake suitcases that Yeva and I had accidentally happened upon on Tuesday, two days ago. (Two days ago?) Hilke had arranged for a photographer to meet us there. She wanted a photo of me to accompany her newspaper article for Holocaust Remembrance Day in the *Stuttgart Zeitung*.

Once again, the sky is slate gray, pouring rain, and the air biting—a mirror of my soul. As usual, although I have been up for hours, I am running late. The earlier I wake up, the later I am.

Today is my last time on this train from Stuttgart to Ludwigsburg. I am thinking again of my father making this very trip. I feel him on this River of Time; his presence, his pain, his fear; going back and forth to Ludwigsburg as the letters indicate, in the autumn of 1949; to get his visa, to get his passport, to sell his car, and to say goodbye to friends. I imagine him—anxious, angry, frustrated, uncertain, alone—being swept down the raging river. Toward what? What end awaits him? He doesn't know, but I do. I know, and yet I cannot help him. I cannot pull him from the water and save him. It is too late to save him.

I am broken too.

I finally arrive at the "suitcase" memorial. Hilke, Hardy, Mrs. Hardy, and this hip rocker-type photographer are already there, waiting. I apologize for my lateness. I'm introduced to the photographer. Bloody hell, he is a Brit! He speaks English without a German accent! Hooray! This makes me enormously and surprisingly happy. I didn't realize how "Other" I had felt here. The German-accented English of the past week was infused with a slight smell of burning flesh.

I didn't admit that to myself until the photographer grinned broad and wide, and chatted in his gorgeous East End accent, and reminded me of the other thing that I had been missing. A fucking sense of humor! Irony! Sarcasm! The Germans didn't seem to have that, at least not in English. This Brit and I were laughing conspiratorially within minutes—hearty, robust, welcome, and much needed.

Hilke wanted to stage some photos. She wanted me to walk around the memorial, looking tearfully at the brown metal suitcases, modeled after the luggage left behind by the never-to-return refugees.

The photographer snapped as I walked back and forth, up and down the outlined square of the destroyed synagogue, and pretended to wander through the assorted suitcases, sitting on this one or touching that one, gazing off through the drizzling rain, looking tiredly into the past.

Afterward, the photographer showed me the photos he had taken. It wasn't until then that I saw how absolutely ravaged I looked: thick, puffy black circles under my eyes, sorrow on my face, and my skin ashen, a pall to match the color of the day.

Hilke was not happy with the photos. They looked staged, she said. Yes, that's because they were. I didn't have any more authentic misery left in me.

Or so I thought.

The next item on the itinerary was the Staatsarchiv, where, just yesterday, Yeva and I had found the Holocaust motherlode. When we got there, we learned that the archivist was sick and had to cancel. (There was a God!) I certainly would have been interested in learning more, but the thought of not having Hilke, and Mr. and Mrs. Hardy looking over my shoulder was definitely a consolation.

Except for grabbing a coffee with the man in Ludwigsburg associated with the "stumbling stones," nothing else was left on Hardy's itinerary—oh, except for one more visit to yet another Holocaust memorial: this one at the precise place of transport. Great. I am so done.

Hardy asks Hilke if she would mind taking me to that site, as it was in Stuttgart. I guess Hardy had had enough too. Hilke said she didn't mind. I gave her ample opportunity to decline, but she wouldn't hear of it. Hardy would see us both that evening at some restaurant for authentic local food, which he seemed very proud of.

Since she had no one to walk her dogs today, Hilke asks if I'd mind stopping at her house, which was on the way. No problem, and off we go.

Now it's my turn to ask her questions.

Hilke was fifty-five years old, ten years my junior. She looked younger, I thought. I asked what growing up had been like for her. She told me about her youth, that she was always a good girl, never had any arguments with her mother—who was still alive. (I am always amazed when a contemporary has living parents.) Hilke was not rebellious as a teenager, she said. She and I were very different in that regard. I was a solid member of the sex, drugs, rock and roll generation. I had been in a big hurry to grow up and make my own way. I moved out of my mother's apartment at seventeen, soon after I started college. Girls didn't do that in those days. (My poor mother. Her life's ordeals will be for another day.)

We got to Hilke's place, a 1970s fenced-in two-story brick house with a bit of a garden. "Don't let the dogs frighten you," she said. "They are big but harmless." She opened the door, and three hefty dogs clattered down a steep flight of stairs. They were a gaggle of friendly mutts, one clearly an older boy, hard of seeing and walking. They all bounded out the door and went every which way, urinating all over the yard like there was no tomorrow. Only when that need was satisfied did they become interested in me, nuzzling and sniffing. I rubbed and patted them and enjoyed the humanity of it—of life and love and care.

"Would you like to come up?"

"Sure." I was curious to learn about her, to see how she lived, who she was. Who was this woman who could be stern and pushy and concentrated yet also soft and empathetic and open?

With the dogs underfoot, we walked up the flight of stairs to the main part of the house. A functional eat-in kitchen with a wooden table and chairs. I didn't see paintings or photos. Nothing that really caught my eye. Except for the shelves. Shelves, shelves, and more shelves covering all the walls. Everywhere, from the floor to the ceiling, filled with books, CDs, and DVDs. "Wow," I said.

"Yes," she said, "my partner is a film and music reviewer." She didn't say more than that, and I didn't ask.

Then we said goodbye to the dogs, who followed us down the stairs, surely hoping for more daylight and perhaps another chance to water the trees. I felt a little sorry for them, that they were going to be shut in again. But Hilke told me that all of them were rescue dogs, so as survivors with a rough past, their present was not too bad.

Hilke entered the address of our next—and last—adventure into her GPS. The Transport Memorial, it was called. She had never been there and was not familiar with the neighborhood. I told her again that I was grateful for her company, but if she didn't want to *schlep* me to yet another memorial, I would understand. It had been a long two days, even for her. She assured me again that she wanted to go.

Twenty minutes away. We used the ride to speak more about ourselves. Non-Holocaust content, thank you very much. Definitely a relief.

I mentioned that I was a bit nervous about her upcoming article. After all these years in show business, I had become wary of press, even though I would seek it out. It was rare, I said, that any interview with a reporter was conveyed accurately. I promised myself regularly that I would avoid doing interviews, only to fall into its seductive clutches again and again out of my desire for self-promotion, fame, and attention. Why did I think that was, she asked.

"Probably because I usually just say whatever comes to mind, and my words, when printed, seem to lack context and seem to leave out what was most important. I have tried to be more careful," I said. She hoped I would not feel that way about her article. (Yes, I hoped so too.) It was scheduled to run while I was in Israel. She would send it to me, she said.

She asked about my early years, about college, about how I had found my way to the theatre. I told her that politics had played a large part during my college days and that street theatre accounted for my beginning. Theatre was about making revolution, I said, not a career. I didn't know what a career was in those days. I lived in the moment, as only a college student in the 1970s could do. Then someone gave me a real job, acting in a play—for real money—which changed everything. Forty years later, unanticipated and unintended, it had become my career. One of the many miracles of my life.

Hilke expressed disappointment in her early life: that it was neither exciting nor particularly interesting. "Not like yours," she said. "Was there a highlight for you?"

There had been a few, I told her. I guess my favorite was when I "made out" with Bob Dylan. "What?!" She nearly stopped the car and demanded, in her sweet-yet-pushy Teutonic way, to hear all of the details. I told her everything about meeting Bob Dylan. Except, like with my father's story, I left out the seminal event, in part because I feared she would think that I was a slut, and in part because my memory was suspect. I was drunk that night. So drunk that I didn't remember? Had Bob and I indeed been drinking Jack Daniels in his hotel room and somehow wound up naked in bed, kissing? And then did he really fall asleep without anything being consummated, and I dressed and left as he snored away? Really? Is that what happened? That's certainly how I remember it. For sure I was there, for sure in Bob Dylan's room at the Henry Hudson Hotel on West 57th Street when I was twenty-eight years old. No, I was not an innocent, promiscuous teenager. I was a not-so-innocent promiscuous adult.

She was beyond giddy. She loved this story. Dylan, as it turned out, was her favorite artist. Hilke now looked at me with a new set of eyes, with a kind of admiration. It was funny. I had become more than the daughter of a tragic Holocaust survivor. I was elevated to a Bob Dylan groupie.

Her GPS indicated that we had arrived at our destination, but we didn't see any kind of memorial. We were in an industrial park, an unlikely place for a memorial, and we saw no train depot.

She parked the car and we got out into the never-ending rain. She walked one way and I the other, looking for this memorial. After a few minutes of wandering, she called out to me from where she was standing and pointed to the right.

There. A gray cement wall, about seven feet high, a few city blocks long. We walked over to where it seemed to begin.

I immediately understood what it was—reminiscent of Maya Lin's Vietnam Memorial in Washington. A communal tombstone. I left Hilke and began walking down the platform alongside the wall. On it were engraved names. Jewish name after Jewish name. In alphabetical order. I walked down the long platform, not really looking for anything specific, except when I came to the letter "*S*." Then I walked slower. Much slower. Then came names beginning "*Sc*."

Go on, Eleanor. Right foot, left foot. One heavy step at a time. I was looking hard at this wall, and it was looking right back at me, daring me to continue. And I do. *I am not afraid of you, Wall.*

Then "*Sch*." There were so many names beginning with those three letters.

And then, there it was. "*Schl*." Full and dead stop.

"Chana Schlüsselberg"—my father's first wife. Next to her name, "Frida Schlüsselberg"—my father's first daughter. Harry's mother and sister.

No breathing. No sound. Just the soft, cold pings of the steady rain.

161

I stared. At them. At their names. At my own last name. *Schlüs-selberg*. Scratched into this cement, waiting for me. I stood there humbled, and as bereft as I had ever been.

And then it registers—for the first time in my life—that Frida was not only my father's daughter and Harry's sister. She was my own half-sister. I had a half-sister. She was the same relation to me as Harry and Seymour. I had never thought of her as *my* sister. She was Harry's and my father's. Not mine.

But now I have a half-sister, I mean, had.

I couldn't move. I was done for. I just wanted to stand in front of that wall, as I had stood in front of my father's casket. I press myself against the wall and try to subsume myself into it.

Eventually, Hilke walked over. She stood quietly, just looking at me. "Is this emotional for you?" she asked softly. It was such a disconnected question. Perhaps it was the translation, in the way German translated into English, that made that question sound so detached, yet innocent and ridiculously obvious. To give dear Hilke the benefit of the doubt, I will believe it was in the translation. And perhaps in the discomfort that she was feeling, watching me decompose right before her eyes; witnessing such a private moment that she was both embarrassed by it and yet curious to be privy to it.

What could I say to her, as I stood there being held up by this wall of the dead? My whole life had been held up by these people: these silent screaming names, innocent human beings who came here to be transported, who never returned, whose life and death were responsible for my own life. It was their death, the murders of Chana and Frida Schlüsselberg, that literally made space for me. Their absence was my presence, the next/other Schlüsselberg daughter. I would fill the void that they left. The Replacement.

Hilke then asked if she could take a photo. Of me. A photo of me: weeping, grieving, standing drenched to the bone at this hallowed site. It felt crass, like taking pictures of mourners at a cemetery or a funeral. But better to say yes than no, I decided. *In general, Eleanor, better to say yes.* Yes, Hilke, you may take a photo.

I stand, leaning against the Jews, looking directly into her camera, broken and indignant. They are all gone, but I am here. I am them.

I ask if it's okay to stay here for a few more minutes. Neither of us had an umbrella, and the rain knew no end. But I didn't want to leave. Would I ever? She understood and walked away to the overhang, where there were glass displays with information about this place.

This is why I came to Germany. I didn't know that before, but I know it now. I came to find the dead. And I found them.

Ten years ago, I played the title role in *Yentl*, Isaac Bashevis Singer's play about a young girl who pretends to be a boy so that she can express herself to God freely, as only men are allowed to do in Orthodox Judaism. For that role, I had to learn to say *kaddish*, the memorial prayer for the dead. I still remember it.

Only immediate family are supposed to say *kaddish*. Who would have said it for Chana and Frida? Certainly not Harry. Only my father would have, but that was more than forty years ago. I believe that no one else had ever said *kaddish* for them. And so, on this day, I do. For

Chana and for Frida. I stand and rock and cry and pray. I look at the wall, touch it, lean against it. I put my lips to it and kiss it.

Yes, this is why I came here. Bless them. Amen.

I look around. Where exactly are we? Where is this transport station that from 1941 to 1943 carried off Jewish men, women, and children; thousands of them? My head floods with images and I careen from one thought to another.

Perhaps let us just stop for a moment. Just stop reading and imagine. Close your eyes, if you dare, and imagine the sounds, the smells, the children, the women, the weeping, the primordial existential fear, being torn from home, torn from family. The precipice—they were on it. Give it a second. I know that we must look away at some point so that we can continue to live. I know that we, *even I*, cannot stay here with them for too long. But neither should we leave them too soon.

I look around. The houses, the apartments whose rear windows face out onto this place—bedroom windows, I suspect—looking on to this transport cemetery, this killing station. I wonder about them, the people living here today. Do they know what had occurred here? Just a generation ago? Right outside their windows?

Then, I think about the people who lived here eighty years ago, when *they* looked out of *their* windows. They actually saw what was happening here—the trains, the transports, the mothers, the babies. Did they do anything? Was there anything they could have done? (We currently have our own refugee transports and hellish incarcerations. Is there anything that *we* can do? What do we see from *our* bedroom windows and televisions and newspapers and internets, and what do *we* do about it? My own answer saddens and disgusts me.)

It is getting late, and even I know that it is time to go.

The rain has soaked through everything: my vest, the parka, my jeans. I join Hilke under the covered roof with the display cases. Behind the glass are old photos of the people of Stuttgart—the Jewish people—about to be deported, standing in the exact spot we are standing now. None of them returned. Not one.

"Who shall live and who shall die?" Jews ask every Yom Kippur. When do we know? The last time we will go home? The last time we will see each other? Kiss each other? Feel warm? Eat? Breathe?

I stare at the photos of these people, familiar strangers, their lives captured for this one last blink. They thought/hoped/prayed that tomorrow they would be saved. But we know better. We know the future.

This is the most authentic remnant of my staggering journey. The beginning of the transport, for me—and for everyone else—is the end of the line.

In the last of the glass display cases are two poems in German, both by Erich Fried, an Austrian Jew by birth.

"Gesprach mit einem Überlebenden"
Was hast du damals getan
was du nicht hattest tun sollen?
"Nichts"
Was hast du nicht getan
was du hattest tun sollen?
"Das und das
dieses und jenes
Einiges"
Warum hast du es nicht getan?
"Weil ich Angst hatte"
Warum hattest du Angst?
"Weil ich nicht sterben wollte"
Sind andere gestorben
weil du nicht sterben wolltest?
"Ich glaube
ja"
Hast du noch etwas zu sagen
zu dem was du nicht getan hast?
"Ja: Dikh zu fragen
Was hattest du an meiner Stelle getan?"
Das Weiss ich nicht
Und ich kann uber dich nicht richten.

Nur eines Weiss ikh:
Morgen wird keiner von uns
Leben bleiben
wenn wir heute
wieder nichts tun.

I ask Hilke to translate.

"Spoken to a Survivor"
What did you do then
that you should not have done?
"Nothing"
What did you not do that
you should have done?
"This and that
and some other things"
Why did you not do it?
"Because I was afraid"
Why were you afraid?
"Because I did not want to die"
Did others die
because you did not want to die?
"I believe
yes"
Do you have something to say
about what you did not do?
"Yes: I ask you
what you would have done in my place?"
That I do not know
And I cannot judge you.
I only know one thing:
Tomorrow none of us
will be alive
if today
we once again do nothing.

His other poem:

"Vielleicht"
Erinnern
das ist
vielleicht
die qualvollste Art
des Vergessens
und vielleicht
die fruendlichste Art
der Linderun dieser Qual

Hilke's translation:

"Perhaps"
Remembering
this is
perhaps
the most agonizing way
of forgetting
and perhaps
the kindest way
to relieve this agony

Hilke drove me back to my hotel. Dinner tonight with Hardy and his wife was all that remained. Thankfully, Hilke was joining us. I knew her for only two days, and now she is a party to my life, my discoveries, and my history. I would have preferred to go out alone with her—eat, talk, and look into her curious, sympathetic face. She is a good woman: thoughtful, smart, and thankfully, a persistent witness. She wanted to see. She would not be denied. Good for her.

We would be friends if we lived on the same continent. Perhaps we will be anyway.

There was nothing more for me in Germany.

CHAPTER EIGHTEEN

Israel

I land at Ben Gurion Airport at 3:30 p.m. on Friday, January 19th. My cousin Ronnie is good enough to pick me up at the airport and bring me to his spotless eat-off-the-floor, interior designer-decorated four-bedroom condo in the suburbs of Tel Aviv. I will spend one night with him and his wife, Smadar (Hebrew for "the blossom of the grape"), and with whichever of his three terrific kids are around.

Ronnie and I are second—or third—cousins, depending on whom you ask. Although we're the same age, my father was *his* father's uncle. Our families were quite large at one time, before The Catastrophe, with the norm being anywhere from six to ten children. Because of inter-marriages between relatives in those days, our family tree is confusing and few of us who are still living really understand it.

Wintertime in Israel looks like springtime everywhere else. After the wet, cold, gray, grim, bitter days in Germany, this was clearly where the Garden of Eden was located. The sky is blue, the light invigorating, the temperature embracing and warm. I feel such relief to be with my family; however distant, they are very much beloved.

Ronnie is good-natured and extremely kind, a salt-of-the-earth kind of guy. If you ever needed someone to save your life, he would be there on a dime. However, even though he is very smart and empathetic, his mindset can sometimes be narrow and tough. Ronnie only looks forward, rarely back. Perhaps those traits are necessary to live in the embattled, complicated Middle East: modern, yet still tribal and ancient.

Spending my first night with Ronnie and the family is perfect. I pat myself softly on the back for arranging my trip in this way over a month ago.

In his bright, modern apartment, I excitedly tell Ronnie about my discoveries in Germany.

"Why do you bother with this?" he asks in his thickly accented English.

"What do you mean?" I ask.

"I mean, who cares!" He laughs. "What difference will it make? Who will care about this after we are dead?"

"Your kids?" I answer.

"Ah, what will they care? They will not care."

"That's too bad for them and for everyone who came before them and everyone who will come after them," I say seriously.

He laughs even harder. At what, exactly, I don't know. At me, I guess. He loves me but likes to laugh at me, tease me. That used to bother me, but it doesn't anymore.

We agree to disagree. I am disappointed that my laborious efforts and discoveries seem to have zero interest to the first audience I encounter, not to mention someone who is a relative.

The next morning, Evan picks me up at Ronni's. Like winning the lottery, I get two weeks at Evan's artist residence/retreat in Acre. Perfect.

In the front seat of Evan's car is Briar, one of the two other resident artists. She is a Maori filmmaker from New Zealand whom Evan had met on one of his writers' retreats, this time in China. (Lucky bastard.) Briar has just arrived after a day-long flight from Wellington. She too is knackered.

Evan dominates the conversation for most of the ninety-minute trip to Acre. He drives fast. I'm in back seat of his little car, trying not to get nauseous. He asks me one perfunctory question about my journey, and then he moves on to other topics. Maybe it's the quality of my responses, but does no one give a shit about what happened to me in Germany?

We arrive at the stunning port city of Acre. I was here a number of years ago when I directed a play for the Yiddish theatre in Tel Aviv—but only for one day.

The air is salty and delicious—good enough to eat. It smells of sun and sea. From the parking lot, the ruins of the ancient ramparts are just off to our right. I seem to remember that they were built by the Crusaders and destroyed by the Turks. Or maybe it was the other way around. Ah, details.

We pull our luggage out of Evan's car as he makes a phone call. A few minutes later, a smiling young Palestinian Muslim bounds out of an alleyway. Evan introduces us. Mahran. I make a note to self: Think of the capital of Iran in order to remember his name. Mahran. (This will prove to be a mnemonic failure for me.) He will show us the way to the retreat/residency/boutique hotel while Evan looks for parking.

After a short walk through a maze of narrow alleyways, again *schlep-ping* the evil rolling luggage over spitefully bumpy stones, we come to Arabesque, Evan's 300-year-old restored, renovated hotel/residency. We enter the great lobby—and it is "great," as in larger than life—and also beautiful. The high-ceilinged room is perfect—airy, light, so tastefully appointed with contemporary and classic pieces: local arti-facts, paintings, touches of past-and-present Arab/Israeli/Palestinian details; a symbol of the dream here. There is an open kitchen, a huge wooden dining table that can seat twenty, and a baby grand piano. An open door points us to a breezy courtyard with huge ceramic pots of colorful flowers and fruit-bearing trees. Fresh kumquats! I pluck a few off the trees. Delicious. The perfect combination of sweet and bitter.

Our rooms are located off this courtyard; the creamy-blue bedroom doors are all open. The rooms seem medieval: cave-like and Turkish. One of the bedrooms is significantly larger than the other two. Of course, I want that room, as I suspect Briar does as well. We wait for our host to decide, and soon he arrives. Since Briar has traveled the farthest, Evan says, she will get the largest room. I'm hurt for a few minutes, but then I fiercely tell myself to get over it. And I do, although for the next two weeks, I make jokes about it.

I will be perfectly happy in my beautiful room. I am beyond grateful. This is a gift from God, in whom I don't believe. And from Evan, in whom I do.

The other artist, Nurit, a photographer from Tel Aviv, will begin her stay next week, although she will join us tonight for a welcoming dinner that Evan has arranged with his Muslim, Christian, and Jewish friends from the community. We three girls are the very first artists in what he hopes will be yearly residencies.

I am in a hurry to get to work, yet I don't know how to begin. *Just begin*, I tell myself as gently as possible. *Start somewhere. On something. Begin.*

Most of the letters have been translated but not all of them. Remarkably, I am still missing about fifteen of them. Knud, the retired professor from Colorado, is holding me up. I've written to him a bunch of times only to keep hearing "tomorrow" or the day after tomorrow. When is tomorrow? (Unfortunately, I learn later that Knud had been suffering from serious health issues.) Plus, the documents that Yeva and I requested from the Staatsarchiv in Ludwigsburg, including my father's thirty-page testimony, have begun arriving. Jesus H. Christ, we selected so many documents! All in German. All needing translations. Yeva had been correct to have them sent online rather than getting hard paper copies.

Doing the research was the easy part. Knowing what to *do* with the research is another matter entirely. How do you say chicken bones in German?

To add insult to injury, I hadn't heard from John for a few days. When we spoke on my last night in Germany, he told me that this coming weekend he was going to take a drug-induced journey with a shaman-type fellow whom we knew. John was always curious about discovering that special something inside himself—that thing that made him tick—which was very seductive to me. For me, brains are hot, plus it didn't hurt that he was handsome as all hell. John's plan was to take the drug MDMA, also known as Ecstasy, which he and I had experimented with together in the past. It brought out deep expressions of love, and a euphoric, holistic sense of being-as-one with each other and with the world. Ergo, its name. I was looking forward to speaking to him after the weekend, two days from today, to see how it went. There was so much I wanted to share with him.

My dark, cavernous room, with its high ceilings and the weight of history in each ancestral stone, would be my home for the next two weeks. There are no windows except for a small one in the bathroom and two ceiling-high windows covered with fabric to help mask the sunshine for sleeping. The only light is electric, which might prove difficult for me. I need real light, a window or something, to connect me to the world.

I rearrange the room a bit. I move the desk to face the door, which, if left open, would bring some daylight into the room.

I set myself up at the desk like a young girl on the first day of school. I put my pencils and pens in a lovely piece of local pottery. I organize my legal pads for notes and whatnot. I take out the FedEx envelope with the photos and lay them all out on top of the chest of drawers under a protective glass. I create a montage of the past, hoping the faces will shout out and guide me. I put the paper clips, scotch tape, highlighters into a basket. I take out the file of letters, which I have not looked at since Hilke gave them back to me three days ago. I am ready. My chicken bones are now out of their plastic garbage bag and arranged in neat piles on the table. What am I going to do and how am I going to do it?

Before I left New York, I pictured how I would work here: how I would write, make sense of the information, how I would tell the story, whatever it was. In my chicken-bone imagination, I would tape my father's letters in chronological order to the walls around my room like a huge whiteboard that would envelop me, that I could refer to freely and easily. Like evidence in a TV crime show, the letters would offer up clues for my investigation of the past.

I was very excited to begin. I tape the first letter, dated 24 July 1949, to the stone wall behind my desk.

Here's some valuable information for you: Scotch tape does not stick to decomposing stone. Just in case you were wondering. Idea number one, shot down immediately. The letters would have to remain in the folder.

So, now what?

"*Something, Eleanor,*" I mutter impatiently to myself. "*Come on, do something.*"

Okay. Well, what? What task could I possibly accomplish?

I decide to create a day-by-day summary/reminder of my time in Germany. I kept a daily journal and my recollections were still fresh. Each of those days felt like a year. I could, at least, record all of that before it was forgotten and became a bunch of nonspecific memories. Maybe that would take me to the next step, whatever that was. Right foot, left foot. Come on.

My first two days in Acre were spent that way: gently, one step at a time. First, breakfast. At that beautiful table every morning with Briar, prepared by Mahran or Evan's grown sons—Micha or Hagai—we'd have fresh Israeli-Arab salad of chopped tomato, cucumbers, peppers, and a variety of small dishes—cheeses, olives, eggplant,

eggs—all so fresh and tasty, all in beautiful Middle Eastern ceramics. After a strong coffee or two, we'd go back to our own rooms to work, where we'd stay for a few hours until lunchtime, followed by a walk. Then more work and then dinner.

Briar and I would walk to the sea. Why go anywhere else? The sea, from whence we came. Nourishing. Eternal. Hopeful even.

We'd walk through the *shuk* with its men hawking their wares as they had for hundreds of years: a kaleidoscope of sweets, lush fruits, crisp vegetables, clear-eyed fishes, aromatic falafel, soft hummus, ever-tempting halvah, and magical pyramids of spices. Briar had never been to Israel before. I got to look at it through her eyes and she through mine. It would take us a few days, but we would become good friends.

Late Monday afternoon, nearing the end of my second day, I phoned John. I was hungry to speak to him. During our few years together, he had been a strong sounding board and comfort to me. When he picked up the phone, his voice sounded detached and distant. I asked him how his MDMA trip went and what he learned. He was still coming down from it, he said, and processing what had happened. It would take a while for him to understand, but he did feel all kinds of love. *Love?* I thought hopefully. *Could that be about me?* I dared to wonder.

No. It made him want to call his nephew in Mexico, he said, and tell him how much he loved him.

"Great," I lied, pressing my hand against a tiny new wound. Just a small gash. And then, as they say, I stepped in it.

"Hey," I ventured stupidly. "Did you think of me at all?"

His response took less than a second. "Does it always have to be about you? You want me to tell you that I was thinking about you for the last six hours?"

A solid thwack to my heart by a two-by-four.

"I can't tell you what you want to hear just because you want to hear it," he went on.

"Um, no," I said. "I did not ask if you were thinking of me for six hours. And if you don't want to tell me what you don't want to tell me, you don't have to tell me."

"I'm going to need some time by myself, Eleanor. I'm sorry but if you could just leave me to it for a while, I have my own journey to take. Plus, I don't want to get in the way of your journey. I'll contact you when I'm ready."

Wow, really? You don't want to get in the way of my journey? Well, too late, pal.

At that moment, everything changed. Again. And whatever was hard before, just got way harder.

CHAPTER NINETEEN

My Office

The first few days, I worked in my room, sitting at my desk. It was windowless, dark—in the room and in the work. I was trying to record the events of my time in Germany: everything that had happened, everything that I had learned and when. The room, however, was making me stir-crazy, and the absence of natural light was adding to the blackness in my soul.

On this particular morning, Mahran had the breakfast shift. He is the son of Evan's next-door neighbors: Hayat, pious and kind, and Muhammad, a totally alpha male but friendly and warm, as was everyone I met in Acre. The feeling in that town is different than in any other Israeli city I've been to. The lack of Arab/Palestinian hostility toward Jews and vice versa is hopeful and energizing. It stands as an example of possibility, of what Israel could be: Arab, Palestinian, and Jew living peacefully in paradise. Oversimplified, I know, but still possible. It was not like that in Jerusalem, Jaffa, and other cities, where the tension is palpable.

Here, each morning, I am awakened at five by the passionate voice of the muezzin calling Muslims to prayer, ringing through the old town, sounding so familiar, like his biblical brother, the Jewish chazzan. During my stay in Acre, one of Evan's friends, Jamal, who by night waited tables in a scrumptious innovative seaside restaurant and by day was a filmmaker and screenwriter, showed us a short documentary film that he'd made about this muezzin: a young husband/father who, between his many daily calls to prayer, was training to be a competitive bodybuilder! Yes, talk about possibility. The film was eye-opening about the devoted life of a muezzin, but also about the enormous conflicts and pressures facing this young man who had a passion for both Allah *and* bodybuilding. He found spiritualism in both. It was an inspiring portrait of a man trying to expand the boundaries of his too-small envelope.

After breakfast, I ask Mahran if there is a café or coffee shop where I could bring my computer and work. "Oh, of course," he says. "Do you want me to show you?" Yes, thank you!

We go to the place where he first met us when we arrived in Acre, by the ramparts. We walk a short way along the sea wall and he points me to this restaurant. Prime location, tables outside, just overlooking the Mediterranean. *Al Fanar.* In Arabic, it means "the lighthouse." Brilliant.

The tables are all empty. It is January, so thankfully, the tourists have not yet begun to flock to this paradise. I choose a table closest to the sea. I ask the waiter, a friendly young Palestinian fellow, if I could sit here for a while. "Pleasure," he says sweetly.

I order my Israeli-Arab version of a tall cappuccino, open my computer, and sit there for the next three hours. The waiters are kind and their English is good. I wow them with my infantile knowledge of Arabic, which they appreciate for the effort and also makes them laugh. From that day on, I would get there by ten-thirty and stay until after one. Sometimes, I'd have lunch, their delicious Arab salad. Other times, just a coffee. Usually two. I returned there every day for the remainder of my stay.

I didn't always write about Germany or the letters. Often, I wrote in my journal about John, trying to make myself strong and give myself comfort to ease the sting of his abandonment. This was not the first time that he'd decided to toss me overboard. The last time, about two years ago, he did it in an email. In it, he said that I did not have the *sine qua non* that he was looking for. I just hate it when guys break up with me using words I have to look up. I know Yiddish, not Latin. *Sine qua non?* "That essential element," said the internet. What the fuck did that even mean?

Well, whatever it was, he wanted it and I didn't have it.

His exit caught me by surprise again. I was more vulnerable than usual because of my time in Germany, and the horrible new details about my father and family. I was inconsolable. Weeping and enraged—at myself as well as at him. I even scheduled a few Skype sessions with my therapist, who, unfortunately, was of minimal help.

But Al Fanar, that was another matter. Facing west, accompanied by the eastern sun and the calm sea, that place was my solace, my therapy. I'd stare at the horizon, agog at the azure water and the cerulean sky. Wave upon wave, gentle, idyllic, where the heavens met the earth. Between John and Germany (not meaning to equate the two, but both painful nonetheless), this café was my balm in Gilead.

It was sometime at the end of this first week that I got an email from Hilke with the link to her soon-to-be-published article in the *Stuttgart Zeitung.* I open the link nervously.

There it was. A full-page story. Across the top, covering a quarter of the page, was a color photo of me from my last day in Germany at the transport memorial, leaning against the water-stained cement wall, looking wasted—wet and weary, like a refugee myself—in front of the names Chana Schlüsselberg and Frida Schlüsselberg.

There were other photos too: of my youthful father from before the war (that Gudrun had commented on); a small portrait of my beautiful raven-haired young mother from post-war time; and finally, that photo of Harry, age five or so, in his lederhosen, standing tall behind his little sister, still in her baby carriage. Heiner and Frida.

But Heiner's name is not engraved on that memorial wall, thanks to my father and who knows who else.

Gedenkentafel am Stuttgarter Nordbahnhof. Hier findet Eleanor Reissa die Namen ihrer Halbschwester Frida und deren Mutter Chana Schlüsselberg.

Fotos: Sartorius/Gérarddile (3), Hilke Lorenz (2)

Jiddisches Heimweh

Suche Mehr als 40 Jahre nach dem Tod ihres Vaters macht sich die New Yorker Broadway-Sängerin Eleanor Reissa auf, seine Spuren in Stuttgart zu finden. Hier hat er gelebt, gearbeitet, geliebt, von hier wurden er und seine Familie ins KZ deportiert. Und als einziger Überlebender ist er zurückgekommen. *Von Hilke Lorenz*

Ich war 17 Jahre alt, da hat mir mein Vater einen Volkswagen geschenkt." Volkswagen, das Wort klingt in Eleanor Reissas deutsch-jüdischer Aussprache noch ein bisschen schriger, als es ohnehin eingebettet in ihr amerikanisches Englisch anhört. Chaskel Schlüsselberg also, zu diesem Zeitpunkt um die 70 Jahre alt, schenkt seiner Tochter das deutscheste aller Autos. Einen beigefarbenen VW-Käfer. Er, der in Polen geborene, lange Jahre in Stuttgart lebende und dann im Februar 1943 von dort nach Auschwitz deportierte Geschäftsmann, kauft ein Auto aus dem Land der Täter.

Das alles geschieht in New York, genauer gesagt in Brooklyn, in der Nachbarschaft von Hispanics, Italienisch-Stämmigen, Afroamerikanern und überlebenden Juden, wo Eleanor Reissa aufgewachsen ist. Wegen ihrer vielen Locken nennt man das Mädchen hier nach dem US-Kinderstar Shirley Temple, sie würde man ihr künstlerisches Talent bereits ahnen. Chaskel Schlüsselberg jedoch hat in dem New Yorker Stadtteil niemals richtig in ein altes Leben zurückgefunden. Nicht beruflich und auch nicht als Familienvater. Seine erste Frau Chana und die sechsjährige Tochter Frida wurden im Holocaust ermordet, den Chana und er mit einem Kindertransport hatten, überlebte, wollte er seinen neuen Elten bleiben.

Eleanor entstammt seiner zweiten Ehe. Aber auch diese Beziehung steht unter keinem guten Stern. Die Eltern lassen sich scheiden, als ihr einziges gemeinsames Kind sechs Jahre alt ist. „Es ist ein Zufall, dass es mich gibt", sagt Eleanor Reissa mit einem Grinsen und fasst damit das innige und zerrissene Verhältnis der nationalsozialistischen Rassenanimus in ein paar wenigen Worten zusammen. Sie bleibt bei ihrer Mutter. Ihr Vater stirbt 1976 mit 73 Jahren. Er bleibt immer ein Außenseiter in den USA. Ihre Mutter stirbt 1986 mit gerade einmal 66 Jahren.

Eleanor ist beider Augenstern. Sie bricht mit 17 mit ihrem VW-Käfer auf in ein eigenes bis auf den heutigen Tag umtriebiges Leben, will erwachsen werden. Das Mathematikstudium lässt sie schnell wieder sein. Sie macht lieber politisches Straßentheater, kellnert, spielt Theater, singt bei einer großen Musicalproduktion vor, schafft es, eine Rolle als Chorsängerin zu bekommen, übernimmt, als die Hauptdarstellerin krank wird und als Chorsängerin krank wird, schließlich rettet so die Produktion. Um Geld zu verdie-

nen, singt sie schon lange jiddische Lieder in Clubs. „Jiddisch war meine erste Sprache, mein Herz schlägt auf Jiddisch", sagt die Frau, die cleverar ein Multitalent ist, Theaterstücke schreibt, Broadway-Musicals inszeniert sowie mit Frank London und den Klezmer Brass Allstars tourt. „Das Jiddische", sagt sie selbstbewusst, „ist mein Alleinstellungsmerkmal." Und wohl auch ihre Kraftquelle, ein Stück Heimat und zugleich Ausdruck von Verbundenheit zu denen, denen sie nachfolgt. Egal wie viele Kilometer sie mit dem VW gefahren ist, er hat sie nie forttragen können von ihren Wurzeln.

Wäre sie nicht gerade in Deutschland und Israel unterwegs, sie wäre natürlich mit den Hunderttausend anderen in den amerikanischen Städten auf die Straße gegangen, um gegen Donald Trumps Politik zu demonstrieren. „Fahr ihr eine Couch für mich, wenn Trump wiedergewählt wird?", fragt sie scherzhaft. Doch der bittere Unterton ist unüberhörbar. Es sind politisch aufregende Zeiten. Damals wie heute.

Damals, Ende der 60er Jahre, führen die USA Krieg in Vietnam, in den Straßen protestieren nicht nur die jungen Menschen. Und ein Holocaust-Überlebender kauft einen VW-Käfer. Welch tiefgehende Verbindung zu dem Land, das ihn verraten und fast seine komplette Familie ermordet hat, muss er trotz allem in sich getragen haben?

Während Eleanor Reissa von den Widersprüchlichkeiten und Zerrissenheit jüdischer Leben erzählt, sitzt sie in einer Bäckerei in Ludwigsberg, und Tische nur, Selbstbedienung an der Theke. Sie hat das erste Dokument, das für die Reise durch das Leben ihres Vaters und ihrer Mutter zugetragen hat, vor sich liegen. Freunde von Freunden haben einen Treuter für sie in der Zentrale Stelle und in der Außenstelle des Bundesarchivs vereinbart. Drei Seiten umfasst die Auswage, die Chaskel Schlüsselberg einem deutschen Staatsanwalt 1948 in Stuttgart zu Protokoll gegeben hat. Dorthin, in die Stadt, wo er Freunde und Familie hatte, ist er zurückgekehrt, als er Auschwitz und den Todesmarsch ins Konzentrationslager Buchenwald überlebt hatte. In der Silberburgstraße 58 wohnte er damals. Eleanor will die Orte sehen, will sich vor Augen führen, „dass das wirklich wahr ist".

Immer wieder muss sie sich jetzt die Augen reiben. Nicht nur, weil der Jetlag ihr auch am dritten Tag in Deutschland noch in den Knochen steckt. Was sie über das Leben ihrer Eltern, überhaupt ihrer großen Familie weiß, war immer „ein großes Durcheinander". Wie ein pointillistischer Maker setze sie nun mal dort einen Punkt und mal dort. Sie wisse, dass das Bild nie vollständig werden kann, sagt sie. „Ich weiß ja gar nicht, was ich nicht weiß."

Wie du überhaupt suchen? Die mehr als 50 Briefe, die ihr Vater ihrer Mutter von Stuttgart nach New York geschrieben hat, waren letztlich der Auslöser, diese Reise nach Deutschland zu unternehmen. Mit „Liebste Ruth" oder „Liebste Ruthe" beginnen alle diese Liebesbriefe, die Eleanor Reissa nach dem Tod ihrer Mutter in deren Nachlass gefunden hat. Sie sind in schönster lateinischer Handschrift und auf Deutsch geschrieben, so wollte der Schreiber sich selbst beweisen, dass er wieder so deutsch wie die anderen ist. „Pass gut auf dich auf", schreibt er immer wieder, das Paar, das als Cousin und Cousine entfernt verwandt ist, hat sich nach dem Krieg im Displaced-Persons-Camp in Ulm, in der Donaubastion, getroffen. Mitte 1949 lässt Chaskel Schlüsselberg seine erste Frau und seine Tochter schließlich für tot erklären. Ruth ist nun seine Zukunft. Ein paar Monate nur fran erhält sie ihr Visum für Amerika. 1950 folgt er nach, und sie fangen ein gemeinsames neues Leben an.

„In diesen Briefen sprechen die Toten", sagt Eleanor. 30 Jahre hat die Tochter diese Schriftstücke nicht angerührt. Lange kommt

für das wie eine Grenzüberschreitung, wie ein Eindringen in die Privatsphäre ihrer Eltern vor. Im letzten Herbst hat sie die Briefe dann übersetzen lassen – von mehreren Übersetzern, so dass keiner die ganze. Wahrlich kommen kann. Von diesen Briefen will sie nach treiben lassen. So viele Namen von Freunden der Eltern stehen darin. So viele Unbekannte, die ihr inzwischen doch auch ein klein wenig vertraut geworden sind. So viele Orte. Bislang fehlt ihr der Kompass, sie zu ordnen.

Natürlich besitzt sie Genau-Beschreibung. Schwarz-Weiß-Fotos, auf denen vor allem Menschen zu sehen sind, die nicht mehr leben. Gudrun Schretzmeier, die Stuttgarter Kostümbildnerin und Ausstatterin unzähliger Theaterproduktionen, schaut die Fotos mit ihr durch und bestätigt, was Eleanor innerlich nie gewusst hat: Ihr Vater war ein Mann, der sehr viel Wert auf sein Aussehen legte und mög-

Reissas Mutter Ruth 1949, kurz vor ihrer Ausreise in die USA

Vor und nach dem Krieg. Und die Tochter von Josef Warscher, dem Vorsitzenden der israelitischen Gemeinde Stuttgarts nach 1945, berichtet über von ihrem Vater. Die beiden Männer waren damals befreundet. Da ist Nähe. „Es ist mehr, als ich erwartet habe", sagt Eleanor.

Aufgewachsen ist sie mit drei Halb-Geschwistern. Der ehemalige Häftlingsnummer, die ihr Vater auf dem linken Unterarm trug. Sie weiß, dass er im Konzentrationslager immer auf seinen Schuhen und seiner Kappe geschlafen hat. Nun liegt vor ihr die Aussage Chaskel Schlüsselbergs über sein Leben vor und während der Deportation. Im Juli 1938 muss er seinen Lumpenhandel in Bad Cannstatt aufgeben. Im Februar 1943 wird er mit seiner Familie nach Auschwitz-Birkenau deportiert.

Er berichtet von Müttern, die auf der Fahrt im Güterwagen ihren durstigen Kindern aus Verzweiflung den eigenen Urin zu trinken gegeben haben. Bei Dunkelheit werden die Ankömmlinge von den SS-Wachleuten brutal aus dem Waggon getrieben. Eleanor Reissa tippt die englische Übersetzung des Schreibens in ihren Laptop. Sie weiß, dass sich die Spur von ihrer Halbschwester Frida irgendwie hier verliert. „Meine Frau und meine sechs Jahre alte Tochter wurden von mir getrennt, ich habe sie nie mehr gesehen", ist das der Moment, in dem Eleanor Reissa das Schreiben unterbricht.

Und dann will sie am Ende ihrer drei Tage in Stuttgart dorthin, wo alles sehr wahr wird, zur Gedenkstätte „Zeichen der Erinnerung" am Stuttgarter Nordbahnhof. Die Namen aller etwa 2600 Deportierten kann man dort lesen. Ganz langsam nähert sich Eleanor Reissa dem Buchstaben S. Bei Chana und Frida Schlüsselberg bleibt sie stehen. Zärtlich streicht sie mit den Fingern über die Namen. Jetzt ist alles ganz nah und ganz wahr. Eilige Winterregen weht ein. Zeit zu gehen.

„Worum fragen immer alle nur, was meine Eltern in dieser Zeit gemacht haben?", sagt sie. Denn auch das gehört zu ihrer Spurensuche: das geduldige Beantworten von Fragen. Dabei würde sie so gerne zurückfragen: Was haben deine Eltern getan in dieser Zeit? Oder einfach mal etwas anderes erzählen. „Zum Beispiel, wie es war, als ich Bob Dylan getroffen habe", sagt sie später auf der Fahrt zum Hotel. Aber das ist eine ganz andere Geschichte aus den Zeiten des VW-Käfers.

Der Vater: Chaskel Schlüsselberg Ende der 20er Jahre

Frida starb in Auschwitz, ihr Bruder Heiner überlebte in England.

180

The article is in German, so I don't yet know what it says. But I feel like I want to share this with Harry. I mean, I want to share it with *somebody*. I feel so alone in all of this. But I am not sure if it will upset him too much. He is eighty-six years old, and maybe he doesn't want to open that Pandora's box anymore.

Harry no longer has an online account, so I email his wife, Joyce. I write her that I have an article and photos that Harry might find interesting, although perhaps unsettling or upsetting. Would she ask him please if I should send it?

I hear back from her quickly that Harry would like to see it, so I attach the article, and click "send."

An hour later, I get a phone call from Harry. His voice is heavy and thoughtful.

"My goodness Eleanor, how did you find that place?" he asks. "It's remarkable."

I tell him a bit about my journey. He listens intently. He is the first person who has wanted to know.

And then he says, "You know, if you need some money to help you with this, with the translations or whatever you need…."

I begin to cry. "No, Harry. Thank you so much for offering—that means so much to me. But I'm okay, it's alright."

"You sure?"

"Yes, yes, Harry. If I need, I'll let you know."

Of course, I could have used the money, but I didn't really need it. I just needed—what? Him. His interest and encouragement. His offer to help me. That was enough.

I call a friend in New York, who gives me a quick, rough translation of the article. It is indeed thoughtful, moving and charming. Hilke even includes the part about me and Bob Dylan. I am neither ashamed nor embarrassed by any of it. I am pleased and grateful, and I write Hilke to thank her.

The translations of my father's thirty-page testimony begin trickling in by email from the various translators I had parceled them out to last week. Besides Yeva and Daniela—my German-American hairdresser in New York—I sent some pages to Frank London's German-born wife, Tine, and to Lutz, who had kindly offered to translate. The task was too massive not to take them up on it.

I look at the transcript for the first time. Page one is dated 3 March 1967, with a stamp showing when it was officially received, the eighth of March. The name on the letterhead? Dr. Hans Worner, whom I look up but find no information about. The address? Simply Stuttgart.

I don't know what to make of this. 1967?

In 1967, my father was living in Brooklyn. My parents had been apart for seven years or so. I was fourteen.

I have a vague, distant memory that my father went to Germany sometime in the '60s. Of course, I didn't know why: that he was trying to get blood money from the German government. We weren't living with him at the time, so I didn't keep track of his travels or where-abouts. All his trip meant to me was that I would not have to visit him on those Sundays—a Get-Out-of-Jail-Free card. Yes, I'm sorry about that too, but my visits with him were mostly sad and strained and effortful. I had the job of clown and storyteller, with one foot out the door.

The title of the first page of this transcript says, "*Nervenfächarz-tliches Gutachten*"—which translates to "Neurologic Expert Opinion."

Okay. Now I understand the function of this document/testimony. It was to present my father's pain and suffering to the German government so that he could get additional reparations, *Wiedergutmachung*, a.k.a. "Cash for Suffering." But—and this is important—only if he could prove it. It's like if you can remember Woodstock, you weren't really there.

In 1953, the German government, under the terms of their Federal Compensation Law, agreed to pay reparations to the following groups:

- to the direct survivors of the Holocaust—also known as the people they were unable to murder;
- to those who were made to work as forced labor—also known as slaves;

- to Jews who were interned in camps or ghettos—a.k.a. prisoners;
- to Jews who were obliged to wear the Star of David badge;
- and/or to Jews who lived in hiding—if you can call that living.

A person could fit into all of the above categories, but the catch was you had to provide the evidence. Aye, there's the rub. That was what those documents that Yeva and I discovered in the archive desperately tried to do.

And now my email inbox is filled with the translations of my father's sworn thirty-page testimony, attempting to prove the unprovable.

CHAPTER TWENTY

The Testimony:
Of Chaskel Schlüsselberg to Dr. Hans Worner, Government Appointed Psychiatrist/Evaluator

(Words in italics are the English translation of the German psychiatrist's evaluation of my father's testimony. Non-italics are my summaries of his testimony, as well as my own two cents, hopefully worth more.)

Schlüsselberg is claiming damage to his health in the form of a heart condition, as a consequence of the persecution. The damage can be traced back to a time of discomfort in the years from 1933 to 1945.

Discomfort? Yes, I'd call pre-war Germany and nearly three years in Auschwitz *"a time of discomfort."* And, oh, can he prove that persecution adversely affects a man's heart? Is that what is meant by "heartache"?

On the occasion of meeting with former Auschwitz inmates on 20.3.1960, the old memories distressed him so much that he suffered from a heart attack the following day.

Uh-oh, reminiscing can be hazardous to your health. (Okay, spoiler alert: the purpose of this testimony is to "prove" that Germany ruined my father's health as well as his life and that they should pay him something for having had that privilege.)

March 20, 1960. I vaguely remember his heart attack. I was seven. I remember him returning home from the hospital, thin and gaunt. Somewhere, there is a photo of him from that time. Maybe that's what I remember.

The first pages of this document include statements from my father's American cardiologist and internist confirming this diagnosis, including dates of other heart attacks—which I knew nothing about—and confirming that his incarceration from 1943 to 1945 contributed to them.

The next section is titled "Family History." This portion tries to establish that my father's health issues are not genetic but rather the result and the direct responsibility of National Socialism. As always—and impossibly—proof is required.

In this family history section, my father speaks of his father, who was a merchant and the owner of a large textile and egg business in Strzyżów, Poland. He says that he learned his father was murdered in 1942 in Rzeszów, Poland at the age of eighty. (How did one learn such things? Someone saw? Someone said?) His mother died of supposedly natural causes at the age of seventy-five, one year before the beginning of World War II. My father says that he was the seventh of nine children: six brothers and two sisters. Three died as a direct result of what they are calling "the persecution." Two others died shortly after the war, and three survived into the 1960s.

I knew nothing about my father's father or mother—my paternal grandparents. Nothing. Just their names—which I only knew because in prayer, my father was referred to as *Yecheskel Ben Nasanal*—Ezekiel, the son of Nathaniel. I knew his mother's name, *Alte Rishe*, because I am named after her. Her name is my Yiddish name.

I did not know that he was one of nine children, the seventh youngest. I had actually met his three surviving siblings and their children when I was a young girl, including his sister Toni, who lived in the Bronx and whom I remember as a burgundy redhead with tight curly hair and a warm intelligent smile. Shortly after he gave this testimony, my father took me to Israel during my summer vacation—my first time on an airplane—where I met his remaining older brothers, Chaim and Eli. It was on that same trip that we stopped off in England, where I met Harry and his family for the first time.

The testimony goes on to speak of my father's first marriage to a Jewish woman from Munich, one year younger than he, and that there were two children from that marriage: one son born on 8 November 1931 and a daughter born on 17 July 1936, both in Stuttgart. It says that his wife and daughter were murdered in Izbica, Poland at a time unknown to him. He was able to send his son to England on a children's transport. The son still lives there, it says, but there is no contact between them.

Until Yeva and I went to the Staatsarchiv, I knew nothing about Frida and her mother's deaths. Harry believed that they had died in the concentration camp Treblinka. At the time of this testimony in early 1967, my father had not yet reconciled with Harry, to whom he had stopped speaking in 1953. That meant that Harry knew none of these details about his mother or sister. He lived with his own impressionistic picture of their fate with whatever shards he could piece together.

Schlüsselberg then sums up his more modern history: a second marriage in 1951 in the USA to a Polish Jewish woman, ten years younger than him.

Not until this translation finds its way to me do I learn the year my parents married. I never saw a marriage certificate, photo, or anything that documented or commemorated that happy event.

Why he needed to make my mother ten years his junior rather than the twenty years that truly separated them, who can know. Lying beats truth-telling in my family. Better "they" shouldn't know the truth. That was always the message to me.

A healthy daughter resulted from this marriage on 11 May 1953.

Wait. Stop. I'm in this document? Even though I know it's written in 1967, it never occurs to me that I will be a character in his tragedy. But of course, I am. Directly implicated. I owe my life to the death of others. As I said recently to a friend—also a child of survivors—it's amazing that we are able to walk upright.

He has been living separated from his second wife for six years. When he got sick and was unable to work, she left him.

She left him because he was unable to work? Really? She left him, I thought, because he beat my half-brother, Seymour—often, I was told—although he never raised a hand to me.

He denies any incidence of previous nervousness or mental diseases, seizure disorders, vascular diseases, tuberculosis, diabetes and blastoma related to his family and relatives.

This is pro forma and repeated over and over in this document. No other way to get money—although it is probably true.

Then comes a section called:

His History

Schlüsselberg was born in Strzyżów, Poland, near Krakow, and grew up with his parents as the seventh of nine siblings. The parents were wealthy people. The father was an Orthodox Jew who not only strictly followed the Sabbath but went to the synagogue every day. The parents owned a spacious house with a large garden.

My father, during all of his days—even in the nursing home—was a pious Jew, with all that that entailed. I never understood how deeply-rooted it was, that he came from such a devout home. In his letters to my mother, he speaks often about the Sabbath and his involvement with the religious community, helping them in their search for a chazzan and with their rebuilding challenges. He prays for God's help a lot. (In Yiddish, we say: "*Es vet helfn vi a toytn bankes,*" meaning, "That will help about as much as putting leeches on a dead person.")

With regards to my grandparents' wealth, I remember meeting some Schlusselberg cousins who said—with certainty—that an enormous amount of money was hidden under my grandfather's house,

and if any of us dared to go back to Poland, we would surely find gold buried under the porch. To the best of my knowledge, none of them dared.

> *As a child he was well and never suffered from any hardship. As far as he knows, he did not suffer from seizures and developed normally. There was no nocturnal enuresis, fear of darkness or any other early psychopathic patterns.*

No *pishing* in bed. Well, that's a relief.

And no "psychopathic patterns." Imagine, a victim of the Holocaust has to defend *their* mental health, when it was the Nazis and their supporters who were the psychopaths.

> *From the age of three, he went to a Jewish religious school. Then at the age of six, he attended a Polish elementary school for six or seven years, until he was thirteen years old. Additionally he attended the rabbinical school where he learned Hebrew and Yiddish. He was an average student and never had to repeat a school year.*

In July of 2018, a year after this journey, I was invited to sing at the Jewish festival in Krakow, Poland. While I was there, I hired a guide and made the two-hour drive to my father's hometown of Strzyżów. Although the town had been rebuilt, the dead continued to speak. Surprisingly, there in a museum, we found my father's Polish report cards! School records from 1907, 1908, and 1909; as well as those of some of his brothers and sisters.

L. p.	Imię i nazwisko ucznia (uczenicy):	Imię i nazwisko, stan i miejsce pobytu ojca matki lub opiekuna:	Imię i nazwisko, stan i mieszkanie odpowiedzialnego nadzorcy:
65	*Eliaschel Schliesselberg* ur. d. 22 stycznia 190_ w *Strzyżowie* rel. *mojżesz*obrz.	*Lewel Schliesselberg handlarz Strzyżów*	

Rok szkolny 190 7/8	I. półrocze:		II. półrocze:	
	I. kwartał:	II. kwartał:	III. kwartał:	IV. kwartał:
Obyczaje:	*chwalebne*	*chwalebne*		
Pilność:	*mała*	*mała*		
w nauce religii:	*/.*	*/.*		
w czytaniu:	*niedostateczny*	*niedostateczny*		
w pisaniu:	*dostateczny*	*dostateczny*		
w języku polskim:	*niedostateczny*	*niedostateczny*		
w języku ruskim:	*/.*	*/.*		
w języku niemieckim:	*/.*	*/.*		
w rachunkach w połączeniu z nauką o formach geometrycznych:	*dostateczny*	*dostateczny*		
w wiadomościach z geografii i historyi (w klasie V. i VI.):	*/.*	*/.*		
w wiadomościach z historyi naturalnej i fizyki (w klasie V. i VI.):	*·/·*	*/.*		
w rysunkach:	*/.*	*/.*		
w śpiewie:	*dostateczny*	*dostateczny*		
w robotach ręcznych:	*/.*	*/.*		
w gimnastyce:	*/.*	*dostateczny*		
Postęp ogólny:	*niedostateczny*	*niedostateczny*		
Porządek zewnętrzny:	*niejednostajny*	*niejednostajny*		
Liczba opuszczonych godzin szkolnych:	usprawiedl. nieuspraw.	usprawiedl. nieuspraw.	usprawiedl. nieuspraw.	usprawiedl. nieuspraw.
Uwagi nauczyciel klasy:				

Uwaga. Zaczął uczęszczać na naukę codzienną w szkole ludowej _2_ klasowej *mies.* w *Strzyżowie* dnia *1 września* 1907 *...* *...ennie uczęszczał do klasy I __ w 190_*

And?

He was an average student—at best.

Shortly after his graduation from school, in 1914, the First World War broke out and the Russians entered his hometown.

So, now I know that my father had seven or eight years of public school education. Until he was thirteen. That was it.

The family was able to escape just in time to Teplitz-Shönau, where they lived in a spacious emergency accommodation for a year. He withstood the escape well. After the Russians retreated to the Carpathian Mountains, the family returned to Strzyżów.

Information about my father and his family from the First World War. I knew nothing about them that went that far back. "*They lived in a spacious emergency accommodation for a year.*" I find myself reading this over and over. What does that mean?

I look up Teplitz-Schönau also known as Teplice-Sanov. Today, it is part of the Czech Republic and credited with being their second largest "spa town." Maybe that accounts, in part, for why he "*withstood the escape well.*" When my father and his family fled there (Mapquest says it's 757 kilometers from their home in Poland), it was still a part of the Austrian Empire. That town had a significant Jewish presence since the 1400s, and unlike the rest of Bohemia and Moravia, the Jews there were never expelled—until, of course, 1938 when it was "annexed" to Nazi Germany.

Four of his brothers were soldiers with the Austrian military from the beginning of the war (because Poland was not yet a nation). Therefore, he had to help with the family business and wasn't able to learn a trade. Primarily he drove around with a carriage and bought eggs. This he did until 1919 or 1920. Then he moved to Germany where several of his brothers were already living in a well manner. For that reason, one brother after another followed, and finally, he himself went.

With each and every sentence, more is revealed to me. Every paragraph and page gives me more details of what I had believed was unknowable, adding on to the pile of last week's mound of information.

And I'm only up to page four—out of thirty!

This is the history of my father and his family—*my family*—as told by him in 1967: about the prehistoric times of 1907–1920, until he was nineteen, when he left Poland to find something more exciting for his young life than "*to drive around with a carriage and buy eggs.*" Stuttgart was 1182 kilometers away from home; a major hub, where he hoped to make his way in this wide world, after the war to end all wars. *Such possibilities*, he must have thought.

Suddenly, I come to a bizarre conclusion, hard to believe yet true: Going to Germany in 1920 saved my father's life. Every member of his very large family who remained in Poland was killed. Every single one.

My father was a child during World War I and an adult during World War II. Both he and my mother were born precisely in the wrong place at the wrong time. Unlike mine, their lives were the opposite of good luck.

After a short stay in Cologne, he went to his favorite brother Max (Moishe) in Stuttgart where he worked at his brother's rag trade company on Gutenberg Street 24 for approximately a year. Probably around the year of 1925, he started his own rag trade business on Muehlstreet 6 in Zuffenhausen.

If Yeva and I had read this testimony while we were still in Stuttgart, we surely would have tried to find these many addresses mentioned in this document. We passed Zuffenhausen on the train from Stuttgart to Ludwigsburg every day. It is also the town where Hilke lives.

From the start, he continually employed six or seven women as rag pickers. He didn't collect rags himself but bought them from scavengers and rag pickers. He made a good living with this occupation and earned between 100 to 200 RM a week.

In the 1920s, with four Reichsmarks being worth one dollar, he earned approximately fifty dollars a week—the equivalent of seven-hundred dollars today. And even though running a rag business does not sound exotic, being a vibrant young man in Stuttgart sure sounds a lot better than riding around Strzyżów in a horse and buggy selling eggs.

In 1930, he married the daughter of a Jew from Munich, named Rubin.

Like him, his first wife was not born in Germany but in Rzowitz, Poland, which was news to Harry. When I tell him this, he seems a bit disappointed. He believed—or preferred to believe—that she was German, not Polish. A classier heritage? Maybe.

Because his wife didn't like the rag trade business—it was too dirty for her—he closed it down shortly after they married, as she urged him to do. He does not remember the exact date. He joined his father-in-law's business in Munich as a travelling salesman, within Baden-Württemberg. As such, he made a good earning, considering the times. He earned between 200 and 250 Marks a week. He held this position until 1932. In the same year, he opened an egg business on Schiller Street 36 in Ludwigsburg, and shortly after, a second one on Gutbrod Street 11 in Stuttgart.

I never knew or understood what my father did for a living before reading this document. Now I know. He was a businessman; he was a salesman; he travelled through Baden-Württemberg, the third largest state in Germany, bordered by the Rhine and the Neckar Rivers, home of the beautiful Schwarzwald, the Black Forest. I have my father's photo inscribed in German by his friend, Josef Warscher, "remembering our time in Schwarzwald." I calculate that his earnings then had the current buying power of approximately $1,000 a week.

In Poland, my father's parents had been well-to-do merchants. In Germany, before the war, my father was a successful businessman; he was entrepreneurial and a go-getter. In America, after the war, he was a greenhorn sweatshop-worker; uneducated, with dye-stained blackened hands, and a thick accent. My life was shaped by that image and by many other false assumptions of him.

His very competent wife helped him with the businesses and after a short period she had her own egg stand on Feuersee Square in Stuttgart. These businesses ran successfully until the boycotting against the Jews started in 1933.

Before the war, high interest rates made Germany very attractive to investors from around the world. However, the stock market crash in the fall of 1929 caused American investors to call their loans to Germany. Then in May of 1931, the bankruptcy of the major Austrian bank Creditanstalt, led to the suspension of all payments to Germany and sent shockwaves throughout Europe. Germany's banking industry collapsed and in January 1933, with unemployment at more than six million (irony noted), Hitler became chancellor.

On 1 April 1933, the Nazis carried out the first nationwide planned action against Jews: a boycott targeting Jewish businesses as well as Jewish professionals. Like my father, most Jews in Germany were proud to be Germans. His brothers were included in the more than 100,000 Jews who had served in the German army during World War I, with many being decorated for their bravery. On the day of the boycott, Storm Troopers stood menacingly, like so many bullies before—and after—them, in front of Jewish-owned businesses and offices. They painted the Star of David, in yellow and black, across thousands of doors and windows, with accompanying anti-Semitic slogans. The Nazis claimed that German and foreign Jews were spreading "atrocity stories" in order to damage Germany's reputation. Like today's claims of "fake news," it was the liars who were spreading the lies. Laws were passed, one after another, making lawlessness legal. It became legal to restrict Jewish employment, restrict Jewish access to culture, restrict education, transportation, and more. It was the beginning of the end.

Right at the beginning of the boycott against the Jews, his wife's egg stand on Feuersee Square was overturned, and she was verbally abused in a very humiliating way.

How frightened she must have been. How frightened I would have been; how frightened I *am*, even though this did not happen to me. The slightest whiff of fascism and racism and authoritarianism triggers the hell out of me and sends me down the dark rabbit hole, wondering when to flee or who will save me or hide me. But little did my father's wife—or anyone else—know what all of that would lead to, that they would slowly boil to death like frogs on a low flame. When do we know? Ever? Even when we see the future repeating the past, we never think it will happen to us. If we did, what would we do then? Still nothing?

At the same time, his sales in both stores declined so rapidly that within fourteen days, he lost his livelihood completely. He had no choice but to close both stores, experiencing a big financial loss. He couldn't find any work and was forced to join his brother Nathan's rag trade business in Stuttgart–Bad Cannstatt. There, he was partly a worker and partly a commissioned wholesale buyer of rags. He earned an income of about 80 Reichsmark weekly. After the boycott actions in 1933, the collecting and trading of rags were one of the very few jobs the Jews were still permitted to have.

That was barely one-third of what he had earned before the boycott. But at least Jews were still allowed to be rag pickers.

In 1937, his brother lost his business license, and he was forced to sell it. That left Schlüsselberg with next to nothing. Nathan got deported to Poland in 1938. Shortly before his deportation, Nathan authorized Schlüsselberg to have access to his bank account in Stuttgart which contained over 10,000 Reichsmark.

"*Nathan got deported to Poland.*" I would have assumed that meant the end of Nathan. Remarkably, it was not. Somehow, he did manage to get to United States, but unfortunately died a short time later of tuberculosis. My father never saw him again.

From the end of 1937, he was unemployed and lived on his brother's money, which he spent very carefully. Every attempt to find work, no matter of what nature, was pointless for him, since he was a Jew. Although he didn't have a job, he would keep himself busy, taking care of the empty, not yet sealed, apartments of Jews that had been evacuated, and sending them their belongings. The eviction of the Jews happened so suddenly and quickly at that time that they could only take the most essential things with them.

Yes, what did happen to those Jews and their belongings when they were summarily and speedily deported? Well, now we know something we didn't even think to ask. Their desperation and fear meant that everything was for sale; that the seller, as well as the "caretaker," would squirrel away what they morally—and immorally—could. I suspect that there were some ethical as well as unethical choices, behaviors, and actions taken by my father that he fails to mention in this testimony. He was a man, not a saint.

> *Approximately in the spring of 1939, the Gestapo ordered him to start working as an unskilled worker at a factory on Tauben Street 4 in Stuttgart as a press operator. The general hourly wage for that job at that time was 85 pennies. For a Jew, it was only 45 pennies.*

You do the math.

> *Because he was a competent and able worker, the director of the company promoted him to be an incentive operator, which led to higher earnings. About twenty-two Jews worked at the factory and for the most part, they had difficulties doing the work. He didn't only help out the Jews at the factory but others there as well. Schlüsselberg tells this in a believable and convincing way: how he had helped and supported older Jews who hadn't yet been evacuated to the East.*

I choose to believe that what my father says is true; that he helped. Maybe he did, maybe he didn't. But he was a God-fearing man and although he surely did whatever he had to do to save his own life, for which I am obviously grateful, perhaps he helped others too when he could. "Judge not," said Jesus, and I'll go with that.

> *In 1940, he was forced to leave their flat in Silberburgstraße.*

Before I left for Germany in January, I asked Harry what he remembered about his life in Stuttgart during his seven years there. One of the things he told me was that he had some memory of the street they lived on. "Silver something," he said.

> *The Gestapo gave him a flat with two rooms in the Rosenbergstraße, which was the area in which the Gestapo concentrated all Jews of*

196

*Stuttgart. There was no barber in the area, and so he decided to cut hair
for the Jews after his work in the factory. He says he earned more money
doing this than from his job in the shoe factory. But on the other hand,
there was nothing he could buy for the money.*

Aha, gotcha! *"But on the other hand, there was nothing he could buy
for the money."* Catch-22 over and over again.

*In April of 1942, at the order of the Gestapo, he and his wife and daughter
were to be deported to the East.*

The East was Poland. The East was Czechoslovakia. The East was
concentration camps. The East was death. Usually.

*Because of an intervention at the factory where they made military
supplies, he was spared from that transport at the order of the Gestapo.
However, his wife and five-year-old daughter were transported to Izbica
in Poland. Since that time, he has not heard from them. Despite his
intense efforts, he could not discover their fate.*

Well, there we have it, the answer to the question of why Chana
and Frida were deported without him. Shall we try to imagine that day
in 1942 when my father, preparing to be transported with his wife and
daughter to unknown but certain death, was cherry-picked out of that
human herd at the last minute? From that very transport station I had
visited with Hilke. His daughter and wife forced to go, and he gets to
stay? Should we imagine that? The pleading, the weeping, the silence,
the horror? Yes, we should, and no, we can't.

I sit here, a free bird with my cappuccino and sunblock, in ancient
Acre, in modern Israel, and read his testimony. The Jewish state, with
all its many flaws, did not exist when those atrocities were being
committed. Whatever one's political leanings, however casual or
passionate, we know now—with absolute certainty—that the Holocaust *would not and could not* have unfolded in this one-sided barbaric
massacre if there had been a State of Israel at that time. These masses
of Jews, millions and millions of singular, unique human beings, would
have had a different fate. If only....

I am also thinking of Einstein and the fluidity of Time. I'm reading about the past, about these people—my family and the others—who had suffered and fought to stay alive. All the while, I know their future. I know the end of the story, what happened downstream, what their future—or lack of future—held in store for them. Their past, present, and future tense, their river empties into me. I am their future. And their witness. As are you.

Is my future already written too? I behave as though I am captain of my own life, as others have believed. Before deportation, they all packed and planned for this or that, thinking they were steering their own ship toward a controlled future.

In Yiddish we say: "*A mentsh trakht in Gott lakht.*" Or "A man plans, and God laughs." What a sense of humor, that God. Certainly no one thought their ship would take them up a chimney. Or to the streets of Brooklyn, New York.

After the departure of his wife and his daughter in 1942, he had to leave that flat in Rosenbergstrasse. He was forced to move to the former Jewish school at Hospitalstraße 36, in a big room with other Jews.

Hospitalstraße 36? Where I met with Eve Warscher, at the Jewish Community Center less than two weeks ago? Like a Venn diagram, Time and Space overlap.

At the end of 1942, he had to line up for deportation again in Hospitalstraße. They brought him to Killesberg, and from there with a truck to the northern rail station in Stuttgart.

I look up "Killesberg." The Internet says it has a great park. What Holocaust? No reference to it at all. But Wikipedia says the railway station is beautiful.

There were a large number of Jews assembled: old people, ill people, men, women, and children of every age. Then, just moments before that transport departure, the Gestapo picked him out and issued the order that he had to resume his work in the shoe factory.

Again? Plucked out again? A moment before he was to be transported, his life was saved because he was a good worker.

I sit in my ancient cave in Acre and read these translations as they arrive piecemeal in my emails, sentence after sentence, like a serialized mystery novel. Whatever I learned with Yeva in Germany was receding into the distance in lieu of this new information—not so much new, as unbearably detailed. The devil is literally in these details. There seems to be no end to it, although, of course, there will be.

In the spring 1933, he became a subject of an increasing number of evil defamations because he was Jewish. After a short while, it became difficult for him to read the newspapers because there was not a single day on which there were no discriminations and agitating against the Jews. When he read these articles, it happened more and more that he got sudden diarrhea.

After Kristallnacht in November 1938, the Gestapo arrested Jewish men. But he paid attention to the hours when the Gestapo would come, and he managed to leave the house without being recognized before the Gestapo arrived. Mr. Sparthelf in Obereßlingen, a former customer of his Lumpenhandlung (rag trade) *business, allowed him to stay with him for the necessary time. The arrested Jews were deported to the camp in Welzheim, and they were released after 8 or 14 days.*

I search for the name "Sparthelf" but cannot find him or anything about him. Mr. Sparthelf was one of those godly humans that saved my father's life while surely endangering his own. Whoever and wherever his is, I bless his soul and wish I could tell his family that their father saved my father's life, and consequently my own.

I also look up "Welzheim." Welzheim is a town about thirty-five kilometers from Stuttgart in the Schwäbisch area where Hilke and I went for dinner on my last night in Germany with Cordelia and Hardy Huober. Well, it seems that there had been "a small concentration camp" near that city, simply referred to as "The Prison." The camp held between 10,000 and 15,000 prisoners. Witnesses testified that the camp would regularly hang prisoners on Tuesdays to make room for the next batch of incoming Jews. (For sure, no one there slept well on Monday nights.) There is a memorial to these victims in the churchyard of the town.

I wonder if Hardy knew about this place. How could he not? If he had, why didn't he speak of it or take me to it? Not enough time? Too close to home? Just asking.

> For one or two years after the beginning of the war, he was forced to wear the Jewish star. But he says he has no proper recollection of the exact dates for this aspect of persecution. On that point, when he had to wear the Jewish star (yellow badge), he was no longer allowed to use the tram, he was not allowed to visit a cinema or a pub or restaurant, and there were only a few shops left where he was allowed to buy goods.

To think that my father, my own father, wore a fucking yellow star.... Of course, I should have known that my father wore the yellow star. But I didn't. Maybe I couldn't. I imagined that about the others, the masses of other Jews—but not my father. Perhaps the mere image of that, picturing my father like that, was more than I could consciously bear, although I always believed I could bear anything. I used to search for my father in the faces of all those men in the black-and-white photos of the camps and the ghettos in books and magazines. I'd stare at those faces, looking for him, sure that I would be able to recognize him. But I never found him. And then, I stopped imagining that he was there; that maybe he didn't really experience that time as horribly as all of the others had. In my pathetic defense, who can imagine one's own parent suffering in Hell?

In this written testimony, the yellow star is underlined. From what Yeva and I learned at the archive, it seems that a Jewish victim would get more money in reparations based on how long they wore that star—if they could prove it. It was underlined by whichever German bureaucrats were reading the document, whose purpose it was to determine the amount of my father's reparation. Reparation is defined as "the making of amends for a wrong one has done, by paying money to or otherwise helping those who have been wronged." How in the world can you pay for such wrongs, for such crimes and abominations?

Back in New York, shortly after I returned from Israel, I had lunch with my friend Sam Norich, who had originally given me such valuable information before I left for Germany, including that book, *The Saving Remnant*. He wanted to hear about my trip. We found ourselves discussing reparations. Sam said that he was once on an international committee that decided on the compensation given to Holocaust survivors. He told me that the amount of money paid out over the years since reparations began in 1952 was billions of dollars, to which I said, "Wow." He looked at me hard and said gravely, "That was nothing. It was nothing compared to what they stole—in wealth and in lives. Nothing."

There were Jewish ration cards for scarce allotments. There was no tobacco available for Jews. Cigarettes were available only on the black market, and they cost one German mark each. These discriminations offended him very much.

My father and his cigarettes. Such a seemingly small thing. I hadn't understood that being stingy with them in the nursing home - this one pleasure - was so injurious to him. And such a familiar punishment.

Schlüsselberg says he never gave in or bowed down his head, but that sometimes he was filled with despair. He felt like a slave and worried a lot about the future.

He never bowed down his head, my father. But "*sometimes he was filled with despair.*" Sometimes?! Worried about the future? Talk about understatements. All of this translated testimony is written in the third person; an interpretation by a German psychiatrist.

Despite the stigmatization and branding as a Jew, he was not often persecuted or harassed in the streets. Therefore, he must give good references to the people of Stuttgart. He was persecuted and harassed from time to time by the Gestapo and especially by fanatic party members of

201

NSDAP (Nazi party). *Schlüsselberg remembers clearly that he was able to get off work for two days on the Jewish highest holidays.*

How nice that my father gives *"good references"* to the people of Stuttgart. He was allowed to take off for the high holidays? Who let him do that? I guess it was the person at the factory who saved him again and again by saying his work was necessary. A nameless person who kept my father alive and off the transport trains until 1943. Let us raise a glass to the nameless humans who do such things, again and again—thanklessly and anonymously—to save us. May we be as brave as they were when our time comes.

> *He was a hardworking man and one of the best workers in the shoe factory and even the Gestapo realized that. This was probably the reason why they were leaving him alone and did not bother him and why his deportations were postponed several times.*

Hardworking. Yes. Let that be a lesson...

> *But finally, when Stuttgart was forced by the Nazis to be free of Jews* (Judenrein), *even Jews like him who were used by the Gestapo, had to be deported. This small group of Jews—maybe fifty-sixty people, mostly men—had to show up on 17 February 1943 to the Hospitalstraße in Stuttgart with their permitted baggage of approximately 30 kilograms.*

For the weight-conversion challenged, thirty kilograms is approximately sixty-six pounds. Fifty pounds is the weight of one large suitcase currently permitted by most airlines. That's what the Nazis allowed you to bring on this upcoming journey to the East. Just like taking an international flight. Except that the Nazis would keep whatever you would bring, and, of course, the trip was usually one way.

> *This group, being guarded by the Gestapo, was deported by normal train cars from the main train station Hauptbahnhof in Stuttgart station to Wiesbaden, and then to a small village close by. They had to stay there and had wait for another transport of about one thousand people to arrive. They had to sleep on the bare ground in a barrack.*

Hauptbahnhof was that central train station in Stuttgart next to my hotel, where Yeva and I would come and go during our three days there. Not for a moment did it occur to me that my father's deportation began from that very station.

Then the transport came. The people were pushed together, packed in animal train wagons like sheep, without a possibility to sit or lay down. In these train wagons—they were completely enclosed except for a little gap in the door. In this way, the deportation to Auschwitz took place.

Okay.

I have to stop now. I am afraid of what comes next. I am on the verge of learning what I always thought I wanted to know. "Careful what you wish for" comes to mind. My father waited all this time to tell me; let him wait another day.

I am still in Acre. The end of the first of my two weeks here. This place is beauty personified. I am reinvigorated by the sun and the sea and the hummus and the humanity. Still, reading this unexpected testimony presses against my brain. The details of the abominations are more than I bargained for. The wounds are further salted by John's thoughtlessness. I agree with my father—the loss of love and emotional pain can cause a kind of heart attack.

I reread my journal of my days in Germany, looking for clues and insights. There are plenty of discoveries, but they are soldered with sadness, rampant rage, and brutal loneliness, all tied up with boundless grief. "The dead keep the living alive," wrote Richard Powers in *The Overstory*. He was referring specifically to trees, but he meant people too. The dead are my nurturers, my guides, my companions. Secretly, I tell myself that John is dead too, as though that might give me some comfort. Ha, of course, it does not. This trip was meant to be about my family's journey but has snaked around to become mine.

Dinner tonight, thankfully, is with the other two artist residents and the very generous Evan. Mediterranean Israeli-Palestinian cuisine plus these companions could make a person forget nearly anything.

Tomorrow, I will go on with my father's transcript. I will try to stop interrupting so much and let him tell his own story.

Even though there is not a title for the upcoming chapter, it deserves one. It could be called "The Beginning of the End," but I will be simpler.

CHAPTER TWENTY-ONE

Auschwitz

The transport lasted for six days and six nights. Because there was no water, each day became even more torturing than the day before. There was no place for releasing themselves; there was just a bucket or pot to relieve yourself, and you had to throw the human waste through the small gap in the door. The conditions in the train wagons were terrible. He remembers several little children who shouted and cried because they were so thirsty. And when they did not cry anymore, they started to whimper and moan softly. And then the parents would spit into the mouths of their children to try to reduce their suffering. These terrible and horrifying experiences of the transport to Auschwitz he will never forget.

Until he came to Auschwitz, he was always completely healthy and never ill; he had no accidents or serious operations until then.

The transport arrived in Auschwitz at midnight. Directly after the unloading, the women, children, and men were separated. The crying and screaming of the mothers for their children and of the children for their mothers would be something he would not forget for the rest of his life.

All of the belongings that he had brought with him, he had to leave in the train. After the separation of women, children, and men, there was another selection of the men. He remembers all the details as though it were today. The disabled war veterans—invalids—of the First World War had to give up their crutches and canes and fell helplessly into the snow.

In case we ever wondered what the weather was like in February 1943—which, for some reason, had never occurred to me to wonder about—we now know. Yes, of course it was snowing.

On the same night of his arrival and after the selection of the men, the outfitting of the clothing took place. He had to undress stark naked and got his head shaved and he was tattooed with the number 105151. He received striped clothing with completely insufficient underwear and wooden shoes. Since he was a strong man, he was selected to go to the Buna Factory in Monowitz, a unit about 7 kilometers away from Auschwitz. That departure to Monowitz imprisonment was by foot. He was in a very overcrowded barrack with three hundred men. Three-tiered military beds, each with a straw mat and blanket. The food supply consisted of a portion of coffee substitute and two hundred grams of bread in the morning, one portion of thin soup with a few slices of beets at noon, and one liter of thin soup given in the evening.

Monowitz. For a detailed, extremely well-told account, and corroboration of this unbelievable reality, one can read Primo Levi's *If This Is A Man*. He slaved at Buna too, as did Elie Wiesel, during the same time as my father. Levi explains some of the significance of the tattooed numbers: People marked with numbers beginning 170000, which included Levi himself, were the recently-arrived inmates. Tattoos lower than 150000 pointed to the inmates who had miraculously managed to stay alive for longer than possible—like my father, number 105151. Of the 650 Italians in Primo Levi's transport to Auschwitz, three survived.

Wake-up call would be at five. Then at seven, they would have to be ready for roll call, where there were a lot of beatings. At seven-thirty, they would march in lockstep to work, which was supervised very closely by the guards. At first, he was an excavator, then a mason, and afterwards, he was responsible for the cement. Work in the summer would go until six p.m., in winter until five p.m. During work, they would be constantly hurried on and beaten a lot by the SS, but even worse were the Kapos."

The concentration camps depended on the cooperation of inmates who supervised the prisoners. Known as *Kapos*, these prisoners carried out the will of the Nazi camp guards and were often as brutal—sometimes *more* brutal, my father says—than their SS counterparts. Some of the *Kapos* were Jewish. Failure to perform their duties would have resulted in severe punishment or death. Over the years, many have viewed their actions as a form of complicity. After the war, the prosecution of *Kapos* as war criminals, particularly those who were Jewish, created a dilemma which continues to this day. I do not have the certainly of my own moral character to dare to judge them.

After coming back, they would have to stand for roll call again, where there was hardly a day in which one or more Jews wouldn't be hanged. Gallows stood in the center of the parade ground. After these executions, the inmates would have to march past the gallows. During the roll calls, they would be beaten often with fists or clubs. Although he was still a strong man, he was beaten down to the ground by the force of these blows to his head by the clubs, time and time again. He never lost consciousness either entirely or partially. He got up each time; otherwise, he would have been stamped or beaten to death. These hits on the head, he might have received at least once during work times and probably ten times during the roll calls. He did not suffer from nausea; mouth, nose or ear bleeding; nor dysfunctions of his seeing, speaking, or hearing ability after these abuses.

Soon after his arrival in Monowitz, he lost all sense of time. He would vegetate without being conscious of time and would only orientate himself by the sun for the times of the day. The daily routine didn't differ between weekdays, weekends, and holidays. He worked seven days a week for more than a year.

Every Sunday, each cellblock had to provide eleven men for the loading work. These Sunday draftees had to unload loose cement, iron, bricks, and so on. As a tall and strong man, he would always have to join the Sunday workers. Especially during the Sunday drafts, he would have to labor very hard. He was also chosen to regularly cut or shave off the hair of his fellow block inmates with a hand machine. For this, he received an extra liter of thin soup.

All of this is news to me. News to me that he was a tall, strong man even. My father? The sad-looking broken man sitting at the window, resting his tired arms on a pillow, waiting all week just to make lunch for me on Sundays? Him? Yes. How can you know a man and not know such things about his life? Not just *any* man but your own father? That was my father's life for over two years. Those were his days, his nights, his mornings, afternoons, and evenings.

At some point, during the year of 1944, he was forced to go on the bock.

I have to look up the word. *Bock*, an Old German word, is defined as a "sawhorse or vaulting horse." I find more specific information on a site called Wollheim Memorial, dedicated to survivor and activist Norbert Wollheim. "The 'buck' or 'sawhorse' was a common punishment: up to twenty-five blows with a cane while bent over a sawhorse, often administered by prisoner functionaries (*Kapos*) in the presence of the SS. Many of the abused prisoners lost consciousness even before the corporal punishment was over."

He could not remember exactly when that happened because of a complete lack of a time concept.

To steal a human being's sense of time? Not to be able to discern a minute from an hour from a day or a month? Or a year? A Thursday from a Sunday, a May from a March, a 1943 from a 1945? The sum of our lives is a collection of our catalogued time, marked moments in days and years. The depth of this cruelty and inhumanity—subtle and not so subtle—is ineffable.

Following the distribution of the evening soup, he would volunteer, along with two other inmates, to clean the soup kettles. The reason for this was that these soup kettles contained some thick food scraps at the bottom (surviving remnants, yes), which were worth more than the watery soup they received every day. On this one particular day, in order to avoid going the long way to empty the water in the washing room, he went instead directly to the latrine. While doing this, he was caught by a Kapo, who hit him in the head so violently that he fell to the ground. It was after that that he received the twenty-five lashings on the back. These lashes on his bare buttocks were so painful that he cannot find words for them. Luckily, he did not get lashes on the uncovered kidney area. Especially the first lashes hurt terribly, and it was nearly impossible for him to bite the pain (translation of *"verbeißen"*: to bite your teeth as strong as you can to avoid crying aloud). *But he withstood all the lashes without losing consciousness. His buttocks bled and were heavily swollen. It took weeks and weeks for the pain in his buttocks to subside. But already the next day, he was forced to work again, even though he was hardly able to stand on his feet because of the enormous pain. In that respect, there was not the slightest reprieve at all. Every day, Jews died of exhaustion or in work-related accidents or were beaten to death. When returning from work at night, the stronger prisoners had to drag the dead along with them, and most times he belonged to the stronger ones. Even if only one man was missing during the evening roll call, they all had to stand and wait until he was found—dead or alive. In Monowitz, he was consistently able to maintain minimal nutritional standards and managed not to lose too much weight. As a good and skilled worker, he was popular with the Germans in the Buna factory. Due to his good nutritional condition, the foreman often called him "Der Dicker."* (Meaning: "the Fatso." Oh my gosh.)

More or less, he was able to keep himself in this condition until January 1945. He came to Auschwitz as a strong man, and he never let himself drift like most other Jews, with few exceptions. It took only a short time before he clearly discovered the few chances to survive. He tried to take full advantage of these few opportunities—but certainly not at the expense of other prisoners. In this respect, he has never had to make any accusations against himself.

After a long discussion, asked about this opinion, Schlüsselberg summarizes himself as follows: To survive this concentration camp was, on the one hand, a question of being in a good physical condition

209

plus a certain psychological robustness. Also the ability to exploit all possibilities, and last but not least, having numerous lucky circumstances. (Lucky?) One simply (!!!) had to switch off completely from one's previous life and focus one's entire thinking and aspirations only and completely towards one's own survival.

In Yiddish, we say, *"Men darf hobn a bisale mazel."* This means "One needs to have a little bit of luck." Yes, one certainly does.

Despite all of the isolation, some information about the war situation reached the concentration camps from outside. Although there was only this little information, it was enough to convince him that his enslavement was only a matter of time, and of his ability to survive. But in spite of having the same information, only a small percentage of the other Jews understood that. One simply could not look back but only think forward. Most of the Jews were thinking backwards, not forward. Thinking about the past, and the sorrow for those who had been lost, especially for his relatives, came only after the liberation, and then, very intensively.

A SHORT POETIC RESPITE

I am reminded of two poems we learned in junior high school:

"Man Was Made To Mourn: A Dirge"
by Robert Burns (1784)

Many and sharp the num'rous ills
Inwoven with our frame!
More pointed still we make ourselves,
Regret, remorse, and shame!
And Man, whose heav'n-erected face
The smiles of love adorn,
Man's inhumanity to man
Makes countless thousands mourn!

"Devotions Upon Emergent Occasions: Meditation 17"
by John Donne (1624)

No man is an island, entire of itself.
Each is a piece of the continent, a part of the main.
If a clod be washed away by the sea, Europe is the less.
As well as if a promontory were.
As well as if a manor of thine own
Or of thine friend's were.
Each man's death diminishes me,
For I am involved in mankind.
Therefore, send not to know
For whom the bell tolls,
It tolls for thee.

CHAPTER TWENTY-TWO

This section of my father's testimony has no title, but it deserves one.

The Death March

On 16 January 1945, they were not allowed to go into their barracks after work. Instead, they had to line up for departure. Each prisoner received 1 kilogram of bread and a blanket. Then they walked two nights and two days without a real stop until finally, they were crammed into an open (uncovered) coal wagon transport. The train went through Czechoslovakia to Buchenwald, taking four days. It was freezing cold, and there was a great deal of snow. During this transport, 25 percent of all prisoners died. At the beginning, they simply threw the dead out of the wagon to make room for the living. But later, they stacked the dead on top of each other and used their bodies to sit on them.

Despite the bitter cold, he suffered only slight frostbite. Yet, he quickly lost weight during the transport.

My father's testimony is corroborated, and additional details of the march are provided on the Wollheim Memorial site: "The Auschwitz camps and their sub-camps prepared for 'evacuation' on 17 January 1945. The Vistula-Oder Offensive of the Red Army began on 12 January 1945. In the main camp, the senior SS officer, Richard Baer, ordered the SS column leaders to vacate Buna/Monowitz concentration camp and the main camp, Birkenau."

I look up "Richard Baer." There he is on Wikipedia. Does *every* Nazi have a damn Wikipedia page? (They vetted me for months before mine was finally approved.) "Richard Baer was the German commandant of the Auschwitz I concentration camp from May 1944 to February 1945, as well as a couple of other camps. He died in 1963 at the age of fifty-two. He lived under an assumed name to avoid prosecution but was recognized and arrested in 1960 and died in detention before he could stand trial."

Once they got to Buchenwald, they were immediately squeezed into a barrack. The maximum capacity of this barrack was for about three hundred people, but the barrack was filled with at least one thousand people. Most of the prisoners, including himself, had to lie on the bare floor, so close together that they could hardly turn around. On the second day after their arrival, they received a typhoid vaccination, which some tried to avoid. Each vaccination caused a small mark and afterward, one would get a scoop of soup for it.

Until the liberation, he didn't see any more bread. He realized after a few days here that he would perish if he stayed longer in Buchenwald. So he volunteered for the entrenchment and emplacement construction forces to Schönebeck at the Elbe River. The food they received was half of a scoop of cold soup once a day. After about two weeks, they came under Russian artillery fire. They then were gathered together and started out as a column of 2000 men and forced to march on foot for several weeks all the way to Oranienburg. (310 kilometers.)

They still weren't given any bread. Apart from the little that they would find in the open fields, they would have to share one turnip with five men a day and from time to time, a couple of potatoes.

During the day, they were forced to march constantly. At night, they would sleep out in the open on the fields. More and more inmates died of weakness every day. Any inmate who couldn't drag himself along anymore was shot or beaten to death by the guards.

During the nighttime camping in the open air, he dreamed of his mother in a kind of half sleep.

Stop.
My father dreams.

Oh my God, yes. Of course, he dreams, Eleanor.

Have I ever wondered if my father dreamed? Ever? I feel sickened and ashamed that the thought had never even occurred to me.

My. Father. Dreams.

And of course, he dreams of his mother.

In inescapable Hell, who wouldn't dream of their mother? *"Mother, Mother! Help me! Save me! Please dear Mother, I am your child, your son! Protect me! Save me, Mother!"* Yes, that is what I imagine.

I am named after my father's mother, Alte Rishe. In Yiddish, *"alte"* means "old." In those days, Jewish people often added the word "old" to their children's names, especially if they had been ill, in order to outsmart that bastard, the Angel of Death—who, of course, was never outsmarted and was always the winner in the end.

In *The Man Who Never Stopped Sleeping*, Aharon Appelfeld recounts his own Holocaust horror. He too dreams of his mother. Often. That is why the title character sleeps so much—so that he can be with his mother again and always. Who in the world would ever want to wake up in Hell when you could linger in the soft, strong arms of your beloved mother, even if only in your dreams?

In this dream, his mother told him that he could save himself only if he hid. The next day, he remembered this dream. His mother told him that if he was brave, he could save himself. So, that day he saw a short break in a canal. At the sight of it, he immediately thought of his dream and so he acted. But when he had slipped himself into the canal, it was already full of other Jews. Because of that, a part of his leg was sticking out and visible. As a result, he was discovered by an SS man and pulled out and then hit with the rifle butt against the right side of his head. That caused a laceration in the area of the right cortex area and bled immediately. No actual unconsciousness, only a strong short-term rumbling in the head and then some time of light dizziness. No vomiting and no nausea. No bleeding from the nose and ears, but bleeding from the mouth. The force of the rifle butt caused six or seven teeth to loosen and the lower and upper gums to bleed on the right side. No impairment in sight, smell, speech, and hearing. No paralysis. The other Jews received pistol beatings as well.

Okay. Imagine you get emailed a bunch of pages. You don't know what's in them. You start reading, not knowing what's in store for you. And then you read the words, your father's words; words attached to other words attached to sentences attached to paragraphs. It's a history book—the history of my father—and of the Jewish people. But it reads like a horror novel. The leading character is someone you know and love. Each sentence walks across the page/screen. One nightmare sentence after another. You don't see it coming. You don't know what the next sadistic act of inhuman brutality will befall our beloved leading man. Your father. My father. In fiction, events are only as possible as the author's imagination. Here, in these nonfiction pages, reality transcends the lowest depths of human imagination.

I reread the paragraph. "Six or seven teeth." That's one-fifth of his mouth. I note, *"laceration in the right cortex area."* My father would never have used such words, even in German. That's the clinical phrase attributed to whatever human condition my father described to the German psychiatrist. A more human description for "laceration" might be: *"cutting open, cleaving, gashing, slashing, tearing, ripping, mangling, maiming, mauling, stabbing, splitting, hacking, butchery."* My father must have used one of those words.

This whole paragraph—his entire testimony—is reported so clinically. But these events happened to an actual person—to my father, Number 105151.

And so, now I understand something else: When your name and identity are taken away, when you are forced to become *a thing*—a number—you will always, from the moment that you are free, sign your full damned name to everything, to everyone. "Your father, Chaskel Schlüsselberg." *Yes, that is my name. I am a man. I am not a number.* It's like speaking about the murder of the six million as though they were a generic numeral figure. No. They were humans. It was not the murder of a number. They were not six million, they were one; each one, an individual; a One; a one and only. A singular life. A you. A me. A him.

I look up "right cortex." The right cortex of the brain coordinates the left side of the body. When my father had his many strokes in the 1970s, the damage occurred in that very same right cortex, which resulted in the left side of his body being paralyzed. Hmm, coincidence?

One last thought about this section: When I was eight or nine years old, after the divorce, I went on a little weekend vacation with my father. We went to this hotel in the Catskill Mountains, a place called Avon Lodge—more exotic-sounding than it was. It was the first time I'd been alone with my father on any sort of overnight since we'd left him. He and I shared a room with two single beds and a nightstand in between. On that trip, I learned that my father had false teeth, full dentures. He put them in a glass of water on the nightstand that separated us. It was, of course, very creepy to me. Until today, I had believed that he had dentures because he hadn't taken good care of his teeth. What shall I say about that now? That I wish I could see him and hold him and tell him yet again that I am sorry.

Shortly thereafter, it was announced that the Jew from the sewage pipe had to come forward. Because of his heavy bleeding and head injury, there was nothing else left for him to do but comply. An SS man brought him to the commander, who called him "too filthy of a Jew to be touched." He was excluded for three days from meals and was chased away. Following those three days, he still wasn't allowed to get anything to eat. While trying to pick up something edible on the ground, he got hit on his hands by the guards. Nevertheless he was able to pick up dirty beet skins from the other inmates.

After this incident, they marched eight to fourteen more days, until they reached the empty concentration camp, Oranienburg. There they got again some watery soup and one pound of bread for the rest of the march. He thought that for sure he wouldn't survive the marching because of his exhaustion, and believing that the Russians were close by, he hid under hay bales nearby. When he didn't hear any noise after a couple of hours, he left and ran into some other inmates. Then he didn't have anything to eat for three more days until the Russian cavalry arrived on 23 April 1945. During that time, during those days, while they waited for the Russians, he ate young pine cones which were bitter as bile. Finally, the Russians arrived. From the Russians—who didn't have much themselves—he got some bread and a cigar. While smoking the cigar he felt sick and nauseous after only a few puffs.

On the day of the liberation on 23 April 1945, he was lice-infested, anemic, exhausted, and almost reduced to a skeleton in a way that all his ribs were visible.

Germany would unconditionally surrender on 8 May 1945.

And that is how my father, Chaskel Schlüsselberg, survived the death march from Auschwitz in 1945.

CHAPTER TWENTY-THREE

The Beginning of the Aftermath

I have a few more days left in Acre. Being here has been a remarkable gift, calming and restorative, although my heart is raw.

The translated emails keep on coming.

> *After two days, he left the barracks. Looking around in the area, he found an empty settlement with plenty of supplies. He was still so depressed and apathetic that he returned to the camp. But because of the comparably scarce supplies there, he quickly returned to the aforementioned settlement, where he stayed for about four weeks.*
>
> *During this time, he finally had enough to eat, as the Russians would bring him food supplies time and again. Every second day, he would have to report to a Russian doctor who treated him very well but didn't allow him to return to Stuttgart until he was healthier. It was only a short time after the liberation, and his entire body was still so swollen that he almost looked like he was inflated like a balloon.*

This bloating is also called refeeding syndrome. Sam Norich had told me about it before I left on my journey. It occurs when food is suddenly reintroduced to people who have been starved; their dehydrated withered cells lack necessary electrolytes, such as potassium and magnesium, which absorb nutrients into their system, causing bloating, stress, organ failure. Unless treated properly, it can be fatal. If years of starvation didn't kill you, days of over-eating would. Yet another cruel joke.

He still he had a bit of water in his feet and in the lower part of his ankle, meaning that he had pain and pressure when he walked. After approximately six weeks, he felt strong enough to make his way towards Stuttgart with a bicycle that he found in the settlement.

This testimony was given ten years after the war ended. Is my father's recounting of time accurate? Was it four weeks? Six weeks? Does it matter? The Nazis stole Time itself. All we can be sure of is that this took place after liberation—which was when? The world seems to celebrate—or better, commemorate—International Holocaust Remembrance Day on January 27th, which some also call Auschwitz Liberation Day, although my father and the others were still marching long after that date. I guess it's good that there is a day of obligated remembrance. I might suggest that Remembrance Day be every day.

The dictionary defines liberation as "the act of setting someone free, from imprisonment, slavery or oppression; release." My father began the death march in January 1945 and was "liberated" in April of 1945. But was he ever set free from Holocaust? No. Not until December 1976, when his body and soul finally experienced the ultimate liberation. It is for my father's sake that I hope there is a God.

Then, *after* imprisonment in Auschwitz, *after* surviving the death march, *after* liberation, he "found" a bicycle and was ready to ride it from Oranienburg to Stuttgart, a mere 411 miles! Like a sick, starving, beaten yet loyal dog who will do anything to go home.

But shortly after that, just outside of Berlin, Russian soldiers confiscated the bicycle.

Yes, of course, they did.

He then managed to get down to Stuttgart in a few days with the help of Russian and American military vehicles. He arrived in Stuttgart sick and exhausted, to such a degree that he could barely stand on his feet. In Stuttgart, he was taken in immediately by acquaintances who took care of him for weeks.

In the letters, there are many references to friends, including Josef Warscher and others, with whom he spent time and who were terribly sad to see him leave Germany in 1950. I wonder if they were the people who "took care of him." Let's add this to the list of the thousands of things that never occurred to me about my father—about the life he gave up in Germany in order to be with my mother. He had an Actual Life in Germany, not a mere survival life—which is how I would describe his time in America. There, he had friends who knew him, cared for him and about him, whose language he could speak and read and write, where he knew the territory, the ins and outs, how to get around, and was respected even. In Stuttgart, he was "a something." In America, he was a nothing. (What did that make me?) In all the time I knew him, he *never* had any friends. Not any. Except for me, he was alone.

He goes on to say that he was given an apartment by the Jewish community. I learned from Eve Warscher that her father, Josef, had been the president of the Jewish community organization at that time. Well, there was a bit of luck. Finally.

Gradually, the swelling receded. He received medication from Doctor Mantel from Reinsburgstraße, now deceased, to get rid of the excessive water in his body. At that time, he still suffered from powerful headaches since the beginning of 1945, when he had been hit with the rifle butt in the head. It was so painful that he could hardly turn his head.

Soon after his arrival in Stuttgart, he found work with the Jewish religious community as a helper in the synagogue. The UNRA (United Nations Relief and Rehabilitation Administration) *supported him financially. After receiving a trade license as a traveling salesmen in the first months of 1946, he could sell textiles and eggs, which secured him a decent income. In 1947, he tried to get a trade license for local and tropical fruits from the Ministry of Agriculture, but his request was turned down. This was his final reason to immigrate to the United States."*

His final reason to immigrate to the United States? Really? No mention of my mother or their relationship as his reason to immigrate?

My family's recurring trait in black-and-white—lying by omission. Something that I still do, although I try not to. Nature or nurture?

> *He felt totally numb for quite a while after the liberation. Schlüsselberg said he simply couldn't comprehend that he was suddenly a free person again who was allowed to move around and behave as one.*
>
> *Shortly after that, he experienced anxiety attacks, especially during the night. He didn't dare to go out at night alone in Stuttgart, as he felt far too unsafe for that. He suffered from nightmares that were linked to his persecution.*

The "persecution?" This psychiatrist uses that word again and again. I don't know why "holocaust" is not used. "Holocaust" means destruction or slaughter on a mass scale. That sounds about right, so why "persecution?" I go back to the original German testimony and find their word, *verfolgung.* "*Verfolgung:* persecution—hostility and ill-treatment, especially because of race or political or religious beliefs." Yeah, okay, I guess you could call the Holocaust "hostility and ill-treatment because of race."

Steve Friess, in an article in *The New Republic*, discusses when the word "holocaust" came into fashion, as well as whether it should be capitalized or not. (Yes, everything you always wanted to know about holocaust grammar.) According to Friess, "The lowercased 'holocaust' generically defined as a large-scale calamity usually involving fire, became the proper noun used specifically to name the period of Nazi genocide against European Jews only after the war's end…Yet for decades after the war, that specific genocide lacked any formal title in English except, 'The Final Solution,' the term the Nazis used. In Hebrew, the calamity quickly became known as the *Shoah*, which means 'The Catastrophe.' But it wasn't until the 1960s that scholars and writers began using the term 'Holocaust,' and it took the 1978 TV film *Holocaust*, starring Meryl Streep, to push it into widespread use."

Television put the capital "H" in Holocaust. Go know.

Even though his condition slowly improved, the nightmares never vanished entirely, and he wasn't able to laugh since the persecution and was carrying a certain sadness with him.

Yes, I knew that always. Intuitively. From my lunchtime visits on Sundays as a child, to my daily visits to the nursing home a decade later, his *"certain sadness"* was palpable. I would tell him a story or a joke to try to distract him or make him laugh. Sometimes I succeeded.

My father goes on to say that he went to Bremerhaven in late '49, where he had to stay for some weeks in lousy camp-like accommodations until his departure by ship to the United States. In this testimony, he completely omits the parts that he described in the letters: the frustrating red tape as well as his life in general from those years. There is no mention of going to England to fetch his son or his love affair with my mother. There is no mention of my mother, period, until he marries her in America.

In my father's very last letter to my mother from Bremerhaven, dated 12 January 1950, he writes:

"My beloved Rukhchu* and Shamale! (*"Rukhchu" is an endearing nickname.)

Today's letter, I assume, will turn out better for you than all the other letters from Bremen. Now the transport is confirmed, and today I have shipped my luggage, so we can assume that my departure can only be a matter of days.

Then yesterday there was a block lockdown. One couldn't leave the block all day, because in one block, luggage had been stolen. At 2 p.m., a division went around and searched. They arrived in my room at 4 p.m. They made random searches of everyone. When you are in the camp, you have to be ready for anything. But that too passed.

I hope that you, my Rukhchu, are doing well. What more I can report about myself? I am so happy that my long wished for dream will become reality. I conclude that you don't have much time, my Rukhchu, because of your sparse letter correspondence. I never got your last letter to Stuttgart, because I didn't give anybody there my address in Bremen. I didn't want to tell anyone how I was doing here, and also I didn't want to receive mail from anybody but you, my Rukhchu, which was very hard for me. I made my peace with that. A hungry man does not believe an overfed man, an old saying that proves to be true. I am demanding the inhuman from you, my Rukhchu, you have to work all day long—which, by the way, I envy you for, because the hardest work is to do nothing. My days are twice as long and the nights also. I hope to fill the days to come differently than here, this boring life, where one has no tasks. Altogether I had work here twice, four hours each time. The work is very primitive, basically one just has to show up. I imagine that you envy me because I don't do anything here and you, my Rukhchu, have to work so hard there. My conclusion is that not working is the hardest thing, and with this occupation of not working, I have been occupied for several months already, which has been very difficult for me.

The weather here is also different each day. One day you need the summer coat, the next day the winter coat.

Learning English is not easy for me, because I have to stay in the block the whole time. The people here are very malevolent, and one has to watch over one's possessions. I hate to be afraid to come home and find things missing. So far, bless God's name, I have been lucky.

Today, a big transport is leaving for the south with approximately 1200 people. With my transport, 1,280 people will be leaving. The ship is called the S.S.M. CHO, and that is my transport.

People say that when one arrives in America, they would have been better off to have stayed here. You, my Rukhchu, know best about that, and I trust you completely. I am the green one anyway. But one doesn't stay a green one forever. You, my Rukhchu, I'm sure, are already like an American citizen.

Now let's put an end to the old stories and hope for the best in the future. My Rukhchu, until a speedy reunion in a few days, I kiss and hug you over and over.

Your loving Chaskel Schlüsselberg."

Perhaps, as they say in Yiddish, I am mixing kasha with borscht by including his letter from 1949 here, mixing it with his testimony from 1967, but those were his own words before he knew what would befall him in these United States.

The transcript of his testimony has, till now, taken us up to mid-January of 1950, when Chaskel Schlüsselberg discovers America.

CHAPTER TWENTY-FOUR

America—Or At Least, Brooklyn

He arrived in New York in mid-January 1950 where he has stayed since that time. He received financial aid for about 4 months from the JOINT (Jewish Relief Organization). *It was difficult for him in the beginning since the language was foreign to him. After about four months, he found a job at a brush factory as an unskilled laborer with a weekly pay of thirty dollars. This was below the union wages and too little to pay for all of life's expenses. He had to put in a lot of overtime. And even though he still kept the Sabbath, he often worked up to seventy-two hours a week. With better English skills, he was slowly able to work his way up into the brush industry and was able, after a couple of years, to raise his weekly wage to fifty-eight dollars.*

The brush *industry?* It was a fucking factory.

After eight years, in 1958 or 1959, he left his first job and entered another brush factory where he began with a weekly wage of ninety dollars.

In the spring of 1950, he married an eighteen-years-younger, widowed Jewish woman from Poland, who brought a fourteen-year-old son into the marriage.

He doesn't mention that he knew her—and wooed her mightily—in Stuttgart, before he came to the U.S., that she was actually twenty years younger—earlier in this document, he said she was ten years younger—and that her son was actually nine when they married in 1950. And didn't it say earlier in this very document that they married in 1951? Which is it? My mother, when I was a young girl, used to warn me: "Never contradict me in public." To them, truth was fluid.

The next pages of this testimony are about my parents' marriage. It is filled with my father's complaints and accusations against my mother—things I have never heard before. The words of love in his letters from 1949 have crumbled like the paper they were written on.

His second wife had an apartment and worked as a seamstress in a clothing factory. They had a good relationship in the beginning. As he had to work a lot from early mornings to late at night, she took a good friend as her boyfriend, which he found out about only years later when he became sick.

My mother had a boyfriend? Then? So soon after they were married? Did I know that? No. Not then, anyway. Later. Much later.

He was a cousin, Leo (Leibish)—related to both my father *and* my mother—who were themselves second cousins. (Which may explain all you need to know about me.) Leibish was also a concentration camp survivor—the only member of his large immediate family not killed, except for an older half-brother, Felix, an elegant, pinky-ringed, bespectacled gentleman. Leibish was a short, tough, smart, funny, angry soul: daring and bold. He was hungry to live and fearless like a Chihuahua.

His identifying tattoo? He's been dead for more than thirty years yet I remember it: it was just the letters *KL*, closer to his wrist than his forearm. It was from the concentration camp Flossenbürg, where he was imprisoned as a teenage boy. It was a small camp in Germany near the Czech border. Leibish had told me that his job there was to build airplanes—*Messerschmitts*, I remember. I have photos of him just after the war; one at an American Army base wearing fatigues, at the top of a simple pyramid of men, like a proud mascot.

They had given him, that orphan boy, work and food and shared their provisions with him. They rehumanized him. Leibish used to say that he loved the American soldiers more than anything and that he would never forget them for what they did for him. I knew Leibish for most of my life and loved him very much. There's a whole other book that could be written about him: his struggles, bravery, resilience, and his lust for life. He died due to inadequate medical care in a hospital in Brooklyn in 1990. Alone.

It wasn't until the early '80s, when my mother was already ill and I was in my thirties, that I learned—from her—that she and Leibish had been sleeping together for years! All that time, I thought they were just good friends. What a dope. Who ever imagines their mother having sex? I missed it completely.

I am so sorry for them—for my mother and my father and for Leibish. They deserved so much better.

In this next section of the testimony, my father complains about my brother, Seymour:

Schlüsselberg paid for the entire engineering education of his stepson, for which he was repaid with ingratitude. The stepson didn't even invite him to his wedding and won't even look at him nowadays.

It never occurred to me that my father was not at Seymour's wedding. But indeed, he was not. Who knew that he cared? That it hurt him? I was twelve years old. I don't remember noticing.

And then my father says:

In 1953, his daughter was born, who he is close to up until today and who is his everything.

Imagine I'm reading things about my mother and my brother, and then, out of the blue, my father points to me. And I'm his *"everything,"* no less? Me? Who wants to be *anyone's* everything?

In truth, I always did feel like his *everything,* consciously and not—as in, his only person. His only joy, caretaker. His only love. His only reason for living. I felt it, but I couldn't name it or understand it. I was "it," as in "tag, you're it." The pressure, demand, and responsibility of being someone's *everything*? Right from my very beginning? Yes, I'd call that a heavy load. It always was…and still is.

He goes on to speak about "his son from his first marriage," and briefly about what he knew about him and what had happened to him in England:

At the age of seven, he was taken in by an English family who raised him together with their own children. From 1939 until sometime after the war, [Schlüsselberg] *didn't receive any messages from his son. He only knew that he attended different schools and finished his education as an agricultural administrator or inspector. In 1949, after receiving the compensation money on behalf of his "Freiheitsschaden"* (money for deprivation of freedom), *he immediately used part of it to visit his son in England.*

So that's where some of my father's early money came from. I had no idea. In the letters to my mother, he recounts how long he waited for the visa to England and how he was stymied by all the red tape. His trip was repeatedly delayed, and he was terribly disheartened by it all. Eventually, in 1949, he was able to get to England.

Because the son spoke almost exclusively English, communication with him was very difficult, and he needed an interpreter for their meeting. Probably due to this reason, he never could really connect with his son. Despite his repeated pleading, his son refused to go back to Germany with him.

Some people are able to connect even though they don't speak the same language. That was not the case with Harry and our father. Harry had been with this non-Jewish English family from the time he was seven, for nearly ten years—much longer than he had spent with his birth parents. No, Harry would not leave them, the Wrightsons; he would not return to the painful world that he originally came from. Who could blame him?

After this visit, they exchanged letters from time to time over a period of six or seven years. He always wrote more often than his son, and his son answered less and less frequently until the letters stopped coming entirely.

He found out about his own son's wedding only by chance. He could forgive the fact that his son didn't ask for his permission to marry, but that he didn't invite him to the wedding still hurts him today. And then, his son took a different, English-sounding name. The English family, who raised him, was now reimbursed for it as good as possible.

How many blows can a human being bear? Clearly, a great many more than we might imagine.

What was the greatest hurt? That Harry wouldn't go with him when he came to get him? That he married a non-Jewish woman? That he did not invite his father to his wedding? That Harry rejected his own father's surname?

My father's sarcastic dig surprises me. "*The English family, who raised him, was reimbursed for it as good as possible.*" Yes indeed, they *were* "reimbursed for it." They got themselves a son, albeit someone else's, to carry on *their* surname since they'd only had daughters. Who would carry on *my* father's name?

Harry's life was saved because he was put on that train to England by his birth parents. But, it was also saved by the family who cared for him during wartime. He is "very sorry for Charlie," Harry says often—and means it. And in the same breath, says that he has "no regrets" about his decision to remain in England. The Wrightsons gave him a life he wouldn't trade for anything. Yes, I understand that. I swear I do.

I used to believe that people who suffered through war could not be blamed for what they did—that war itself was to blame, and we all just do the best we can when conditions are cruel in order to survive in the moment, which will hopefully lead to another moment and then to another after that. Yet there are some people who act in extraordinarily selfless and brave ways when daring challenges knock on their door. Others act more in their own interests. Sometimes, it's hard to tell the difference. Nothing is simple and no good deed....

> *Schlüsselberg was asked about why he didn't mention his son in the "Wiedergutmachungs Angelegenheit"* [concerning the reparations claims he made] *by Dr. Sachs from the federal state office for "Wiedergutmachung"* [reparation payments]. *Schlüsselberg is fairly uncomfortable with this question and explains that this didn't happen in any fraudulent way. He had his reasons that become obvious looking at his previous statements.*

Yes, well, speaking of behaving in one's own interest.... Yeva and I had also wondered why we found no mention of Harry in any of my father's documents when we were at the archive in Ludwigsburg. Whatever this psychiatrist may think, I think that my father did not mention his son due to a kind of greed and resentment; the saving of his own skin, getting more for himself and his own empty life. "The hell with my son," he might have thought on some level, after this boy, whose life he saved, paid him back with abandonment and rejection. (Or perhaps I'm projecting. It's certainly possible and probably even likely.)

Despite all his disappointments with his son, he is planning to make a stop in England to visit him on the way home to the U.S. [from Germany where he is giving this sworn testimony]. *Although he can now communicate in English without any problems, he doesn't expect much from this visit. He still wants to try everything he can to have a connection with his son because of his responsibility towards his first wife who died because of the persecution, at least to re-establish some kind of contact with him.*

I have lived for sixty-four years never knowing anything about my father's feelings toward his first wife or his first daughter; that some of his actions—who knows how many—were driven by consideration of them and love for them.

That's a lot not to know.

Schlüsselberg repeats again and again, that not mentioning his son in his "Wiedergutmachungs Angelegenheit" [application for reparations] *did not have a fraudulent side to it."*

Methinks the gentleman doth protest too much.

CHAPTER TWENTY-FIVE

My Father's American History

He bought a house big enough for three families in Brooklyn in 1953 [the year I was born], *for which he had to take out a big loan. It is custom in the USA that the owner had to provide janitorial services and clean the facilities.* (Really? Who told him that?) *His wife didn't support him in this at all. In 1958 or 1959, he was able to buy another house across the street in Brooklyn, fit for six families. With this second purchase, he didn't have to take out such a big loan as with the first one.*

I guess he wasn't doing that badly as an unskilled factory worker. Although I wonder if he had been getting reparations from Germany by then. And, he did work his ass off.

This modest wealth must have gone to his wife's head. He was working so hard and instead of supporting him, she played the Grande Dame and didn't economize well with the money.

"Grande Dame?" If you knew my mother, that would make you laugh. She was a sweatshop-worker for all of her days in America— and she worked her ass off, too.

Then he became sick in 1960. In the morning after getting up, he suddenly didn't feel good and had trouble breathing and felt a pain around the heart area. The doctors who were being consulted, Dr. Ernstoff and the cardiologist Dr. Elster, in Brooklyn, hospitalized him to the Mount Sinai Hospital in New York, where he stayed for six weeks in stationary care.

I do have some memory of this time, but the six-week hospitalization is a surprise to me. Dr. Ernstoff was the doctor who delivered me, and who features prominently in the mythology of my birth, when my parents wanted to name me "Old Rishe" after my father's mother. Ernstoff, who would remain my father's doctor and ally all his life, suggested "Eleanor." The way I tell it, Dr. Ernstoff said I would have enough to overcome in this world without carrying the name "Old Rishe" around my neck. Eleanor is not a name that my parents would have come up with on their own, except perhaps as an homage to Eleanor Roosevelt. But their generation of Jewish people were not particularly big on homages, except to dead relatives, of which we had plenty to choose from.

There he was diagnosed with exhaustion and a dysfunction of cardiac blood flow. Whether or not he suffered a stroke, he doesn't know. His blood pressure was approximately 170 or 175. During his hospital stay, his wife wouldn't leave him alone until he signed the six-family house over to her. After signing the papers, she practically stopped taking care of him. Around that time, he found out about her boyfriend. Since that time, he doesn't care much about her, and they live separately.

My mother wouldn't leave him alone until he signed the house over to her? Can you imagine reading that about your mother?

Up until now, he didn't want to get a divorce, because he has been afraid to lose his daughter from this marriage, who is very attached to him and he to her. Earlier, it must have been more of an obligation for her, but now she likes to come every Sunday to stay with him. The attitude of this child towards him makes him very happy, and that's why he does everything he can for her.

He was right; it was an obligation to me. How did he know? I'm not sure when that changed, but it did at some point. I always felt bad for him. As well as responsible. For as far back as I have memory.

He wasn't able to keep the three-family house because more and more Negroes moved into the neighborhood, and the property lost more and more of its value. That's why he sold it in 1961 for a small profit. Since then, he has a small two-room apartment with a kitchen. He interacts very little with other people except for on Saturdays at the synagogue. He's a religious Jew and keeps the Sabbath strictly.

This is all true. He had little to do with anyone else. There was only work, synagogue, and me.

He goes on to say that he had been having heart troubles beginning in 1960, which I knew nothing about, which cost him work and wages. Then he had heart trouble again in 1964, during his night shift. I didn't even know that my father worked a night shift.

He suddenly didn't feel good around three o'clock in the morning. Afterward, he had a strong headache and pain in the left arm, so much, that he left early from work. Going home with public transport was very difficult for him.

"Public transport" meant the subway from downtown Brooklyn to East New York. At 3 a.m. Not a short trip.

When he went up the stairs in his house, his legs suddenly became weak, so that he had to sit down. Simultaneously, he couldn't talk properly anymore, only mumble. His left arm and left leg became paralyzed, and the left corner of his mouth dropped. He was rushed immediately to the Associated Hospital in Brooklyn, where he stayed for ten days. During this time, he says an EEG and repeated ECGs, as well as a pneumonocentesis, were done. He received massages and different injections of unknown natures to him. After a couple of days, the paralysis of his left side and his speech improved. This improvement went on for about eight weeks, and since then, his condition stayed unchanged. Until today, his speech is a little unclear, and his left foot remains a little weak, as well as a certain clumsiness of his left hand.

By 1964, we had already moved out of his house and into that six-family house that he had, unbeknownst to me, signed over to my mother. I always thought that his first strokes were in the 1970s when I took care of him.

After about three months, he returned to work at the brush factory, where he works up until today.

"Today" being 1967…

He stayed in the continuous care of Dr. Ernstoff, who sends him for ECGs every six weeks to the cardiologist, Dr. Elster. He can't remember any other serious illnesses or any other accidents. He didn't have any operations. No venereal diseases.

Well, how do you like that? My father had no venereal diseases. Good to know.

CHAPTER TWENTY-SIX

The Results of the Psychological Examination

The report concludes with details of his current medical condition, which includes painful recurring headaches, neck stiffness, and other medical tidbits. It culminates with the doctor's psychiatric report:

Schlüsselberg is a sixty-five-year-old simple, neatly dressed man who is open and willing to give information. One can connect with him quickly and well. He is polite and friendly and behaves appropriately and correctly within the given situations. (Oh brother.)

Schlüsselberg speaks perfect German, although with a strong American accent. He suffers from a slight motor residual aphasia, which causes him to stumble from time to time at the beginning of a word. At these occasions he likes to fall back on the English equivalent. He seems to speak English perfectly as well. (Perfect English? Obviously, this guy had no idea what perfect English sounded like. My father spoke English like a refugee, barely intelligible, always.)

One learns from him that he is an observant Jew, who strictly keeps the Sabbath.

He prefers to recall the time before the spring of 1933 and talks about it enthusiastically. (Really? You mean he prefers to remember his life before the persecution?)

In contrast with that, Schlüsselberg reluctantly recalls the time of the persecution. He would prefer not to talk about it at all as it upsets him very much and stays with him for days. That is the reason why he has avoided speaking about the persecution for quite a while already.

Schlüsselberg talks about everything that happened to him and his family just after 1933 in a fairly straightforward manner. He tells of his transport to Auschwitz, and not in relation to himself, but in relation to the infants in the wagon which torments him still. In this way, he tells how he had experienced the arrival of a transport with war victims and toddlers in Auschwitz and how exactly they had been dealt with. When he is asked the question of what happened in this regard to his wife and the daughter born in 1936, he suddenly starts to cry and sob loudly, and he is not able to calm down for a long time. His deep emotional outburst is devoid of any theatricality and in every way real. After he has calmed down again, he apologizes and hopes that you will excuse his lack of control. When he thinks about the persecution, but especially about the fate of his wife and daughter, something like that happens to him again and again. The pain of the loss of these two relatives is still deep inside him, which sometimes makes him unable to control himself. He surrounds the deceased wife and daughter with a halo, and he still mourns them to the very bottom of his heart. About his second wife, he barely cares. With much love, however, he speaks of the second marriage which gave birth, in 1953, to his daughter who, unconsciously for him, was a kind of reincarnation of his perished daughter.

Stop.

"A kind of reincarnation of his perished daughter." What shall I do with that? Is it a surprise? Am I shocked? Yes, but only because it is in print for all to see. Secretly, I have thought this for decades, ever since I found out about Frida. Sometimes I felt like I *was* her; the replacement, and, yes, the reincarnation; the regrouping, reorganizing, and repurposing of her cells into what has become "me." And here, in 1967, this doctor says so too.

Looking at this, one can extract that Schlüsselberg has very much tried to overcome and block out the experiences of the persecution, which obviously worked out for him but only in a very limited way. Schlüsselberg is bitter about his fate as a Jew during the years 1933–1945. He says that he simply cannot overcome what was done to him because he was a Jew. Because of this persecution, he lost his best years as a man and simply couldn't continue with his previous life after the liberation. During the difficult years of the persecutions, something simply broke inside of him and didn't allow him to find his way back into his old entrepreneurial spirit and former vitality.

My poor broken father.

Then the psychiatrist goes into some clinical details and comes up with his diagnosis:

Schlüsselberg clearly must have been a very vital man which is apparent from his background but now is less so and in a more bleak way. His mood is mostly gloomy, with a hint of sub-depression.

A *hint* of "sub-depression"?!

Reading these words, this entire damned testimony, devastates me, although I wonder what it actually means to be truly devastated. It's not that I can't go on as I sit here in the Acre sunshine. It's not that I can't eat or sleep (even though I do take meds to sleep because indeed, I cannot sleep). Devastation, the dictionary says, causes severe and overwhelming shock or grief. Oh, okay, then yes, I am devastated.

What am I supposed to do with this information? I always thought I wanted to know who my father really was, how he felt, what he did before the war, what happened to him in Auschwitz, and his life afterward.

Great. So now I know.

And now you know too.

CHAPTER TWENTY-SEVEN

The End?

While in Acre, in that second week, my longtime beloved friend from Jerusalem, tour guide and know-it-all (in the best sense) Ron Perry, came to visit me. Sitting with him for lunch, at a popular restaurant, he listened to my story of John's exit with needed sympathy; his kind eyes and heart providing a comforting shoulder for me. But as a history maven, that Ron, he really wanted to hear about my father's letters and learn what was in those remaining untranslated German documents. He understood that I was overwhelmed and he wanted to help me.

He knew of a nearby kibbutz that housed German students. He contacted them on my behalf, and within two days, a young man and young woman were sitting with me in the great hall of Arabesque. With me and my computer sandwiched between them, these two young people and I looked at documents from my grandfather's file—my mother's father, Isak Hoff—who spent the war years in Uzbekistan. They too had applied for reparations, which is why Germany had files on them, but they were never approved. Their suffering was either deemed not horrific enough on the scale of tragic inhumanity, or they missed the deadline, which was always changing, or a paper was returned for a missing signature, or someone forgot to dot the "i" or cross the "t." For these and other ridiculous reasons, their request for reparations was denied. But their testimonies in these documents revealed painful details about their time in Tashkent—another part of my family's past (from 1941–1945) that I knew nothing about. My grandfather testified in heartbreaking detail of the death of his son, Moishale, my mother's youngest brother, who I now learn had died from typhus. My grandfather wrote of having to dig the grave himself to bury his son. He wrote also of their starvation; the cold, the beatings, wounds, and enslavement.

The young people translate thoughtfully, and I sit like a robot and type. For hours. Is there no end to these German documents?

Enough! This is enough. More than enough. Stop now, Eleanor. It's time to go home.

And indeed, it is time. My two weeks in Acre are done.

My time there was as rejuvenating as any place could be, and for that (among other things, including his unconditional friendship), I will always be indebted to Evan Fallenberg. But the profound pain of my family's trials and tribulations leave me inconsolable. Adding insult to injury was the loss of John and the manner and timing of his rejection.

I return home, broken. I am my father's daughter.

When I left New York, three weeks ago, I had a batch of unintelligible letters and an imagined family history that had sustained me for the last sixty years. I also had a boyfriend, lover, and best friend. When I return from this trip, I have a suitcase filled with new family pain; no longer impressionistic and no longer avoidable. And like my parents, I am alone and abandoned. Someone reading the vast email correspondence with John over the years would have seen the writing on the wall, just as I saw it on the wall of my father's letters to my mother. We were a bad idea and not meant to be. He just knew it before I did.

John and I meet at my apartment a few days after I return to New York. Mostly, he speaks and I listen. He weeps with remorse for hurting me—but not for leaving me. He loved me but was not "in love with me," he says. In our early days, he once told me that when he was done with a relationship, when it was finished, he was able to put the woman in the back of his mind and close that door. When he told me that, I suspected—knew—that one day, I would be that woman behind the closed door.

I am uneasy speaking of him here, in this hallowed space that belongs to my family's sufferings. His absence is flea-sized compared to the enormity of the blows inflicted during in my journey. And yet he was a part of it, and the loss of him in my life felt like an amputated limb. Hard to stop scratching.

But people can get used to anything.

CHAPTER TWENTY-EIGHT

The Letters After All

Ah, yes, the letters. What about those fifty-six letters?

They turn out to be the MacGuffin, a term popularized by Alfred Hitchcock; a common device in film, especially in thrillers. It's the excuse to tell the tale, Hitchcock said, but is not the tale itself.

The letters were my treasure map, my "X marks the spot." They gave me direction, unlocked the door, and led me into the room. I never would have opened the door without them. But what I found in the room was definitely not what I had been looking for.

During much of this time, I lost interest in the letters. They didn't grab me. I didn't understand their content. They contained so many gaps, so much minutiae: details about money or purchases or people, places that I didn't know or care about. Also, the letters were only one-sided. They weren't a dialogue but rather a monologue. Who could know what was in my mother's letters that led to my father's responses? Some letters did not make narrative sense to me and did not seem meaningful or compelling. They were not the romantic novellas that I and everyone else had hoped for.

But now, at the end of my journey, I realize that there was a much deeper truth about those letters: Their content and mere existence were too painful for me. My father's actual words—written in his own hand, from his empty room, with his fountain pen, at his lonely table, day after day after day, to my mother, thousands of miles and lifetimes away, during such a horribly brutal solitary time—were just too much.

I had believed that I was immune, that I had seen and heard it all; my irreverence and my jokes were proof that this Holocaust stuff had no effect on me anymore. Been there, done that.

I was wrong. It was more than even I could bear, and as a result, I found myself unintentionally and unconsciously avoiding them. Auschwitz was one thing, terrible and crushing; but all of this additional heartache—my father's intimate, insecure, needy words from his letters *after* that nightmare—was icing on the tragedy cake that I just could not swallow. My father's doubts and fears about his relationship with my mother were not imagined. They were real and well-founded. His instincts, those invisible signals and signs that saved his life during the war, were correct. That marriage lasted only a few years. After all of that effort to connect and be together and find solace and love even, the whole stinking business lasts for a fucking minute, just long enough to make a baby. A paltry life out of chicken bones.

It was not until I completed a few early drafts of this book that I was finally able to absorb the depth of my father's letters and the subtext of his words. I decided to retranslate some of the letters, those with blurry narratives. That helped a lot. Those letters became clearer, their narratives easier to follow. Everything that happened to me in Germany—the documents, the people, the places—now provided a context and filled in so many of the blanks.

There were some letters that were still mysterious, facts and details I will never know or understand. One, in particular, described some kind of slander, some kind of hurtful information that a friend or relative of my father's had told my mother. In that letter of 26 October 1946, he writes about a letter he had received from my mother's mother, my grandmother. He says:

When I came home from Ludwigsburg today, a lovely (not really) letter from your mother awaited me. I was frightened when I read it, and I am starting to get an idea about the nature of my friendships there. I can understand very well how you must have felt. A written explanation and defense is not a good idea because as the proverb says: one who defends himself must be guilty.

It is very hard to understand that you, who have known me for four years but have just met Rose for the first time, believe everything she says and gets angry about it. Can that be right? Why can't you just write to me about it? If there are good things to write about, the bad things shouldn't be left out.

I'm surprised that she didn't tell you that she has a child from me; that would have driven you crazy. I am sorry that my opinion was so wrong, that you two would get along. If you have any questions, I will answer them for you: anything you would like to know. Let me know if there is anything between 1920 to 1946 that you would like to learn about. Everything that happened after that time is well-known to you. This way you will hear about everything from me personally and not ever again from Rose.

If our friendship is dear to you, I ask you to never speak a word to this woman again. If I will get there, with the help of God, I will finally know what to do.

Forgive me for this letter, which probably sounds a bit cold. You don't understand my situation here, all by myself, with no one to care for me after such a blow.

It was intrigue like this, which I had imagined the letters would contain, that would make them interesting, a novel piece of personal history. But instead, it made them agonizing. The letters were the literal manifestation of all of my father's isolation and sorrow. He was so vulnerable. From pre-war to war to post-war, again and again, he was beaten further and further down. And alone. Always alone.

Worst of all is that I know how it ends. I am on the lower part of the river, looking upstream. Reading his letters is like watching a car crash in slow motion. And I can't prevent it. He was right, my father, to be worried and uncertain about his future with my mother. He was right about being a *greene*. He would never, ever be more than a *greene*, an "Other." I wish I could warn him, like in a time-travel movie. "Turn back, Dad!" I would shout. "America will eat you up and spit you out. You will never belong here, Dad! Not ever! Stay in Germany! Or go to Israel! But don't come here."

He would have had a better life in Israel, a land that would welcome him, speak his language, where there would be so many others like him. He could have had a daughter there, in that Jewish land, carved out of fury and in retaliation to National Socialism and anti-Semitism. Maybe a son, too.

But then I wouldn't be here.

CHAPTER TWENTY-NINE

The Takeaway

It's been more than two years since I was in Germany. Before I went there, I knew nothing. Now, I know a little bit more than nothing. But still not everything.

The darkness that has been with me all of my days is clearer now, more defined, based on facts rather than shapeless shadows. The sources of my sorrow are labeled and filed and have a beginning, although not an end. That will die when I die.

There is also a reawakened paranoia. My senses are more alert to nationalism and bigotry. The sound of marching boots and the smoke in the distance make me wonder about packing my bags, and where and when to flee if the bastards get too close again. What means "too close"? I am witnessing history mutate and repeat. So soon?

I did not imagine this new heavy pall. My parents were married for a short time, six years only. I knew my father for twenty-three years, a small part of my life and an even smaller part of his. I spent little time with him: just those Sunday lunches, and then visits to the nursing home, and then that was that. He has been dead for more than forty years, two-thirds of my life. But even without his physical presence, my father and his holocaust are scratched onto my skin. He is my tattoo.

Here are my takeaways:

I am certain, even though I am not a scientist and even though I have done little research—I am consistent in that regard—that my own rage, of which there is plenty, and my existential fear and consciousness of death, and my sarcasm and greed and empathy, all of these things and more, come directly from the womb in which I was born. My genes contain the chromosomes of memory. *Their* memory. My parents' memory. Inherited trauma. My chromosomes remember. The years of starvation, the years of freezing, the years of beatings. The constant flinching waiting for the next blow, preparing for the pain. The trauma of being whipped on the bock. The hiding and the smoking and the clipping of hair and sleeping on the wooden shoes, and the being secretive and being wily and being scared to death and scared of death. My radar is locked onto the stink of anti-Semitism and racism, as well as the cruel arbitrariness of extermination—a simple turn to the right or the left can hasten the end, or can *equal* the end. How can you *ever* be careful enough?

Even as a girl, I sensed death hiding in full view just around the corner. I used to joke that my mother had an expression: "Every silver lining has a cloud." She never really said that, but that was how I felt. You can be happy, but don't be *too* happy—which she did say—because evil and danger are ever-lurking, waiting to pounce as soon as you let down your guard.

When I was young, at the time of the chicken bones, someone gave me a very pretty, girlie phonebook for my birthday, to enter the names and addresses of friends and relatives. On the very first page, I wrote, "When I die, please call everyone in this book." I was eleven.

That my father felt that I was the reincarnation of his first daughter, Frida, saddened and surprised me—and yet I felt that too; that I had been given her life, that all of her bits and pieces had magically, karmically recombined to become me; that the Cosmos would not permit her to die forever because her life was stolen. The crime was corrected.

I am the correction. I am Frida's justice. Frida's Revenge. My life is revenge.

That's one part of this takeaway, the part about me; about how and who I am and why. Is my anger and irreverence a bit more understood now? Forgiven? Gosh, I hope so.

There is something else, though. Something I have been holding inside for these two years, waiting for this moment to say, here and now. I will repeat these words again and again until the very end of my days.

My father and the others, who lived and died during that time, in that place, were not survivors. No. I reject that term. Those people did not survive. Dogs survive. Cows survive. What those people did—all of them—not just the ones in the ghettos or the forests or the basements or the camps—was fight. They were fighters. Whether they lived or were killed, they fought. With every molecule of their breath and brain and brawn. They fought. To live. With all their might and their heart and prayers and selflessness and selfishness and guns and books and pens and bread. They were Holocaust fighters, not survivors. In the cattle cars, up the chimneys, in the attics and tunnels and sewers. They fought for their lives. For our lives. For my life. I am not the child of Holocaust survivors. Fuck that. Fuck that passive, minimizing, head-bowing term. My father never bowed down his head, he said. Well, why should I? Why should we? Words count. I, Eleanor Reissa Schlusselberg, am the daughter of Holocaust fighters, courageous humans who fought the Devil like hell for life to the death.

Can you imagine if the world had called them Holocaust fighters? To have been the daughter of fighters rather than the daughter of survivors? I would have been Supergirl, for goodness sake. Strong and proud rather than an ashamed, hidden light.

In its early days, the State of Israel marginalized Yiddish. In fact, there was a time that it was forbidden. It was considered a joke language, a language of the victim; it reflected a time of weakness, when Jews went like sheep to the slaughter. From today's observatory, that looks like arrogance and gall. Perhaps it was just ignorance. Or blindness. The tenacity and resourcefulness of the Israeli rests squarely on the unacknowledged shoulders of those people who were hunted, starved, burned, shot, gassed. I spent my life as an embarrassed child of an "Other," of a man I perceived as a powerless victim with false teeth and a funny accent, who accidentally had some good, horrible luck and lived. Sheep? No way. Tenacious. Instinctual. Smart. Brave. Greedy to live. That is where I come from, who I come from, who so many Jews come from.

Can this new perspective impact my life so late in the game? The thought of it makes me chuckle as I weep.

What is the daughter of a survivor entitled to? Nothing. Not a thing. Whatever I had was more than I needed and way more than they had. It was all gravy. My life was gravy and that was enough.

But the daughter of a fighter? What is the daughter of a fighter entitled to? Everything! Every damn thing! They fought for a full, rich, worthy life and anything less is to spit in their sweet loving faces. That is my inheritance.

There's a Yiddish expression: "*Az men est khazer, zol es rinen fin mol,*" meaning: "If you're going to eat pork"—which as a Jew, you are not permitted to do—"eat it with gusto and with appetite and let the juice run freely down your chin." They gave me appetite, my family. To live. That is what they birthed, these fighters.

And Frida? My half-sister Frida?

I understand now why Harry still cries for her, eighty years after her murder. I cry for her now too.

Here's what I think about her. She would not go gentle into that good night. And I don't blame her. She has secretly given me the permission to rage against the dying of the light. I got her life. That is what I allow myself to believe.

Does it matter if I am her reincarnation or not? Does it change anything? For me or for Frida? For her, unfortunately not. For me? The jury is still out.

So, we're done.

Here were some letters that my father wrote in 1949, seventy years ago, that my mother kept for twenty years after their divorce, and that I let languish for more than thirty years after my mother's death. Why didn't I have them translated years ago?

I guess because I just couldn't. Until now.

What else?

My parents' lives, did they have meaning? Was their struggle worth it? In 1976, when I phoned Harry to tell him our father had died, he said, meaning no disrespect, "Poor Charlie, he was rather an unlucky chap, wasn't he? If you think about it really, nothing in his life went quite right. Except for you, that is."

I am their fruit. I am the meaning of their lives. I got to live the life *they* deserved to live.

And my life? What about the meaning of my life?

I recently bought a house for myself. Although I am alone, without a partner or lover, I spent my money, some of which is a remnant of the safety-cushion that my ingenious, careful, clever, beautiful, fierce, beloved mother—the sweatshop worker—saved for me. I bought myself something that they never had—a home. A log cabin on a lake. For my parents' daughter, because she is entitled: Entitled to be happy, to have something she dared to dream about, to have something she doesn't need but actually wants. I'd like to think they would have said "Do it." Although, like me, I suspect it would have made them nervous and afraid. Afraid of having too much; afraid of too much joy and happiness which is so impossible to maintain and will only lead to disappointment. Ah, my mother's voice....

Also, recently, I took an actual vacation—not to visit a friend or relative, or a journey attached to work, but a real vacation—a hiking trip to the Dolomites in Italy with my loyal friend, Elizabeth. On the fifth and final day of the trip, the hike was the most difficult, with the furthest distance to cover and the highest altitude to climb. It was a beautiful day, in a beautiful place with warm, blue skies, vistas, and natural magnificence all around me. I don't know what other hikers were thinking that day, but I found myself thinking not of hiking but of marching; of my father and his march out of Auschwitz. Was there anyone else in the Dolomites on that beautiful day in July of 2019 thinking about the death march in frigid, starving February of 1945? If there was, I sure would have liked to meet them. I made a little joke to myself that day: What's the difference between a hike and a march? Snacks.

In my hiking boots and walking sticks, and my backpack filled with bottled water and sweet-and-salty chocolate-covered nuts, and with regular stops for lunch and espresso, I thought of my father, marching nearly to death and hiding under a bale of hay with some bread in his hands, determined not to die with an empty stomach. After about five hours and nine miles, long after the rest of the group had already finished, I finally reached the summit. I looked out at the glory and awesomeness of this world, of this godly spectacle, and I wept. I wept for my father and for my mother and for myself and for the "Others." *Look at my life*, I thought. My little victory is their victory. The vista of my life is their vista. I wish they could have seen it, lived it. Their lives were so hard, *too* hard, and yet so driven, so strong and relentless and determined, so that I could have this moment.

Lastly, it seems that after decades of shoveling coal into the engine of my career, the locomotive has enough energy to chug along on its own. I have work. In English *and* in Yiddish. I've always had a difficult time categorizing myself. I understand now that I am a storyteller— from acting to singing, directing and writing—just different muscles to tell the story.

Most recently, a new engagement: I'm the host of a podcast from Yale University's Fortunoff Video Archive called *Those Who Were There: Voices of the Holocaust*. Ha, perfect. Exactly where I am meant to be. God is laughing their nonbinary head off. I can run, but I cannot hide. Just as well. I really want to talk: to kids, fans, anti-Semites. Whatever. I'm the tip of the ever-melting iceberg, still attached to the body of people who came before me.

I knew them. They still have so much to say.

ACKNOWLEDGMENTS

Circumstances miraculously came together and made this challenging journey fall right into my lap. Or so it seemed. As my supportive and thoughtful editor, Debra Englander, said, it seemed like someone was watching me from above. Yes. Who do you thank for that?

I can and always will begin with my family, who are mostly gone but for as long as I am here, they are here.

All sorts of gratitude:

To Yeva Lapsker, Frank London, Lutz Engelhardt, Hans-Dieter Huober, and Hilke Lorenz for taking me, guiding me, and offering me unimaginable possibilities.

To Amy Schecter, Susan Gallin, Burt Rashbaum, Betsy Howie, and Julian Schlossberg, whose friendship, insights, and care for me and for my family's story, held me up when I needed holding up. To Marita Gochman, Linda Friedner, Tony Phelan, and Robert Aronowitz, who tried to lend their hands to help this story see the light of day. To George Eltman, who tried to get me to tell the story without cursing so damn much.

To Seth Rogovoy, an honest and critical reader, as well as a loving advisor and friend. To Heather King, who patiently navigated my book down the publishing river. To Bob Stern, who focused his sharp, clear eye and talent on this book.

To Evan Fallenberg, my friend who opened his residency to me, and read and reread, who understood and walked me through this process, and who "coincidentally" and separately from Susan Gallin, connected me with my incomparable agent, Deborah Harris—teacher, comrade, leader, and friend.

Finally, to my cousin Ellen Harris, who laughed when I wept (which was just what I needed), and my aunt Pauline Froster, who is a reminder—if one needed any—of those who should be here with us now, hugging us, cooking with us, teaching us who we are and where we come from.